"Need a hand?" Those emerald  Jason—and he shifted u

"No, thanks."

No anger or resentr
nation. Like Mady didn't

That should have mad

But what it did was bug him. Big time. She was his partner. If she needed help she should just say so. He opened his mouth to tell her that just as she planted those small hands on the top of the log and vaulted over it in a surprisingly graceful motion.

Almost. One foot didn't quite clear the obstacle. It grazed the slick surface of the log, sending her flying.

Jason dove, catching Mady like a wide receiver snagging a throw just before it hit the ground. They landed hard—Mady cocooned in his arms, his shoulder digging a rut in the decaying leaves.

They lay there for a heartbeat, then he looked down—and found his nose buried in a mass of sweet-smelling curls. He couldn't stop himself. He drew in the fragrance that was purely Mady. It went straight to his head. His eyes drifted shut, his arms tightened.

"I..."

"Hmm?" he mumbled into her hair.

"I...can't..."

His heart ached. *I know. Me neither. I can't take this—*

"...breathe!"

His eyes flew open and he sat up quickly—which resulted in her sitting in his lap, cradled against his chest...which definitely was not acceptable. Not with her looking up at him like that, with those wide, hypnotic eyes.

Jason vaulted to his feet, pulling Mady up as he rose.

She stared at him, then her lips tipped slightly. "Relax, Jason. I'm not going to attack you."

♛♡ *Palisades Pure Romance*

WILDERNESS

KAREN BALL

Palisades is a division of Multnomah Publishers, Inc.

This is a work of fiction. The characters, incidents, and dialogues are products of the author's imagination and are not to be construed as real. Any resemblance to actual events or persons, living or dead, is entirely coincidental.

Although the author did research wilderness expeditions into the North Cascade region, some creative license has been taken for the benefit of the story.

WILDERNESS
Published by Palisades
a division of Multnomah Publishers, Inc.
© 1999 by Karen Ball
International Standard Book Number: 1-57673-552-4
Design by Andrea Gjeldum
Cover illustration by Aleta Jenks
Cover image of woman by Digital Stock
All Scripture quotations, unless otherwise indicated, are taken from:
Holy Bible, New Living Translation (NLT)
© 1996. Used by permission of Tyndale House Publishers, Inc.
All rights reserved.
Also quoted:
The Holy Bible, New International Version (NIV) © 1973, 1984 by
International Bible Society,
used by permission of Zondervan Publishing House
The Holy Bible, King James Version
Palisades is a trademark of Multnomah Publishers, Inc., and is registered in
the U.S. Patent and Trademark Office.
Printed in the United States of America
ALL RIGHTS RESERVED
No part of this publication may be reproduced, stored in a retrieval system, or transmitted, in any form or by any means—electronic, mechanical, photocopying, recording, or otherwise, without prior written permission.
For information:
Multnomah Publishers, Inc.•PO Box 1720•Sisters, Oregon 97759

99 00 01 02 03 04 05 — 10 9 8 7 6 5 4 3 2 1

To Dad, a true shepherd, a man of God. You taught me the meaning of obedience, of success in God's eyes. May He show you how much you've touched and changed the lives of those around you. I see Christ in you every day, Daddy. I love you.

To Don, the Master Brainstormer. You're a genius, hon! Thanks for all your help and patience and wonderful suggestions. I never would have made it on this one without you.

and finally,

To our wonderful church family at Blessed Hope Fellowship. You took my family and me into your hearts and homes, making us feel welcome and loved. Thank you for forty years of living your faith, of reaching out in love, of teaching me the joys of an extended family. Every minister should have a congregation like you. You are a part of my heart, and I love you.

"He led his own people like a flock of sheep, guiding them safely through the wilderness. He kept them safe so they were not afraid."

PSALM 78:52–53

❧ 1 ❧

It takes the night to bring out the stars.
ANONYMOUS

This isn't how it's supposed to be!

The miserable thought just kept running through Mady's mind, over and over, like a mantra.

Or an epitaph.

She turned her face and rested her forehead against the cool airplane window. The early morning sky was dark with storm clouds. Flashes of lightning lit the haze, giving the entire scene an eerie, almost supernatural feel.

Please, Lord, please...no more turbulence. It's like a roller coaster—her stomach churned—*and You know how much I hate roller coasters!*

Of all the things she hated in life, those particular devices of torture were right at the top of the list. Oh, she'd tried riding them. Twice. Once when she was seven and at one of those temporary open-up-on-Friday, close-down-and-hit-the-road-on-Sunday carnivals. She'd screamed so loud and so long that the operator had finally shut the thing down and pulled her off.

The other time had been during spring break when she was in college. She'd gone with a group of so-called friends to Disney World, and the rats had convinced her to try Space Mountain.

"It's really neat," one young man had said, his arm around her shoulders, his smile broad and coaxing. "You ride this little car and see all the constellations...."

Like a fool she'd believed him. She'd been so immersed in flirting with him that she missed the signs telling pregnant women and people with back problems to turn back. Within the first few seconds of the ride she'd known she was in hell. She had to have been. Nothing else could be that completely, utterly, no-doubt-about-it terrifying.

She'd never spoken to that young man again.

Now she wished she had. Wished she'd made peace with him...because she was having serious doubts that she'd ever get the chance to do so.

She bit her lip, forcing away the waves of nausea, grateful for the cool feel of the window on her face. She'd prepared for this. Knew she hated to fly in the best of conditions. Didn't care how enormous the plane was, whether it had one level or twelve. Every plane she'd ever been on still left the perfectly good, solid ground and vaulted with audacity into the wild, blue yonder.

"Amazing, isn't it? That something this large, this heavy can stay up in the air?"

Mady twisted in her seat, glancing behind her between the seats. A pair of dark eyes smiled at her.

"Unbelievable is more like it," Mady muttered, and the man's mouth lifted in a smile full of compassion.

"We will be fine."

She almost believed him, until a sudden drop in altitude jerked her around again to face forward.

Oh yeah, they'd be just fine.

Breathe, Mady. Slow, deep breaths. Licking her lips, Mady obeyed, willing herself to remember the relaxation exercises she'd practiced over and over until they had supposedly become second nature.

Unfortunately, her first nature—utter panic—wouldn't back off enough for her to get her breath.

A jolt of the small craft threw her forward, smacking her nose against the seatback in front of her, then bouncing her back in her seat. Her stomach lurched as the plane dropped momentarily, then stabilized.

Oh no…no, no, no…

Mady drew in slow, steady breaths. *I am not going to be sick!* Not that she wasn't prepared. She had the little bag clutched in her fingers…the one with Wyatt Urp printed at the top and a picture on the front of a cartoon cowboy, complete with buckling knees and spiraling eyes.

She was prepared all right. But she'd be darned if she was going to use the thing. Compound terror with humiliation? No thank you. She rubbed her temples, trying to ease away the cobwebs of near panic cloaking her mind.

Where were all the verses she'd memorized for just such occasions? Verses about fearing not, about God being a refuge in trouble, about perfect love casting out fear?

Mady didn't know for sure, but they weren't anyplace where she could get ahold of them. And about the only thing even close to being cast away right now was the sweet roll she'd unwisely inhaled at the airport.

Pressing her lips together, she fought the frustration and disappointment with herself. *Just…back off.* She dug her fingers into the armrests of her seat. *I'm not in the mood, okay? I don't need to hear how far I am from what I should be right now.*

Before the chorus of condemnation could begin, she sat up straighter in her seat. With sheer force of will, she pushed away the queasiness, swallowing fast and drawing in deep breaths.

Maybe she'd get lucky and hyperventilate. Pass out, even. The thought made her smile.

Clenching her teeth, she grabbed the emergency procedure brochure from the pocket in front of her and fanned herself furiously. Distraction. She needed a distraction.

Fortunately, in a plane this small, it wasn't hard to find something—or someone—to look at.

A young couple was seated one row in front of her. They were turned to face each other, hands clasped with careless ease, smiling into each other's eyes and sipping from bottles of Evian.

They'd been like that earlier, too, when Mady arrived at the boarding gate in Seattle that morning. Six people had been sitting there, waiting—these two among them. The first word that came to Mady's mind as she studied the happy couple was *young*. Very young. Wide eyed and freckle faced, even.

Seeing the way they gazed into each other's eyes, the adoration in their expressions, a second description sprang to mind.

The woman looked up then, and her gaze collided with Mady's. Far from glaring at Mady for staring, the young woman's face had colored prettily.

"Oh, I'm sorry. Did you want to sit here?" She glanced at the seat next to her, and Mady shook her head quickly.

"Uh, no...no, that's fine." The last thing she needed

was to sit next to a pair of honeymooners. They had to be. No one else had that slightly dazed, ain't-life-just-glorious? kind of look.

Mady moved to another aisle, easing into the hard chair to wait for her boarding call. Definitely honeymooners. She recognized the look on their faces well. She should. Hadn't she seen that very same look on most of her friends' faces as they'd gotten married over the last several years? All of them. One by one. Except for her.

Mady slanted a glance at the second couple. They were seated near the doors leading to the runway. These two looked close to Mady's age. The woman was beyond beautiful. Stunning. Gorgeous. Catwalk material. She had a Mediterranean look about her: high, exotic cheekbones; delicate features; thick, dark lashes.

This was no pale English rose; this was one of those vibrant, fascinating dazzlers who tanned easily to a deep, golden glow and thrived on sunshine and admiration. And from the look of her, she got plenty of both.

What Mady wouldn't give for that kind of skin. Instead, she had to run for the sunscreen if the overhead lights were too bright.

Then there was the woman's hair. It was a mass of cascading curls, black with cinnamon highlights, and it looked as thick as it was luxurious.

Mady sighed and reached up to tug at her cap of blond, short-cropped curls. No one would ever covet her hair. No way. Nor would they call her beautiful. Oh no. She knew what they would call her. What they *had* called her all her life.

Cute.

Just the thought of it pulled a woeful sigh from her.

How many people—men and women, young and old—had said that to her?

"You're a real cutie, you know?"

"You sure are cute."

"You're so cute I could just eat you up!"

The worst part of it all was she knew they were right. She *was* cute. Short and petite, with pixieish features and a set of dimples that outdid the Pillsbury Dough Boy.

Another sigh. *You know, Lord, I really don't see how it would have hurt anything to let me be sultry. Or elegant. Or lovely...*

Anything but cute.

The sound of flipping pages drew Mady's attention to the man sitting next to Miss Gorgeous. He had the same black hair, the same striking Mediterranean features as the woman next to him.

"Do you mind?"

Mady jumped slightly, then exhaled in relief when she saw the comment was directed at the dark-haired man, not at her. The woman beside him gave him a peevish glare, poking at his arm on the armrest between them.

He ignored her with casual disinterest, which only served to irritate her further. Lips tight, eyes narrowed, she reached out to shove his arm off the rest.

"What are you doing?"

His outrage was met with a cat-who-ate-the-canary smile and a half-lidded regard. "This—" the words were clipped and dripping with disdain—"is mine." She pointed to the armrest on the other side of him. "That is yours. Kindly refrain from hogging what is mine."

His reply was succinct. "Brat."

"Boor."

"Witch."

Red heightened the color in the woman's high cheeks. *"Skilos."*

Mady had no idea what she'd said, but apparently it was far from complimentary. With an angry wave of his hand, the man turned from her abruptly, and Mady bent her head in case one of them should happen to glance her way. She didn't want them to spot the smile she was working so hard to restrain.

Brother and sister. They have to be.

When the boarding call had come for her flight, both couples had joined her in walking out to board the ten-passenger, twin-prop craft sitting on the runway.

As they'd tromped through the early morning mist, Mady thought the plane looked small. Really small. Miniscule, even. She'd never been in such a small plane before. Unlike the massive airliners, you felt every bump and shift and drop in altitude.

No, no, no, Mady. Forget the plane. Don't think about the plane. Distractions, remember?

Mady drew a breath and nodded. Right. She glanced to the side. Just two rows forward sat the last member of their group—a man who seemed utterly immune to the small plane's aerobatics. He'd no sooner taken his seat when he pushed his cowboy hat down over his eyes, crossed his arms, stretched his legs out, and promptly dropped off to sleep.

He was probably an alien. A Martian in disguise. It was the only way he could be so calm in the face of certain death—

Pick another tack, Mady. This isn't helping.

Okay. So he was an alien. She chewed the inside of her lip, tilting her head for a better view of the man's profile. A very *appealing* alien, admittedly. But an alien all the same.

She'd noticed him almost as soon as she arrived at the boarding gate. Couldn't help it. Not so much because he looked the quintessential cowboy—tall, broad in the shoulders, lean in the hips, square jaw… and he had all the requisite gear, too: hat pulled low over his eyes, duster, worn jeans, denim shirt, and boots.

He looked like he'd sauntered right out of a John Wayne movie.

But that wasn't what had caught her attention. Neither was it the fact that he had amazing blue eyes or dimples when he smiled. Well, not entirely. No, the biggest reason she'd noticed the man was that he spent the entire time they were waiting for boarding talking with a frail, little blue-haired woman.

Mady had heard the woman's nearly panicked tones as she came down the stairs to the waiting area. She'd paused on the last step, scanning to see who was so upset. A tiny, elderly woman whose arms were locked about a quivering furball was standing near the counter, her pointy chin trembling.

"Pookie just *can't* stay in her carrier for the entire flight." For all of her diminutive stature, the dear lady had a voice that rivaled an air horn. "She needs to be with her mummy or she'll be terrified."

Probably closer to the truth that Pookie's *mummy* was the one who would be terrified since she was almost in tears as it was. Compassion swept Mady—after all, the woman was clearly a kindred soul who adored animals and detested flying—but before Mady could head over to comfort the woman, Mr. Dimples, a relaxed smile firmly in place, beat her to it.

He strolled up to the little woman, taking off his hat with what seemed to be a natural kind of regard. Leaning down so he was on eye-level with her, he flashed her what had to be one of the most winning smiles Mady had ever seen.

It was dazzling and mesmerizing all rolled into one. And Mady found herself wondering what it would be like to be on the receiving end of such a smile. Before she could glance away, the man lifted his eyes just enough to peer over the woman's fluffy hair…and locked gazes with Mady.

Finding herself eye to eye with that electric blue gaze, Mady had much the same reaction as if she'd touched her tongue to an empty light socket. While the switch was on. While standing in water.

Jolted out of her fascination with the man, she looked away and stepped out, intending to find a seat and slump down out of his disturbing view.

Unfortunately, she'd forgotten one small fact. She was still standing on the last step.

With a trip and a yip, she went sailing forward, arms flailing wildly, feet scrambling to catch her balance before she did a full gainer into the chairs. Amazingly enough, she managed to grab the back of a chair and thus avoid falling on her face. With a relieved sigh—and the thought that there must have been a platoon of guardian angels on hand for *that* one—she lifted her chin and turned to glide gracefully toward an empty chair.

"Disgraceful! Imagine, a cute little girl like that being drunk this early in the morning!"

At the "Tsk, tsk, isn't it a shame!" comment from little Miss Blue Hair, Mady felt heat flood her face. Oh, if only the floor would open up and swallow her. Not daring to look at the woman or the man with her, she slid into a chair, slumping down, trying to make herself as inconspicuous as possible.

But at the sound of a low, soothing voice, she peeked up. Dimples was talking to Pookie's mummy. Mady couldn't hear what the man said, but whatever it was, it must have been brilliant. Within seconds, Pookie filled one of the cowboy's arms, and the trembling "mummy" was snuggled into the other.

He led the woman to a chair and spent the entire time sitting with her, holding her dog, and talking quietly. By the time Pookie's flight was called, Dimples had convinced the animal's owner that the carrier was, indeed, the safest place for her darling. Mady watched with amazement as the elderly woman stood, her dog safely ensconced in its shelter, then reached a frail, veined hand out to pat Dimple's cheek tenderly.

"You're a sweet boy." She wrinkled her little nose delicately. "If you'd only get a haircut, I bet some fine girl would snap you up!"

Mady didn't know how he'd reacted to the comment, but she almost choked on her restrained laughter. But that was nothing compared to the next pearls of wisdom from the little woman.

She leaned close to Dimples and whispered *sotto voce,* "Just make sure you stay away from girls like *that* one." And she nodded in Mady's direction. "When they're sold out to demon drink that young, well…only misery can come of that, dear boy."

Stunned, Mady seriously considered setting the woman straight, telling her she was not drunk, just…well, grace challenged!

She would have done it, too, if she hadn't found herself caught once more by a pair of deep blue eyes. Dimples held her gaze, a slight smile twitching his lips as he said in a voice taut with laughter, "Don't worry, Eulalie. I wouldn't dream of it."

Mady gave a gasp of relief when he looked away from her to smile at the elderly woman. "Now, careful you don't miss your plane."

Dropping her gaze to her magazine, Mady waited for her heart rate to return to something resembling normal. And only fierce determination had kept her from fanning herself with her magazine.

She'd been surprised and, she admitted, pleased to see Dimples rise and head to the plane with the rest of them when the boarding call came for her flight. She'd intended to tell him how nice he was to help the woman, but once on the plane, he'd made it abundantly clear that he wasn't interested in talking. To anyone.

She'd tried. A couple of times, but he hadn't responded to either overture, so she'd given up.

She didn't let it bother her. It was a simple fact of life that some people just weren't comfortable chatting with strangers. The blue-haired woman with the dog had been in distress, so that qualified as a mercy mission. If Mr. Dimples didn't want to talk with her, that was fine. Besides, she'd most likely have a chance to commend him on his kindness during the week.

That settled in her mind, it hadn't taken Mady long to dismiss the twinge of disappointment that her airport Prince Charming wasn't quite so charming as he'd first seemed.

Tipping her head to one side now, Mady studied his snoozing form, noting that the dip and tumble action of the small plane had no effect on him whatsoever. She nodded. He was an alien all right.

With alarming suddenness, the plane jerked and danced, going through the worst series of bumps and jostled yet. Mady endured the turbulence by gritting her teeth and closing her eyes. She replaced visions of a plummeting ball of flames with the picture of the plane—and its passengers—on the ground, safe and sound.

The next image—her on the phone, locating a train, a taxi, a pack mule, *anything* but a plane to take her home when the time came—actually made her smile.

After what felt like centuries but could only have been seconds, the plane regained its equilibrium. Mady opened her eyes slowly and felt a wave of satisfaction. That last bit of the dipsy-doodles had awakened Dimples. Maybe he wasn't such an alien after all. As he sat there, arms crossed, staring straight ahead, Mady could see a bit of thick, brown hair poking out from under the cowboy hat.

He angled his head a bit, and she got an even clearer look at his face. With his hat pulled low over his eyes, she couldn't see his features well, but disappointment nudged at her again when she realized he looked rather...sour.

Like he's been sucking on persimmons, as Eva would say.

Eva.

Mady turned to stare out the small window again. It was all Eva's fault Mady was here. Eva was her best friend in the world—and she should have been sitting in the seat next to her, suffering at her side. That had been the plan, anyway.

It was an idea they'd concocted years ago when they turned thirty within a week of each other. "Let's make a deal—" Eva had accentuated her proposal by raising her plate of Chocolate Decadence and holding it high—"If we hit thirty-five and we're both still single, no matter where we are, we do something wild together."

"Like what?"

Oh, what a Pandora's box one simple question can open. The twinkle in Eva's eyes should have warned Mady that her friend was cooking up a scheme. Not that a warning would have stopped Mady from forging on.

"Into the fray!" It was Mady's motto in life. Never let limitations—or little things like fear, apprehension, even blind terror—keep you from trying something new. What she loved was having fun, exploring, experiencing, discovering. Those things drew her like a light-high bug to a zapper.

Sure, when it's on your terms.

Mady frowned. What was wrong with that? Reason didn't eliminate risk. It just made it...

Safe? Predictable. Not so risky after all?

Her lips twisted. No. It made it wise. Reasonable. Prudent. All of which Eva's suggestion seemed to fit.

"Like an adventure. Something big. Something... audacious."

"Sounds good." Mady had clapped her hands in anticipation.

This time it was Eva who hesitated. She pursed her lips at Mady. "You have to promise one thing though."

Mady's hands had dropped into her lap, and she'd fixed her friend with an attentive gaze. "Such as?"

Eva sighed. "You'll be careful. Whatever we do, you'll be careful."

"Well, of course. I'm always careful."

"Uh-huh. Sure."

Mady folded her hands together in her lap. "Well…I try to be."

"Mm-hmm. As evidenced by the fact that all of the emergency rooms in town know you by name."

"Not all of them!"

"Most, then."

"A couple." Mady's jaw had jutted out.

Eva's lips twitched and her eyes sparkled. "Several. In town. And a couple throughout the country."

Mady threw up her hands. "Okay, so I've had a few accidents from time to time, but nothing has ever been serious."

"Oh no, nothing serious." Eva held up her hand and started counting off. "Let's see, a separated collarbone when you had a close encounter with a stump while running full-tilt—"

"It was dark and I was in a hurry…"

"A concussion when you missed your step while balancing on a curb…playing follow-the-leader with the high school youth group…in a McDonald's parking lot—"

"A *mild* concussion. Don't make it sound worse than it was."

"Stitches above one eye when you were mugged by a rampant kneeboard—"

"I couldn't get my balance."

"Stitches above the other eye thanks to a sleepy Irish setter whose growls you ignored—"

Mady held up her hand. "Okay, okay, you've made your point. I'll be careful."

"Swear on a stack of Bibles. Swear to me that you'll be reasonable and cautious and look before you leap."

"Fine. Great. I'll swear on whatever version you think would be most binding. I'll be positively boring."

For all her friend's fuss, she knew Eva was only looking out for her. And she appreciated it. Somebody had to.

Before long, she and Eva were immersed in full-blown brainstorming. They schemed and dreamed and discussed. But it wasn't until a few months later, after brainstorming and tossing out ideas, that they'd finally come up with the perfect plan: a wilderness excursion. Eva's cousin, Earl, led groups on wilderness trips and taught survival training in the northern Cascades of Washington state. What could be more exciting than that? Especially for two city girls? So they called him, asked for brochures and ideas, and finally settled on a four-day expedition where they'd learn how to explore the wilderness together.

"Going into the wilderness, facing down beasties and obstacles, and doing it as a team." Eva had chortled gleefully. "Just consider it basic training for when we get married!"

Mady's excitement grew as they talked, dampened only by the fact that she was fairly certain she'd never get to follow through on the plan. After all, by the time she turned thirty-five, her life would be far too busy to go on a four-day anything, even with Eva, dearest friend or no. After all, Mady's time would be taken up with a charming husband, a challenging career, and a dozen beautiful and talented children....

Okay, maybe not a dozen. But at least one or two.

Over the last several months when it became evident that the trip would happen, they'd pinned down more of the details. Eva's tone had risen gleefully as she elaborated. "We'll fly in from Seattle, then head up the mountain on horseback."

"Horseback? We get to ride to this place?"

"I told you it was remote." Eva's grin had widened. "We'll spend the week hiking and exploring and riding horses and fishing and just soaking in the glory of a primitive mountain wilderness."

Mady had paused at that. "Primitive? Exactly how primitive are we talking here?"

"Well..."

"Bathrooms? Will we have bathrooms?"

At Eva's silence, Mady sighed. "I don't suppose there's a hospital nearby then?"

Eva's brows had arched wrathfully. "You promised you were going to be careful this time!"

"I know, I know..." Mady sank deeper into her chair. "It just...well, it's never quite as much fun when you have to worry about things like medivac access and being lifted off of mountaintops by a helicopter—"

"Mady!"

She'd laughed then, holding up her hands as Eva came at her, fingers curled and ready to throttle her. "Kidding! Just kidding! Sheesh! Ever notice how old people lose the ability to take a joke?"

Eva had joined her laughter and leaned down to hug her tight. "It's really going to be grand, isn't it?"

Grand. Mady sighed, leaning her cheek against the window. Yes, it would have been. If Eva were along. It would have been utterly perfect. Eva had a special knack for making anything more fun, more exciting—

The plane shuddered and Mady's ears suddenly plugged, sending a stabbing pain through her head that made her wince. Before she could hold her nose and blow to relieve the pressure, the plane tipped, tilted, and dropped what Mady was sure had to be about two hundred feet!

"Aaaaalililili!"

The strangled cry escaped her before she could clamp her mouth shut, but she really and truly didn't care. Throwing herself back in her seat, her fingers imbedded in the armrests on either side of her, Mady thanked her lucky stars Eva wasn't along.

Right now, the last thing she needed was more excitement.

❧ 2 ❧

Even if you're on the right track,
you'll get run over if you just sit there.
WILL ROGERS

There was one clear emotion running through Mady's body as the plane continued its insane shimmy in the rough air…one feeling that screamed across her nerves and left them ragged and tattered—and her fingers imbedded in the armrest.

Fear. Or terror…panic…the screaming meemees…

Take your pick. She felt them all.

Of course, the sensible thing to do was pray. Beg God to smooth out the air. That, or let them plummet. Either way, the nightmare would be over. But she couldn't get her lips—or her mind, for that matter—to cooperate. All that she could manage was one simple plea.

Help.

Only it came out more like, *OhhelpOhhelpOhhelp*… Like repeating it would make God hear it better or something.

Thankfully, the plane decided she'd had enough and chose that moment to level out and fall back into the slight, shuddering mode of travel it had been following almost since they left the runway.

Mady lifted a hand to massage her temples, trying to ease away the weariness in her mind. For all that she was disappointed Eva wasn't with her, she had to admit she was glad she came, nightmare flight notwithstanding. She needed the time away. She needed some time to think.

Time to decide what she was going to be when she grew up. Assuming, of course, she ever grew up.

She knew what she wanted. Knew what she enjoyed and what she was good at. Even knew she was ready to give it a try...sort of.

With a shake of her head, she banished the debate. She'd think about it later. Her eyes drifted to the window, to the storm still raging outside.

She'd think about it once they were on the ground. Once she knew she *had* a future to worry about.

"You'll be glad you missed this one, Eva."

But even as she muttered the words, Mady knew she was wrong. No doubt about it, Eva would be sitting here, telling her how much fun they were having. And she'd remind Mady how ready they were for whatever they encountered. They should be. They'd put enough hours into planning this little venture. And into training for it.

Mady had been surprised when she'd realized they'd have to train. *Physically.* As in exercise. Taking hikes. Even enrolling in a refresher course on horseback riding at the community college.

Now, Mady enjoyed the outdoors and sports as much as the next person, but her head had started to spin as Eva had laid out all they needed to do to prepare for what was in store during the four days they'd be in the mountains.

It was a lot to do on top of working long days.

Not that she wanted to put in more than forty hours

a week at her job. Oh, it was a nice enough place, but working in a clothing store just wasn't what Mady had envisioned for herself at thirty-five.

But the way things were going, she'd probably still be there when she was fifty.

"Why don't you quit that job and go out on your own?" Eva had demanded one night just a week ago. Mady had called her to cancel their evening of shopping for equipment for the trip. One of the other salesclerks had called in sick, and it fell to her to take up the slack.

"And do what, pray tell?"

"Start your own business. As a creativity consultant. You've always wanted to."

True enough. Mady had always had a knack for looking at a room or a yard or a whole house and seeing simple, practical ways to bring out the hidden beauty and personality. And she'd longed to spend her days doing just that, opening people's eyes to simplicity and the lost art of gracious living, drawing beauty and creativity out of people and their homes, changing serviceable houses into cherished havens. But…"That takes money, Ev."

"You've got plenty saved up, Mady. You know you do."

Shifting from one foot to the other, Mady had wrinkled her nose at the phone. Yes, she knew it.

"And you'd be great! God's given you a gift. I've seen your home. It's amazing. Like some kind of restoring, nurturing haven. You've already got customers lined up, clamoring for you to turn their homes into wonderlands. And didn't that customer of yours, that rich lady, say she'd recommend you to any and all of her friends after you came in and worked miracles in her home? She said you were an absolute artist, remember?"

Mady's fingers tightened on the receiver. She didn't want to talk about this. Didn't want to think about making that kind of change. So her job wasn't exactly fulfilling. At least it was steady. Dependable. "This just isn't the time for me to do something like that."

Silence met this pronouncement, and Mady shifted back to her other foot. "Ev?"

"Keep saying things like that, Mady, and before you know it, time will be gone and you'll lose your chance. For good."

With a heavy sigh, Mady leaned her head back in her seat. Those words had haunted Mady for a week now. They gnawed at her, tying a knot in her stomach that just wouldn't go away.

So you've got a knot in your gut. So what? Better that and financial stability than jumping into something that might work…or might not.

Mady closed her eyes on the internal debate. There were some risks it just didn't make sense to take.

Hadn't she faced that last week when she blew out all thirty-five candles on her cake? She'd been surrounded by friends and yet achingly aware that there was no adoring husband beside her, his arm around her shoulders…no children smiling up at her, eyes shining at the thought of blowing out the candles on her birthday cake. Nor was there the likelihood of those voids being filled.

So far Mady had yet to spy a candidate for Mr. Right— or even Mr. I'll-Take-What-I-Can-Get. Her romantic horizon was as bare and depressing as a discarded

Christmas tree. On the curb. Void of needles. In mid-February.

"Take delight in the Lord, and he will give you your heart's desires."

Mady could hear her mother quoting the psalm as clearly as if she were sitting on the plane with her. Oh, how she missed her mother. She could hardly believe she and her father had been gone for over ten years. So much time lost…so much laughter never shared…

The plane shifted sideways, jerking Mady from her thoughts as it swayed back and forth like a toy held in some maniacal toddler's hands.

At the touch of a hand on her shoulder, Mady almost jumped out of her seat.

She whipped her head to the side and found the dark-eyed man from the seat behind her was now sitting next to her, his face filled with concern and compassion.

She blinked. "I…where did you come from?"

His dark brows raised and a small smile tugged at his lips. Mady realized how brusque she must have sounded, and her hand flew to cover her mouth. "Oh! I'm sorry."

He was shaking his head. "No, do not worry. I startled you." He settled back into the seat. "I hope you do not consider this an intrusion, but I heard you cry out." His eyes came to rest on Mady's cheeks. "And when I looked forward to be sure you were all right, I saw you were weeping." He inclined his head. "I thought perhaps company would help calm you."

She tried to pinpoint the man's slight accent as he spoke. His tone was rich and resonant, and the intonation was clearly European. But from where?

Mady swallowed and gave him a grateful smile. "Thank you—" she stopped and peered over her shoulder. The man's companion was seated behind her, her dark eyes closed, her long, manicured fingers digging into the armrests of her seat. Mady felt a wave of compassion.

I know just how you feel...

She turned back to her new seatmate. "But what about your friend?"

His smile was rueful. "My sister, Lea. She much prefers solitude to my company. Particularly when she is uneasy. She says I only irritate her already raw nerves."

Mady smiled at that. "Well, then, I'm happy to have you join me."

A lean hand reached out to her. "My name is Nikos Panopoulos."

Greek. No wonder she couldn't fix the accent. She'd never met anyone from Greece before. "Mady Donovan."

He settled back in his seat, tugging on his seat belt lightly. "You have come on this journey alone?"

"Not on purpose."

His brows arched again at her wry comment.

"A friend was supposed to come with me."

"But?"

Mady leaned back in her seat with a sigh. "She called me yesterday—"

"Yesterday? Such late notice?"

"—with a broken leg."

He lifted his chin in an understanding nod. She leaned her head back with a sigh. "I should have known there was a problem when I answered the phone."

"Oh?"

Mady's smile was rueful. "Eva was hesitant." She met the man's dark gaze, her smile widening. "If there's one thing Eva isn't, it's hesitant. Ever."

"Ah. I see."

Mady sighed again. The whole sad story took all of five minutes to tell. Some guy hadn't seen a stop sign; Eva was riding her bike into the intersection; the resulting collision left Eva's bike in a mangled pile and Eva in a cast up to her thigh.

Mady had felt her lower lip thrust out, felt the frown creasing her brows—and stamped her foot again. *This isn't fair...*

"You could not reschedule for a later time?"

"Twenty-four hour notice required for a full refund. And I couldn't afford to lose the money. Besides, Eva's cousin, Earl, set this trip up special. Eva said he's really gone out of his way for us."

"It is admirable you honored your agreement."

The approval in his tone surprised Mady. "Well, we could hardly leave Earl two people short for the week. Actually, one person."

"One?"

She nodded. "Eva said Earl found someone to take her place. So the group should be the right size."

"Then everything worked out well." Nikos sounded pleased, and Mady didn't have the heart to disagree with him. Besides, he might be right. She might end up really happy that she'd come.

Of course, she'd been anything but happy about it at first. The whole time she and Eva had discussed the issue, her disappointment had been growing. *Eva and I were supposed to do this together! That was the whole point.*

It won't be nearly as much fun without her. What am I supposed to do for a partner? This just isn't fair....

Her emotions must have come through because Eva finally gave a huff. "Mady, come *on*. I know this isn't what we wanted, but that doesn't mean everything is ruined. Remember Who's in control."

She opened her mouth, then clamped it shut. What could she say? It was the same thing she'd been telling herself for the last week. God was in control. She knew it was true.

Mady just couldn't help wishing He'd do things the way she wanted for a change.

"Well, I for one am glad you are here."

She turned her head to smile at Nikos. "Thanks. I think I will be, too. Eventually." Leaning down, she pulled out her camera from beneath her seat. "And I'll be sure to get plenty of pictures for Eva. So she feels like she was here."

"I think perhaps you are a good friend to your Eva."

She laughed. "It's only fair. Eva's a good friend to me."

And she was. A very good friend. Mady could still hear Eva's parting words. "You'll go on this trip and you'll enjoy yourself."

A burst of laughter had escaped Mady at her friend's command. "You sound like a Marine drill sergeant. You *will* do this and you *will* have fun."

"And don't you forget it! Cheer up, Mady. You will have a good time, I'm sure of it. I just know God's got something special in store for you."

Mady yelped as yet another pocket of turbulence bounced the small plane. *Something special, huh? Like what? The plane ride from the bad place?*

She slanted a look at Nikos, who was watching her with a small smile.

"Are you afraid?"

He pursed his lips slightly at her abrupt question, and she liked the fact that he didn't answer quickly.

"No—" he shook his head slowly as he spoke—"but neither am I entirely calm." His teeth gleamed white against his olive skin. "Let's just say I will not need any coffee when we arrive at our destination."

Mady giggled. She understood completely. "Definitely not. I'm hyper enough to fly the rest of the way on my own." She glanced out the window. "Come to think of it, that might actually be safer!"

He laid a hand over hers where it still clutched the armrest. "I'm sure the pilot has our safety well in hand."

"Nikos?"

He and Mady glanced back at Lea Panopoulous. She looked wan and worn out, and the day hadn't even begun yet. Not really. This was just the first leg of their journey.

Lea bit her lip, her velvet brown eyes wide and glimmering with tears. "Would you come sit with me for a while?"

Sympathy swept Mady at the quiet request. Clearly the flight was taking its toll on Lea. Even more than it was on her. She turned to Nikos. "I'm fine. Really."

He lifted her hand to his lips and pressed a soft kiss to the back of it. "You have a kind heart, Mady. I wonder if you know how rare that is?"

She had no response to that unexpected comment, and with an almost courtly nod Nikos rose and moved back to sit beside his sister. Mady watched him fasten his seat belt, then reach out to take his sister's hand and hold it between both of his. She leaned her head back with a small sigh.

Turning away, Mady felt a sting of tears. Nikos and his sister made a striking pair.

A striking pair…

Mady's mouth fell open as realization clicked into place. She glanced at Mr. and Mrs. Honeymooner seated in front of her. Obviously they would be teamed together on this little venture. Which left Mady, Nikos, Lea…and Prince Not-Quite-So-Charming.

A small tingle of alarm shot through her, and she glanced at the man seated at the front of the plane again.

Be reasonable, Mady. You know nothing about the man. He could be utterly charming and gracious, a truly wonderful person.

She started to cheer up at that. It was entirely possible. Maybe he just wasn't feeling well. She knew she was ready to chug a bottle of Maalox after the flight they'd been having. She leaned to the side, getting a slightly better view of the man. Her hopes stumbled as she noted the way his features—what she could see of them, anyway—had settled into scowl, even when he was dozing.

Mady bit her lip. Okay…well, no one had control over what his features did when he was asleep. Most likely he was scowling from a bad dream. Or a bad piece of pastry. Could be he'd grabbed one at the airport, and the way those things sat there, under those warming lights for hours on end…oh yeah, probably a bad pastry.

Or a bad temperament.

Mady tried to ignore the gloomy thought, but she

couldn't. Her eyes drifted to study his profile again.

Oh no...he's a grump. It's clear as the scowl on his face. You wouldn't make me trade Eva for a grump, would you, Lord?

What if their fearless leader wanted a man and a woman on each team? It sort of made sense, she supposed. Balance out the strengths and weaknesses.

Well, surely a brother and sister wouldn't want to be teamed together. She grabbed on to that idea as she turned slightly to consider Nikos through the crack between the seats.

Definitely not a grump. Hadn't he been sensitive enough to know she was frightened...kind enough to try and reassure her?

It was settled. He'd make a fine partner. As, in all likelihood, would his sister once she started breathing normally again. Mady was certain that pasty cast to her complexion was the result of their flight and not because she was a sickly sort.

I'll take either one of them, Lord. Whichever You think is best will be just fine with me.

As though sensing he was being studied, Nikos glanced up, and Mady found her gaze captured by his dark, enigmatic eyes. A slow smile played across his features as those dark brows lifted slightly.

A quick rush of heat filled Mady's cheeks, and she opened her mouth to apologize for staring—

Whomp!

If she hadn't been held securely by her seat belt, the force of this jolt would have thrown Mady from her seat.

"Using seat belts doesn't do much good if you don't use your head as well."

She glanced up at the source of the dry comment. Dimples had spoken! But the dimples weren't anywhere in sight. No siree. The look on his face now was so far from the tender, compassionate expression he'd given Pookie's mommy that Mady suddenly wondered if he were even the same man.

He sure didn't look like it. His face was as full of reprimand as his words. He peered at her sourly from beneath his wide-brimmed hat.

Mady was awash with disappointment. Never mind that she didn't know the man from Adam, she still felt enormously let down. The verdict was in.

Dimples wasn't a prince at all. From the looks of him, he wouldn't even qualify as a court jester.

He was a grump.

Slow down, girl. Maybe he's one of those people who just doesn't express himself well with strangers. A sweet-faced, blue-haired image drifted through her mind. *Unless, of course, they're over seventy. Then he positively shines.* She pressed her lips together. But even as she started to pass judgment, the voice of reason spoke up again.

Just give him a break. Slow to speak and slow to anger, remember? Could be he comes across more abrupt than he intends.

Give him a break? Wouldn't she just love to! But she pushed aside those less-than-sociable feelings, drew a calming breath, and nodded. She even managed a gracious smile. Surely the man hadn't meant to sound condescending. "Um, thanks. I apprec—"

He cut her off with a careless wave of his hand, making Mady feel like a pesky gnat buzzing around his head. He turned to face forward and stretched those long, jean-clad legs out in front of him. "You're not doing yourself any favors fidgeting around in your seat, that's all."

Fidgeting? She wasn't fidgeting. She *never* fidgeted! So she hadn't sat stock still like a comatose alien…like *some* people. But that didn't mean she'd been fidgeting, for Pete's sake.

And it sure didn't mean she needed to be talked to like some antsy three-year-old.

"Excuse me, but I don't believe I was fidgetin—"

He snorted. *Snorted!*

Mady almost choked on her exasperation. This man needed to be put in his place. But before she could open her mouth, he went on.

"So what were you doing? Aerobics?"

Mady pressed her lips together more tightly. All *righty,* then. He *had* meant to be condescending. And the more she talked with him—or rather, was talked down to by him—the more she realized how terribly she'd misjudged the man. Dimples or no dimples, he was *not* a prince. What she had here, plain and simple, was a grump.

Her eyes narrowed. No, a *sourpuss.*

Yes, that fit. Sourpuss. An apt name if ever there was one. As though to prove her case, he gave her one more bit of bothersome banality.

"Anyone with an ounce of sense knows the best thing to do in a situation like this is relax."

Well! So she didn't have an ounce of sense, was that it? Mady opened her mouth, closed it, then leaned forward. Normally she didn't get too upset with people. But really! She'd had just about enough of this man's attitude. "Now, just a min—"

Sourpuss yawned and crossed his arms, evidently scarcely able to keep his eyes open.

Mady clenched her teeth. "Listen, Mr....Mr...."

He shooed her again—and she barely restrained herself from going over and chomping on the fingers waggling at her. "No need to thank me. Just breathe deeply and face forward. We'll be on the ground soon."

Right on cue, the plane pitched, shimmied, then took an alarming drop in altitude. This time even the starry-eyed honeymooners yelped.

Mady pushed herself back in her seat and dug her fingers into the arms. "That's what I'm afraid of."

Her only response as she closed her eyes and sent up a series of very heartfelt, very frantic prayers was another of Sourpuss's snorts.

❧ 3 ❧

We can't all be shining examples, but
we can at least twinkle a little.
ANONYMOUS

Jason Tiber crossed his arms over his chest, refusing to give in to the twinges of guilt nagging at him.

Why should he feel bad? He'd been positively neighborly! He'd tried to help a stranger by pointing out that she might be putting herself at risk, and the silly woman had looked at him like he was some kind of insect. A repulsive one at that. Okay, so maybe he should have known better than to try a logical, reasonable approach with a woman who perched like a wired canary on the edge of her seat—and on the edge of panic.

An unwelcome surge of sympathy hit him then. The flight really had been awful. Fortunately, he liked flying in small planes, actually felt safer in them. So this kind of roller-coaster ride didn't bother him. But if Little Miss Priss back there wasn't a seasoned flyer...well, he could understand her fear.

So if a bumpy plane ride can freak her out, what's she doing on this trip?

He jerked his cowboy hat low on his head. Good question. And the only answer that came to Jason made his jaw tense.

Last night when Earl had called him about the trip,

he should have dropped the receiver back in place. But seeing as Earl was one of Jason's longest-standing buddies—and seeing as he was calling Jason because Jason had asked him to—that hadn't seemed right. So he'd pulled up a chair and listened as Earl told him there was an opening with a group going into the mountains.

"You told me to call you when the next group had an opening, right?"

Jason hadn't thought much about the question last night. Now...

He glanced at the people seated on the plane and grimaced. Now he wondered if his buddy hadn't been covering his behind.

But then, Jason knew Earl was right. He had called him just a week ago, asking if there was anyone going into the mountains.

"Anyone?" Earl's tone had been surprised. "Don't you mean is there a group of extreme adventurers going into the mountains?"

Jason's hopes had perked up at that. "Is there?"

"No."

So much for perking up.

"I'm just trying to figure out what you're asking for, Jas."

He should have ended the conversation then and there. Should have listened to the voices ragging on him, telling him he was asking for trouble. But he didn't. He'd been too desperate to do something—anything—to get away.

"I'll make it simple. I'm asking you to call me when you have an opening. Any opening. In any group that's heading into the mountains."

Pause. Then, "You okay, buddy?"

Jason had gritted his teeth. Leave it to Earl to cut to the chase. "I'm fine. I just—" he rubbed a hand over his eyes, wishing the heavy weariness behind them would ease—"I just need a break for a while."

"Too much time to think, eh?"

He'd almost hung up then. There were times he wished Earl didn't know him so well, didn't care what was going on, didn't see through the front that seemed to satisfy everyone else.

"Do you have any openings or not?"

Another pause. "Not right now. But I will call you, Jas. As soon as something opens up."

Jason had been surprised and pleased when Earl called back less than a week later.

"I've got a vacancy. In a special request group."

That was all Jason needed to hear. *Special request* meant a group ready for anything.

Earl went on. "So, you still looking to get away?"

Was he ever. "When do we leave?"

"Tomorrow morning. You fly in here early and we head out by noon."

As much as Jason hated to admit it, he'd gotten excited. Earl hadn't offered any details, but then Jason hadn't really given him the chance. But he knew the kinds of groups Adventures Unlimited usually drew. Men ready to pit themselves against the elements, to take on the ultimate challenges of wild and rugged terrain.

And there was no better place for that than Earl's. Jason had gone on several expeditions with his friend, each more exhilarating than the last. Earl had a sweet setup—cabins, stables, and a lodge surrounded by towering Douglas fir and western red cedar. The only access to Earl's place was by flying in on a small plane. The only access to the surrounding wilderness was either hiking or riding. The Cascade range was the perfect place for finding rugged, even dangerous, terrain. All of which suited Jason just fine.

What didn't suit him, however, was what he'd seen when he reached the boarding gate. He'd realized within moments of arriving that the people waiting there were about as far from adventurers as it got.

As for a group of men...

Jason's lip curled. He'd wanted to groan out loud when he spotted the young blonde and the sultry brunette. And when he spotted the little lady with the dust mop dog, he'd seriously considered coming down with the flu.

His relief at discovering Eulalie Spaetzel and the piteous Pookie were on a different flight was intense, albeit short-lived. Because right on the heels of this glad news came a small, curly-haired vision tripping down the stairs into the waiting area.

He'd noticed her as she started down the stairs, though he couldn't exactly explain why. She wasn't the kind of woman that usually caught his attention. Oh, she was a cute little thing, sure. Reminded him of his niece's picture book of sprites and fairies. But there was something about her. Something that had nothing to do with her looks. Something captivating...enticing in a way he still didn't understand.

Against the strict training his sweet mother had given him—*"You maintain eye contact with the person you're speaking to, young man. Don't you be glancing up at*

every new person who waltzes into the room"—he'd
glanced up from Eulalie. He couldn't help it. It was as
though he'd sensed the sprite's presence, for crying out
loud. His nerves had practically tingled with some weird
awareness.

And when his seeking eyes had met that wide, startled, unbelievably green gaze...the contact had rocked
him.

Thankfully, she'd broken the connection with her
flying trapeze act. As he looked back to Eulalie, he'd
counted himself every kind of fool.

Sprites and fairies? He was losing it. No doubt about
it.

But that curly-haired package wasn't his only challenge. At first he'd been pretty occupied with poor, worried Eulalie and Pookie, so he hadn't really taken a good
look at the people sitting in the hard chairs around him.
But he'd seen enough to figure these folks weren't out to
pit themselves against anything—except maybe lodgings
without room service.

As he'd talked with his elderly companion, then
helped her slip her quivering furball of a dog into the
carrier, he'd been hoping against hope that he had the
flight time wrong, that his group was still coming.

No such luck. When his flight number was called,
the three women and two men waiting at the gate had
joined him to walk to the small plane.

The first couple was young, barely adults from what
he could see. The woman was blond and tan; the guy
looked like an L.A. surfing bum with those streaks of
white–blond in his sandy hair. Both looked like they suffered from terminal perkiness.

Perky people drove him nuts.

The other woman though, she was enough to catch his interest. And to nail the coffin on his so-called adventure into the mountains. Women who looked like that didn't scale mountains. Not without an elevator. As for physical exertion, she probably thought that meant fixing your own cappuccino.

No, a woman like that wouldn't put herself through the kinds of physical challenges he'd been expecting on this little jaunt. She was too elegant, too exotic, too clearly old money. Too manicured. Those long, elegant nails must have cost a fortune!

He grimaced again. What could Earl have been thinking? Surely he didn't expect Jason to go along with this…to go along with *them*?

You agreed to go. To fill in the vacant spot. Gave your word.

No, he'd agreed to take part in an adventure. From the looks of things, that was *not* what this was going to be. He thought about the woman who'd tripped on the stairs, and groaned. Suppose she did one of her flying squirrel imitations on the top of a cliff? Guess who'd have to dive after her.

Jason's lips pressed together. Earl, that's who. Because he wasn't going to do it. If he went on this trip, he'd end up baby-sitting the entire time.

And he swore off that a long time ago. Earl knew that.

The jolt of the landing gear hitting the runway pulled Jason's attention from his churlish thoughts. He pushed his hat back and leaned forward, peering out the small window. There, just beyond the runway, was the blue van for Adventures Unlimited.

And standing next to the van, a big grin on his face, was Jason's "good buddy" Earl.

Jason narrowed his eyes as he muttered, "Looo-cy, I'm home…and you gots some 'splaining to do!"

When Mady felt the bump of the plane's tires hitting the runway, she exhaled in sharp relief. Safe at last! She unfastened her seat belt with surprising speed, considering how badly her hands were trembling, and sat poised, ready to bolt the minute the plane stopped moving.

The aircraft taxied, then finally came to a shuddering halt. The pilot stepped out of the cockpit and smiled at them. "Welcome to Adventures Unlimited, folks! Sorry for the rough ride here from Seattle, but this early summer weather was being a bit uncooperative."

Mady almost allowed herself a snort at that.

"Fortunately, the weather down on the ground is a bit more hospitable. For the moment, anyway. Just a bit of wind—" he grinned as though he were giving them some wonderful gift—"and the forecast for the week is sun and warmth. So you picked the right week to come. Sure wish I was goin' along!"

"Tell you what, you can take my place."

The words were out of Mady's mouth before she'd even realized they were there. Fortunately, the pilot and the others laughed, taking her comment for a teasing joke. Relieved, she glanced forward and her gaze collided with Sourpuss's. He wasn't chuckling like the others. Instead, his dark blue eyes were speculative. She had the oddest feeling he knew she'd been half-serious and that he looked down on her for it.

"Coward," his eyes seemed to say.

"Sourpuss," her gaze shot back.

Their staring match was broken when the pilot reached to open the hatch so the passengers could disembark. "Now, ol' Buck, the driver for Adventures Unlimited, is out there, ready to meet you all. So gather up your belongings and hop on out. And have a great week. I'll have the cargo hold open in a jiffy, and you can get your gear. And I'll see you on Thursday for the flight back to Seattle."

Mady tried not to think about getting back on the plane. Instead, she stood quickly, ready to get as much distance between herself and the offending aircraft as possible. It wasn't until her head met the low ceiling with a resounding thud that she remembered there wasn't enough room to stand straight. Not even for her.

"Oooooo, that must have hurt." Miss Honeymooner crooned in a sweet, young voice as she slid from her seat. Then she turned to her husband, her freckle-spattered face creased with solicitude. "Be careful when you stand, sweetie. She's just a little bitty thing, and you know how tall you are."

Well, at least she didn't call me cute.

Grimacing, Mady rubbed the top of her head and shot a glare in Sourpuss's direction. He was probably laughing himself silly—

He wasn't there. He'd gotten off already. *Like a rat deserting a sinking ship. . .*

"Did you hurt yourself?"

She started at the low voice next to her ear and turned her head to find Nikos standing behind her. She sighed. "Nothing's really wounded—" she smiled— "unless you count my pride."

His chuckle was deep and rich. "Something most of us can afford to lose, at least in part." His smile broadened, and she caught her breath. *Oh my, he really is something.* It wasn't so much that he was handsome. No, Lea seemed to have cornered the drop-dead gorgeous category in the family. But Nikos was…arresting. His features had a slumbering, smoldering look to them, and his manner was purely male.

Odds were good both he and his sister were responsible for a good number of whiplash cases. People would definitely notice them.

Speaking of his sister…Mady glanced back to find her standing behind Nikos, rubbing her temples with long, tapered fingers.

"Nikos, please, I would like to get off. Now."

"In a moment, dear sister. I daresay you can survive for a few more minutes."

Uh-oh. "Dear Sister" was looking decidedly unhappy with her brother's response. Mady had no desire to get caught in a sibling tiff, so she moved to the side to let them pass. Nikos shook his head.

"No, please." He smiled and inclined his head.

A pleasant warmth crept into Mady's cheeks, and she smiled at him as she moved down the aisle to the door.

Two more points for the charming and gallant Nikos.

Once off the plane, "ol' Buck" greeted them with a toothy grin. "Hey, folks! Glad you could make it. It's gonna be a great week, just you wait and see. Now, go on and grab yer gear off'n the plane and chuck it in the back of the van—" he jerked his thumb over his shoulder toward a waiting maxivan—"We'll do the introductions proper when we get to the ranch house. For now, feel free to exchange names and help each other get this gear loaded." His grin broadened a notch. "After all, the name of the game for the next week is teamwork. Right?"

Someone touched her arm, and Mady turned. Nikos nodded his head toward his sister, who, Mady noted with interest, was heading for the van. Apparently her luggage was supposed to get off the plane and on the van by itself. "I'm afraid Lea was less than gracious as we were departing the plane. I apologize."

Mady grinned, falling into step beside him as they moved toward the cargo hold of the plane. "It's okay, really. I understand. I wanted off, too."

"May I help you with your baggage?"

How sweet. She was liking this guy more all the time. "Thanks, but I think I can handle it. It's not that much. Besides—" she cast a sideways glance toward the van—"I think you'll already have more than your fair share."

He followed her gaze, then lifted his hands. "The sooner one makes peace with certain unpleasant realities in life, the more time he has—" his smile deepened as he looked at Mady—"to enjoy the pleasant surprises that bless his path."

A strangled sound turned Mady's head. Sourpuss. She should have known. Apparently he'd overheard Nikos and he wasn't impressed. In fact, he looked like he swallowed a worm—maybe even a bucket of them—but then, that would make him a cannibal, wouldn't it?

Mady chuckled at the irreverent thought. Sourpuss cast a glance heavenward at the sound, his expression turning even more sour. It took every ounce of her control to resist the almost overpowering temptation to stick her tongue out at the man.

It would serve him right for eavesdropping.

Instead, she settled for turning a high-wattage smile at Nikos. "You're absolutely right." She spoke to Nikos, but met Sourpuss's gaze straight on. "I can't tell you what a relief it is to meet a man of refinement on this trip." She smiled at Sourpuss. "For a change."

The only reaction from her intended target was a muscle jerking in that square jaw, but Mady felt an inordinate surge of satisfaction at the sight of it.

"Which bag is yours?" Nikos directed the question to Mady as he stepped beside Sourpuss, who was pulling a backpack from the cargo hold.

"It's the blue pack." She leaned past her nemesis, careful to avoid any contact, and grasped the strap of the pack, giving a mighty tug.

The bag, which apparently hadn't been as well anchored as she'd anticipated, flew out of the cargo hold—and landed smack dab in the middle of Sourpuss's back.

Mady cried out a warning, but it was too late. Man and pack sailed forward and landed in a heap on the ground. Horrified at what she'd done, Mady stepped toward the fallen man…just as he put his hand out to push himself up.

Directly under her foot.

She recoiled, but not before she'd felt his fingers flatten as she trampled them. Mady jerked up her foot, which only resulted in her losing her balance.

"Watch out!"

Several things happened then in quick succession.

Sourpuss threw his hands over his head.

Nikos grabbed for Mady's windmilling arms—and missed.

Mady cried out in dismay as she tumbled to land in a heap on the ground. Or she would have, if not for the rather solid cushion of Sourpuss's back.

For about three-and-a-half seconds, she lay there, frozen with consternation, sprawled on top of the poor man.

That's when she started to giggle.

"You can get up anytime."

The muffled comment from somewhere beneath her only succeeded in increasing the giggles twofold.

"You...can get up...*now!*"

She could hear the tautness in his words, though she couldn't tell if it was because he was growing angry or because the poor man couldn't breathe with her spread eagle on his back. If only she could stop laughing...but the day had been too stressful and the trials too extreme.

She was gone. Completely gone. Like Mary Tyler Moore at Chuckles the Clown's funeral. Mady knew full well laughter was completely inappropriate, but she couldn't do anything else.

So she lay there, clutching her aching sides, tears streaming down her face, gasping for air...howling.

The least she should do was apologize. She could do it. She knew she could. Just concentrate on getting the words out between the sniggers. "I'm...*so*...so-so-*sorry!*"

The last word came out in a wheezing hoot, completely decimating any hope she'd had of sounding sincere.

She tried to roll over but couldn't find a safe place to put her hands to anchor herself. Every option was…well, unacceptable. The safest spot was the back of Sourpuss's head, but that hardly seemed right. Land on a man's back and then shove his face into the dirt and smother him while you get up?

The thought—and the image it inspired—only made the absurdity of her situation that much more hilarious to her clearly warped sense of humor.

Suddenly her nice, firm foundation shifted. In one, breathtaking moment, she found herself swept up and cradled in a pair of well-built arms. She hiccuped back a half-sob, half-giggle, and turned her face up to the man who stood holding her tight against his chest.

Sourpuss gazed down at her, his expression torn between irritation and amusement.

"I'm not sure whether to drop you or throw you," he muttered, his blue eyes glittering. "Though I *am* sure you deserve both."

"Then perhaps a safe compromise would simply be to surrender her."

This came from Nikos, who stepped forward and, before Mady could express an opinion, slipped his arms beneath her.

Mady felt the muscles in Sourpuss's arms tense as he tightened his hold on her, effectively shoving her nose flat against his flannel-covered chest. Either he was trying to be sure she didn't fall or he was hoping to suffocate her.

Probably the latter.

A sideways glance in Nikos's direction told Mady he wasn't going to back off; and for a fraction of a moment, she thought she was about to become the rope in a testosterone tug of war. Raising her hands, she planted them directly in the middle of each man's chest.

"I have an even better idea."

Two pairs of fierce gazes came to bear on her, and she almost backed down. But she drew a breath and gently pushed at the chests that she was fairly certain would be butting by now if she weren't wedged between them.

They didn't budge.

She cleared her throat.

No movement.

She pushed again, this time with more force. "Put me down!"

Nikos looked down at her then and gave a small, smiling nod. "Excellent solution." He dropped his arms and backed away a step, giving the man holding her a meaningful look.

Oddly enough, Sourpuss continued to hold her, frowning down at her. She applied another gentle push to his chest, pointing down with her free hand. "Down." She wiggled her feet at him. "My feet? On the ground?" She looked from the grass to him, then down again.

With a slight huff, he let her legs swing down until her feet brushed the ground. He kept his other arm around her, just long enough to be sure she was steady. When she looked up at him again, he stepped back.

Mady had heard about locking gazes with someone, read about it in books and magazines. She'd always envisioned it as a slow, almost hypnotic kind of connection.

But it wasn't. It was fast and abrupt and consuming, like a flash fire that wasn't there one second and blazing out of control the next. She felt turned to stone and about to melt all at the same time. That brilliant blue gaze held her captive, and Mady wondered vaguely if an electrical storm were about to break. Why else was the very air about them charged and snapping?

Emotions she couldn't begin to define or understand welled up inside her. She felt a subtle shift, though she wasn't sure if it had happened beneath her feet or inside her chest. Either way, it made her dizzy, and she threw out a hand to steady herself.

Nikos was there in an instant, his fingers cupping her elbows. "Careful, Mady. Are you sure you didn't hurt yourself when you fell?"

She gave Sourpuss a quick look. "Uh…no. I—that is, my landing was…cushioned." She offered him an apologetic smile.

He stepped back, sliding his hands into the pockets of his jeans. "Anytime." His gaze rested briefly on her face, then drifted to Nikos's firm grip on her arms. "Well, you seem to be in good hands, so if you don't mind, I'll go get my things."

With that, he reached down to retrieve his pack and a small case and strolled toward the van.

Mady wasn't sure if she was relieved or disappointed.

"Mady?"

She spun toward Nikos, bumping into his nose in the process.

"Oh! I'm sorry!" She reached up to touch his face gently. "Did I hurt you?"

He grinned down at her. "If I say yes, will you kiss

it and make it all better?"

She swatted at his shoulder and went to grab her wayward backpack. "I don't think so. I've gotten myself into enough trouble for one day."

His deep chuckle followed her as she gathered her things and followed Jason to the van.

"Promise me you'll be careful."

Eva's warning drifted into her mind, and she let out a deep sigh. She *had* been careful. And what had happened? The Texas Two-Step down a flight of stairs...the plane ride from the bad place...verbal fencing with an ex-prince...a flying half-gainer smack-dab into trouble...

If those things were any indication of how this little *adventure* was going to shape up, maybe she should just pack it in and go home. Now. Immediately.

But as much sense as that made, Mady knew she wasn't going to do it. She came on this trip to *learn* something. And so far all she'd learned was that cowboys make poor princes.

But very good landing pads.

She laughed outright at the thought. No, she wasn't going to go home. Not now—her gaze traveled to the van and came to rest on a pair of cowboy boots sticking out the side door—when this trip was just starting to get really interesting.

❧ 4 ❧

*This time, like all times, is a very good time, if
we but know what to do with it.*
RALPH WALDO EMERSON

Jason settled himself into the backseat of the van, pulled his hat low on his head, and did his best to look asleep. Small talk was not on his list of favorite things to do.

Apparently his ploy worked because the others left him alone. After the van started up and they were on their way, he peered out from under the rim of his hat to take another look at his…team.

"Oh look, sweetie! What beautiful flowers."

The young blonde leaned her head on her companion's shoulder and gazed up at him. "They're almost as beautiful as my bouquet was."

"But not near as beautiful as you, hon."

That was flat too much. Jason choked on that one. The others spun around to stare at him as he coughed and gasped for air.

"Need someone to pound your back?"

He fixed the woman sitting in front of him with a watery-eyed glare. "Don't you think you've done enough of that for one day?"

Satisfaction filled him at the pink that tinged her cheeks as she spun, turning her back on him.

"You okay…?"

The young fella let the question hang there, clearly

waiting for Jason to share his name. Well, there was no escaping it. Not without being out and out rude. And he hadn't gotten quite that uncaring of what people thought. "Jason."

"Brian," the young man offered quickly. "Brian Douglas. And this is Heather. My—" a goofy grin twisted the kid's mouth—"my *wife.*"

Heather giggled and planted a kiss on Brian's cheek—and Jason had to fight not to choke again. What *was* it about women that turned men momentarily mindless? Some men, anyway. To his recollection, he'd never let a woman scale the "center of my universe" pedestal.

Of course not. You were too busy being the center of other people's universes. There was no room for the incidentals—a woman, love, children—in your plans. Remember?

He shoved the mocking voice aside. True as it was, he had no desire to ponder his past. All he knew was that there would be a blizzard south of the border before Jason Tiber let a woman wrap *him* around her finger like a pipe cleaner.

Just then, Heather snuggled closer to Brian. "I'm cold, sweetie." She batted those baby blues up at him, her lip popping out in a perfect pout. Right on cue, good ol' Brian slid his arms around her, hugging her close.

Didn't the poor guy know how much trouble he was in?

Probably not. And it wasn't Jason's job to tell him. Not anymore.

He turned his gaze to look out the window, but the small woman perched on the bench seat in front of him caught his attention.

Again.

He frowned. What was her name? He'd heard it when she introduced herself to the ever-present Nikos. It was something odd…not a good, old-fashioned, normal name like Jane, Susan, or Ethel. He shook his head. He missed names like that.

He glanced at the woman in front of him again. Oh yeah, Mady. Mady Donovan.

The woman who'd used him as a landing pad. He couldn't hold back a smile at the thought—but he pushed it away as quickly as it appeared.

Not that he was against smiling. There was just no point in thinking about this wide-eyed pixie any more than he had to.

Speaking of eyes, what color were hers, exactly? At first glance he'd thought they were a kind of mossy brown. But when he'd held her in his arms, when she'd turned to gaze up at him and those bright eyes had peeked out from under her crazy cap of golden curls…

Green. Definitely green.

He could see them now. He'd have sworn they had a mystical kind of glow, like emeralds, so full of life and wonder and warmth they almost stopped his heart.

He frowned, remembering the moment….

He'd really wanted to plant a fist right on Nikos's nose when the schmuck had stepped up and slipped his arms around Mady.

Apparently the good Nikos saw himself as some kind of fairy-tale hero bent on saving the fair damsel from the dragon.

Well, this fair damsel could handle her own, and the dragons had best watch their behinds!

Sure, she looked harmless enough. He let his gaze rest on her, taking in the way she sat there on the bench seat in front of him, gazing out the window at the scenery. She was about as imposing as a pansy. So small and serene, a half smile on her face. Oh, it was a clever disguise. Nothing on the outside gave any warning of the disaster she could single-handedly bring crashing down about the ears.

But she'd felled him easily enough, like some kind of throwback David downing an unsuspecting—and, he might add, undeserving—Goliath.

He glanced down at the scratches on his hand; he could still see the imprint of the *fair damsel's* shoe there. But the stunned amazement he'd felt at finding himself facedown in the dirt—and then at having his hand used as a floor mat—was *nothing* compared to the reaction that had jolted through him when little Miss Twinkletoes had landed square in the middle of his back.

He'd expected her to be horrified. Expected her to leap to her feet, face red with humiliation, sensibilities offended at the admittedly unintentional contact. What he hadn't expected was the giggles.

Waves of them, ringing out, over and over, floating around him until he'd had to bite the side of his mouth to keep from laughing himself. What did he have to laugh about? The woman had knocked him on his face. Nearly broken his fingers. All but crushed his spine.

He made a face at that last one. Okay, there wasn't enough of her to crush anything. But it hadn't felt good. So he was glad he hadn't given in to the temptation to join her laughter. Last thing he needed was some kind of common bond with the woman.

Instead, he'd decided to take matters—and one blonde, walking disaster—into his own hands.

A smile tugged at his lips at the way she'd gaped up at him. Clearly, he'd surprised her. *Keep 'em thinking... that's my motto.* And from the pensive expression on her face right now, he was willing to bet she was doing plenty of thinking.

Probably about ways she could avoid him for the next four days.

Care to explain why you want her thinking about you?

Frowning at the thought, he looked down at his hand again. He didn't. Of course he didn't. What he wanted her to do was think about her own behavior, maybe even learn from the encounter and change for the better.

He pulled a face. It rang false even in his own mind. Better to dismiss the whole topic. The troublesome Mady Donovan wasn't the only person of interest in the van. Not by a long shot...

Jason's eyes drifted to the dark-haired woman lounging in the front passenger seat.

Mady was cute, no denying that. But this woman...well, she was flat gorgeous. As beautiful as they came. Jason grimaced. Probably as high mainte-nance, too. From the cheerless look on her face, she was far from happy to be here, but then, she didn't really fit in. Jason could more easily picture her floating into an elegant hotel or resort, piles of luggage in tow. Limos, five-star restaurants, Rodeo Drive...anyplace that cost lots of money and was filled with people ready and will-ing to do her bidding.

Yes, that setting suited this woman. Not a van

loaded down with gear, hiccuping its way over a gravel road made up mostly of ruts and potholes.

The minute they'd gotten off the plane, the woman had made a beeline for the van, pulling open the front passenger door and sliding into the seat. Hadn't lifted a perfectly manicured finger to help the guy with her when he pulled their bags from the plane. Staking territory. That's what she'd been focused on. Making it clear that she deserved the best seat in the house. Everyone else? They were on their own.

His mouth twitched. She'd be a handful, that much was certain. As for her hapless companion, good old Nikos...well, considering the man's physical similarities to the elegant woman with him, and considering how blatantly uninterested he'd been in her—and how blatantly interested he'd been in Mady—they had to be related. Cousins, maybe. Brother and sister. Something that made them close enough to treat each other with affectionate disdain.

Jason had watched with interest as Nikos zeroed in on Mady, like a hawk at lunchtime spotting a rabbit shivering in the grass. Of course, this little rabbit hadn't seemed at all averse to the attention directed her way. In fact, she'd soaked it up and turned back for more.

She was only doing it to get you riled.

It had worked. More than he cared to admit.

Why?

Jason grasped his hat and pulled it further down on his forehead, cutting off his line of vision. He was getting a bit fed up with the questions those inner voices kept throwing at him. Why did a woman he hardly knew get to him? How the blazes should he know? She just did, and that was all there was to it.

That, and the fact that he wasn't happy about it. Not one bit.

It was Earl's fault.

Like a dog finding a bone he'd been digging for, Jason clamped down on that satisfying fact. He shouldn't have to deal with Mady, or the honeymooners, or Nikos and his out-of-place companion. He should be sitting here swapping stores with a bunch of self-assured, experienced outdoorsmen. Emphasis on *men*.

What he *shouldn't* be doing was worrying about some little puff of a woman and why she got him riled. Why she made him feel peeved and protective all at once.

He shoved his knees against the seat in front of him and pressed himself back in his seat. Hunching down again, he crossed his arms, lowering his chin to rest on his chest. No point in making himself crazy. Mady Donovan would be history soon enough. As would this entire fiasco. Because the minute he hit the lodge, he was hunting down his good buddy Earl for a little one-on-one.

And if he didn't get the answers he was looking for, *somebody* was going to get slam dunked.

Earl Hunter loved what he did. Not just liked it. Not just got jazzed by it. He flat-out loved it.

Truth be known, nothing made him happier than taking people into the wilderness and watching them learn and grow and have the time of their lives. He figured God had made him specifically for this work, and that was why he was so good at it and enjoyed it so much.

This certainty made situations like the one he faced now a whole lot easier to endure.

He met Jason's hard glare without blinking. *Never let 'em see you sweat, isn't that how the saying goes?* But then, he didn't have any reason to sweat. He'd prayed about the group, asked God to show him the right person for Eva's replacement, and Jason's name had come to him as clear as the stars on a summer night.

So hey, this was God's doing, not Earl's. And on that basis, Jason could argue all he wanted, it wouldn't change anything. God wanted Jason here, with these people, in this place. Earl wasn't sure why, but that didn't matter.

God knew. That was enough.

"You tricked me."

It was the third or fourth time Jason had muttered the accusation. Earl noted with wry amusement that he was sounding a little less emphatic each time. He considered the charge thoughtfully. "And I did that…how?"

Apparently Jason found this question just short of absurd. "You're kidding, right?"

Earl moved around to the front of his desk, perched on the edge, and looked down at his friend. Jason was a good man. Had the potential to be a great man for God. If he could just get past who he was—and wasn't. "Not at all. I'd really like to know. How did I trick you?"

Jason threw up his hands. "How about *special request group?*" Sarcasm dripped off the words.

Earl spread his hands out in front of him. "And so it is."

"Come on! Your last special request group was a

bunch of guys into speed orienteering."

"That's what they requested, yes. This group is different."

"No kidding."

At Jason's muttered comment, Earl had to restrain a grin. "But they're a special request group all the same. They're here for specific reasons, Jason. And we need an even number in the group to accomplish what we've set up for them. The fact that they're not exactly what you expected just makes it that much more of an adventure."

Jason's look was about as dubious as it got.

Earl crossed his arms. "Think about it, Jas. Your patience and tolerance will be tested beyond anything you've been through in a very long time."

No response. Just a thinning of Jason's lips as he sat there.

A wave of compassion swept Earl, and he found himself wishing, as he'd often done in the past few years, that he could help his friend. He dropped his hands to his desk. "You said to let you know when the next vacancy opened up, and I did exactly that."

Jason looked like he wanted to argue, but Earl knew he wouldn't. He was too honest for that. Finally he just gave a dispirited nod. "Yeah, I know." He crossed his arms over his chest, looking about as receptive as a brick wall.

"Don't worry, Earl. I won't let you down. I'll do what I agreed to. I'll round out the group and I'll participate in the activities. But I'm not a baby-sitter. These people are on their own."

Earl studied his friend for a moment. "Jason, what were you hoping for when you called me?"

"I don't know. A break. Something to take my mind

off of…" He paused and his gaze swung to meet his friend's. Earl just waited. Finally Jason went on. "Things." He paused again, as though waiting for Earl to comment, but he still didn't say a thing.

Jason shifted in his chair, leaning forward to rest his forearms on his knees. "A challenge. I guess that's what I wanted. Some kind of challenge to overcome."

Earl grinned. "Well, there you go!"

The dazed exasperation in Jason's eyes made Earl laugh. "Think about it, Jas. What could be more challenging than spending four days in the North Cascade mountain wilderness with a group of people you don't know—"

"A group of *inexperienced*, green-as-grass people I don't know." He gave an annoyed shake of his head. "I wouldn't put it past them to waltz right off the edge of a cliff before the first day is over."

"Exactly my point! What could be more challenging than watching out for a group like that?"

Jason stiffened, his eyes narrowing a fraction. "Watching out for them?"

Earl held his friend's ambivalent gaze, not replying. Sometimes silence was the best response.

"Nuh-uh, buddy. Forget it. I already said I am not baby-sitting these people. Not what I signed on for."

At Earl's continued silence, Jason stood and paced. "Knock it off, Earl. I know what you're doing!"

Earl shifted his position, watching, not speaking.

Jason shot him an accusing glare. "You think I don't see what you're up to, but I do. Stick Jason with a bunch of know-nothings, and he won't be able to help himself. He'll reach out, help those poor little lambs, protect 'em—"

Earl almost flinched at the ice in Jason's tone, but he managed to maintain a neutral silence.

"—*shepherd* them." Jason's eyes were as cold as his voice. "Well, no thanks, buddy. Not interested. Never again. Not in this lifetime."

"I didn't arrange this intentionally, Jason."

The room was still for a moment, then Jason gave a frustrated sigh and dropped back into his chair. "I know."

"And, quite frankly, neither did you."

Jason stared at him hard, but Earl just shrugged. "You're here for a reason."

"A reason other than the fact that I wasn't as specific as I should have been?"

This time it was Earl whose expression hardened a bit, and Jason had the grace to look away.

"You wanted a break, well, here it is. So it's not what you expected. At least it's something different. You've done everything else, Jas. At least a couple of times. Rafting, mountain climbing, orienteering, the triathalon, scuba diving, *sky*diving—" he leaned forward, waiting for Jason to break in—"am I missing anything?"

"Quite a few, as a matter-of-fact."

At the self-satisfied reply, Earl was torn between the desire to belt Jason or just to give up. But he knew he couldn't do either. So he just concentrated on staying the course and trying to get through his thick-headed friend's armor. Just a tiny chink, that was all Earl was looking for. One little crack to squeeze through with the truth.

"I'm sure I am, and more's the pity."

He watched Jason hesitate at this, then sit up straighter. "Pity?"

His friend's complete disdain for the word was evident, and Earl held back a satisfied grin. He'd known that would get Jason's attention. He lifted his shoulders in an easy shrug. "I know you can do it all, Jas. So does anyone who's ever met you. So what I'm wondering, buddy, is what you're trying to prove?" Jason's cheeks took on a slight pink tint. "And to whom."

Silence. Earl hadn't expected anything else. He actually knew the answer to both questions, but now wasn't the time to say so. Jason wasn't any more ready to hear it than he was to say it. "Face it, bud, you've done it all. And you know as well as I do that it hasn't been enough. There's still something inside of you pushing for more. More extremes. More challenge."

After a few moments of strained silence, Jason gave a curt nod. "Okay, so you're right."

Earl grinned.

"You don't have to look so smug about it."

The muttered chastisement only tickled Earl even more. "So maybe the problem isn't that your little ventures aren't challenging enough so much as that they're the wrong kind of challenge."

Jason's eyes flickered at that, and he rested his elbows on his knees, eyes intense. "Meaning?"

Time to press his advantage. "Meaning why not try something different? Good night, pal, you've pitted yourself against almost every physical challenge you can find, but you've avoided the greatest challenge of all."

"And that would be, O Wise One?"

Earl straightened, then moved to rest one hand on Jason's shoulder. "People, my friend. You avoid people like the plague." Jason's almost eager air vanished as he stiffened again, but Earl didn't back down. "Don't you think it's time you faced your demons, Jas?"

The silence in the room was broken only by the steady ticking of the grandfather clock sitting in the corner of the room. Earl waited, knowing it could go either way. Jason could still stand up, wish him well, and walk out the door. If he wasn't ready, it wasn't going to happen.

But Earl had a feeling…

A low whoosh of air escaped Jason, and he rubbed a hand over his eyes. "Okay, Earl."

At the quiet concession, Earl let out a breath he hadn't realized he'd been holding. "Okay?"

"Okay. Maybe you're right." He pushed himself back in the chair, his hands gripping the armrests. "I'm not saying you are, mind you. Just…maybe."

He gave Jason's shoulder a pat and moved away. "Good." He kept his voice neutral, even though he wanted to jump up and down and do the biggest victory dance Washington state had ever seen. "So…you're in this for the duration?"

Jason's mouth twisted in a wry smile of amusement. "Up to my neck, it would seem."

Earl's responding grin and laughter were filled with a mixture of relief and triumph. "You won't regret this, Jason. I know it."

The other man just grimaced and rose from his chair. "I already do, old buddy. I already do." He headed for the door, then paused, his hand on the knob. He turned slowly, and for the first time in all the years Earl had known him, there was a flicker of uncertainty on Jason's face. "I hope you know what you're doing."

His response was swift and sure. "Always, old buddy. Always."

It was true. He did. It wasn't hard when all you did was follow the Lord's leading and then hold on.

As Jason pulled open the door and left the room, Earl gave in to the grin he'd been holding back. This time...this time he intended to hold on tight because he had the definite feeling they were in for the ride of their lives.

❦ 5 ❦

For when your faith is tested, your
endurance has a chance to grow.
JAMES 1:3

Mady rocked back and forth in the willow rocker, admiring the view from the porch of the Adventures Unlimited lodge.

Mountains towered all around, craggy peaks reaching up into the clouds like a toddler's fingers sinking into cotton candy. There was still snow in the higher elevations, and she shivered, glad they had opted against going that high.

A blanket of evergreens started at the timberline, cascading down the mountains and spilling into the valley. Just beyond the outbuildings in front of her—the stables and cabins—Mady could see more of the thick undergrowth and flowers she'd noticed when they landed an hour ago.

This had to be one of the most beautiful areas she'd ever seen. She leaned her head back, breathing in the heavy fragrance of evergreen. What must it be like to step out the front door every morning and see all of this?

Heaven.

The thought made her smile. She was taking a four-day vacation in heaven. She liked that.

Casting a quick glance down at her watch, she saw she had another fifteen minutes or so before she would join the others in the large, airy living room.

Earl Hunter, the owner of Adventures Unlimited and their guide for the week, had greeted them when the van delivered them earlier. Tall and lean, with weathered features that gave witness to a life spent in the out-of-doors, Earl was a man who looked able to tackle and overcome almost anything. His plaid shirt and stone-washed jeans gave him a comfortable appeal, and his broad grin was welcoming and amiable. Mady had liked him instantly.

His good-humored greeting still rang in her mind: "Well, folks, welcome to the time of your lives."

When he'd beamed at the group, a giggle had escaped Mady. She'd been trying to keep herself under control since her little outburst back by the plane, but the man's exuberance was positively contagious. He'd continued his upbeat chatter as he showed them the lodge, and before long, even good ol' Sourpuss had a smile on his face.

It had made him so much more attractive.

Earl led each of them to their rooms. "You won't have a lot of time in them today," he'd cautioned cheerfully as they walked down the hallway. "Just long enough to lay out your gear for inspection, maybe to freshen up a bit. It's eight o'clock now. We'll meet in about a half hour for a nice breakfast, then go over the plans for the next few days. Once that's done, I'll check out your gear, and then we'll get loaded up on the horses. Should be on our way by noon or so."

They came to Mady's room last. As Earl unlocked the door then handed her the key, he bent to pick up her bag.

Unfortunately, Mady did the same.

The collision of their foreheads resulted in a dull thunk—and in a series of stars momentarily exploding in Mady's head.

Earl's hand shot out to take hold of her elbow, and he chuckled. "I've heard of a meeting of minds before…"

Thankfully, the stars were dimming as Mady rubbed at her tender forehead. But she almost gave herself whiplash when a low voice behind her muttered, "Sure hope you've had a recent refresher course on first aid, Earl, ol' buddy."

Jason Tiber. Just perfect. Of all the people to be walking by just then, why did it have to be him?

"Just a few weeks ago as a matter of fact," Earl answered, tossing Jason a curious look. "Why?"

Jason kept walking, but his answer drifted back to them. "'Cause I've got a feeling you're going to need everything you've ever learned, pal." He looked up, and the devilish gleam in those blue eyes sent a little thrill of awareness zinging through her. "And then some." With that, he stepped into his room and closed the door.

She jerked her attention back to Earl, hoping he wouldn't ask her what that was about…or why her face was suddenly flaming red. It had to be, if the flash of heat assaulting her cheeks was any indication.

"I'm glad you came, Mady. I know it wasn't exactly what you had planned."

No doubt about it, Earl was a nice guy. She gave him a lopsided smile. "I take it you talked with your cousin?"

"She said you were dauntless in the face of opposition…but that she finally wore you down."

Pure Eva. And pure bunkum. "I'll just bet she did."

"Well…I may be embellishing a bit." His grin was unrepentant. "But I think you'll find you made the right decision." The laughter in his eyes faded, and he looked like a man with a lot on his mind. "God's up to something. I have a feeling this trip…this group is going to be something special."

He fell quiet for a moment, then as though pulling himself out of deep thought, he clapped his hands and directed another of those wholehearted smiles at her. "Anyway, you've got a little time now to get settled in—" He'd started to lean toward her pack, then jerked to a halt, watching her with teasing caution.

Mady stepped back, waving at the pack. "It's all yours."

Hefting it, Earl took it inside the room. "I heard the flight from Seattle was a bit…challenging."

Mady pushed away from the doorjamb. "Good word. Not as good as *horrible, atrocious, nauseating,* and *utterly terrifying,* but *challenging* is good."

His expression said he knew she was only half joking, and his smile told her it didn't bother him one bit. She found that reassuring. He set her pack on the bed. "Look at it this way: Between Eva's accident and the flight, you got the tough stuff out of the way right up front. From here on out things can only get better."

"Any chance you've got a direct line to God on that?"

The smile in his eyes was full of confidence. "No doubt about it. On that and every other issue I bring to Him. But then, so does every believer." He turned to leave, then paused. "Just listen for the breakfast bell. Should be ringing in twenty-five minutes or so. And believe me, you won't want to miss this meal."

Sure enough, the bell sounded right on time. Mady had found the others gathered in the spacious dining room where Earl ushered them to a huge table. Mady's mouth watered at the spread that awaited them. The tempting aromas drifted around her, and her stomach growled in eager response. Lea looked at her askance—obviously well-bred women didn't have gurgling stomachs-but the others merely laughed. Even Jason.

After sharing a hearty breakfast, Earl instructed them all to set out their equipment for his inspection. With the group in tow, he'd gone from room to room, looking everything over, making sure each person had packed only what was needed.

It hadn't taken him long to whittle things down to the basic necessities. Lea's bottle of exotic perfume had been the first item in the discard pile. When she started to protest, Earl just smiled at her.

"Well, you go on and take it along if you want, Miss Panopoulos."

With a triumphant smile she reached for the bottle.

Earl nodded. "Yup, gotta say it's mighty thoughtful of you to attract the bugs and bears so they won't bother the rest of us."

Lea paused in midreach. "Bugs?"

Earl planted his hands at the small of his back and stretched lazily, arching his shoulders back. "And bears. They seem particularly fond of the finer perfumes. Near connoisseurs, I'd say." A slight frown creased Earl's craggy face then as he shook out his arms. "Though I admit I'm not sure if they like the smell or the taste better."

The bottle stayed where Earl put it.

Next went the honeymoon couple's CD player, CDs, and two pairs of heated, battery-powered socks. Heather shrugged, her eyes wide, her cheeks tinged with pink. "My mother gave us those." She glanced up at Brian who was doing an admirable job of not laughing out loud. "To keep us warm in the mountains."

"Well, now, ain't it nice you got each other for that." At Earl's easy response Heather giggled and blushed prettily. The man was really a wonder, Mady thought. He was a veritable fount of knowledge and information, but he was much more than that. The more Mady watched him, the more she realized just how skillfully he handled people.

As the others left the room and headed down the hall, Mady touched Earl's arm. He paused, glancing back at her.

"That was really nice, the way you handled the situation with Heather."

Surprise shone briefly from his eyes, and then a slight blush colored his cheeks. "Thanks, Mady. That's awful nice of you to say so."

She grinned at him. She hadn't meant to embarrass the man, but it did tickle her a bit to see their usually unflappable guide somewhat flustered. She patted his arm. "Just wanted you to know I think you're awfully good at what you do, Earl."

He grinned at her. "Yeah, but you haven't seen me in the wilderness yet." He stepped aside so she could walk out of the room in front of him. "I just might lead you guys off a cliff somewhere."

Mady laughed as they exited the room, then paused in the hallway. Jason was there, leaning against the wall, arms crossed loosely. His considering gaze was on her, and she had the distinct impression he'd overheard her exchange with Earl.

He nodded at Earl as he walked past, but his eyes stayed on Mady. She couldn't read his face, but she thought she caught a glimmer of approval in those blue eyes. The thought both surprised and warmed her, like the sun popping out from behind the clouds when you've resigned yourself to a gloomy, overcast day. She gave him a bright smile, letting her appreciation show. But he'd already turned away.

Mady hurried to follow the group as they went into her room. Earl gave her a thumbs-up on her gear. "Good job, Mady."

Mady sent up a sigh of gratitude to Eva and her guidance. She hadn't been looking forward to discarding any of her things. She thought she'd whittled her stuff down to the bare minimum and was gratified that Earl seemed to agree.

She started to smile, but it stalled when Jason spoke up.

"What about her...books? Seems like unnecessary extra weight."

Mady glanced quickly at the bed where her things were laid out for inspection. She felt her brows gather in a frown. Two books. She had two stinkin' books! And she was pretty sure she knew which one Jason was objecting to.

Earl looked down at them as well. "A paperback on surviving in the wild and a compact Bible..." He reached down to pick them up, holding one in each hand as though weighing them. "They're small and light, not too much weight. And both should prove quite helpful."

"Well, the guidebook, sure…"

Earl fixed Jason with a friendly but firm look. "Which guidebook?"

Jason opened his mouth, then closed it, giving Earl a rueful smile. "You're the boss."

Earl glanced down at the Bible, then back up at Jason. "Sometimes. But if it were me, I'd want both of them on this trip. Never know when you'll need them."

Jason shrugged, but Earl wasn't finished. He reached up to rest his hand on Jason's shoulder as he walked past him. "Nice to have a partner with such foresight, eh, old buddy?"

A ferocious urge hit Mady at Earl's quiet words to toss a smug "So there!" in Jason's direction. It took some determination on her part, but she resisted.

She just settled for following Earl out the door of her room, a pleased smile on her face.

Remembering the brief triumph, Mady smiled again. Planting one foot on the plank floor of the porch, she pushed the rocker back and forth, leaning her head back, soaking in the stillness.

When was the last time she'd just sat and enjoyed silence? She couldn't remember.

The sound of the front door swinging open turned her head, and a small twinge of dismay pulled at her.

Jason Tiber stood there, hands in his pockets, staring at the mountains.

Mady stopped her rocking, sitting as quiet and still as she could. Maybe he wouldn't notice her.

No such luck. With a slow turn of his head, Jason fixed that pensive blue gaze on her. "How's the head?"

Mady grimaced. Oh, to be elegant and graceful. "Fine."

A small smile lifted his lips. "I've got some aspirin if you need it. Hate to have you start the day with a headache."

"It's...fine." Couldn't the man see she didn't want to talk about it?

He shrugged. "Whatever. Just trying to help."

She doubted it. But she resisted saying so. Of course, she wouldn't have had time to do so even if she'd wanted, for Jason had turned and walked down the steps, heading for the stables.

"See ya. Nice talking to you. Thanks for stopping by and ruining what was a peaceful moment," she muttered.

With an impatient huff, Mady pushed herself out of the rocker. She started toward the porch steps but halted when the lodge door opened and the new bride stepped out.

"Oh!" The younger woman smiled apologetically. "I didn't mean to run you over." She stuck out her hand. "I'm Heather Wi—" She shook her head, pink tinging her cheeks. "Used to be Wilson. Now it's Douglas."

Mady laughed. "Don't worry. You'll get used to it."

Heather sighed. "Soon I hope." Her eyes scanned the area. "Were you going to take a walk?" At Mady's nod, Heather's smile blossomed. "Mind if I join you?"

She hesitated, then forced the assent out. "Oh, uh, no, not at all." So much for a nice peaceful walk.

Together they made their way down the stairs, walking away from the buildings. "It's really beautiful here, isn't it?"

Mady let her gaze touch on the scenery. "Yes, it is."

They walked in silence for a few minutes, then Heather paused, lifting her hands high and drawing in a deep breath of air. Her eyes shone when she turned back to Mady.

"Aren't you just *thrilled* to be here?"

Mady laughed. The girl was nothing if not enthusiastic. "Well, I don't know about thrilled, exactly...but I'm glad." She wagged her head slightly side to side and gazed heavenward. She was where she was supposed to be. And she was glad to be here. "I think."

Oh, boy, didn't she sound definite? Mady chanced a look at Heather, but the younger woman didn't seem to notice. She was chattering away about her new husband, their new apartment, and how wonderful their life was going to be.

"And I don't even mind that our place is small, you know?" She waved her slim hands in the air. "I mean, we haven't actually lived there yet or anything, but I'm sure I'll love it."

Something in the girl's voice gave Mady the impression she was trying very hard to convince herself of that fact.

"Your apartment is small?"

"And dark. Really dar—" Heather's hand came up to cover her mouth. "I mean, I'm sure it will be fine."

Mady gave her a conspiratorial smile. "You know, Heather, you don't have to love everything about your apartment. And you can make changes, surprisingly small ones will make big differences."

Heather's eyes lit up. "Really? You know, I've been looking at magazines and things, trying to get some ideas, but it's all so overwhelming." She shook her head slowly. "I just don't think I'm the creative type."

Mady considered the younger woman with compassion. "You don't have to be creative, Heather, just know what you like. What colors, what textures…" Her gaze moved to the tall evergreens, the vibrancy of colors in the flowers, the majesty of the mountains….

"There's so much beauty to be found all around. And not just here. Everywhere. In any location…in people's homes. You'd be amazed at the way each home, each room, has a feel, a personality. All the little changes, the small touches you can make to transform houses into homes; rooms into havens, places of refuge—"

Mady broke off with an apologetic groan. "Oh, gosh, sorry, Heather. I didn't mean to babble." Poor girl was probably bored to tears!

But Heather actually looked delighted. "It sounds wonderful! Oh, I'd love to have you come see what you can do with our apartment."

Gratitude for Heather's reaction filled Mady. "Tell you what, before we head for home, I'll give you a list of easy things you can do no matter how small your place is. You'll be amazed at what a difference it will make."

Heather studied her for a moment, then touched Mady's arm gently. "You must really love doing this for people. Your face is glowing. Is this what you do professionally?"

"No, it's just a hobby."

"Well, anyone who loves it as much as you obviously do should think about doing it full time." Heather's straight, even teeth shone out. "I think you'd be wonderful."

Mady's mouth fell open, and she turned to stare at Heather. "Do you by any chance know a woman named Eva?"

Heather blinked at her like a perplexed hoot owl. Mady grinned and waved the question away. "Never mind."

They started walking again, and Mady soaked up the silence. For a few minutes, anyway.

"So why don't you do this interior design thing? I mean, you could just try it part time, you know."

From the mouths of babes...

Eva had been telling her the same thing for months. "Just give it a try. Just on weekends. What could it hurt?"

"Plenty, seeing as most of the people who want me to come see their homes are customers at the clothing store! If my boss finds out, she'd probably fire me."

"But these women came to you, not the other way around." Eva had sniffed dramatically. "If that's not a nudge from God, I don't know what is."

A nudge into the unemployment line, maybe. But no matter how she'd pushed the idea away, it wouldn't leave her alone. It kept pricking at her heart and spirit.

Follow me.

The words echoed in Mady's mind as they had so many times lately, and her stomach clenched.

She shook the struggle away, tired of dealing with it, but Heather was looking at her with a "Well?" on her face. "I've got a steady job, Heather. That's what counts right now."

Heather's pretty nose wrinkled. "Do you like what you do?"

I like paying my bills.

Mady didn't say it out loud. Instead she just sighed and glanced down at her watch. "We'd better be getting back. Don't want to be late."

Heather clapped her hands together. "Oh, I can hardly wait to get started."

"Me, neither." *Because the sooner we get underway, the sooner we get back.*

As they drew close, Mady saw Jason sitting on the porch steps, his arms resting on his knees, his watchful gaze fixed on her with what looked to Mady like amused curiosity.

It was the same expression she'd seen on people's faces when they watched the monkeys at the zoo.

She should look away. *Just give him a glare and look away.* That's what she should do. But she didn't. Couldn't, in fact. There was something about the look in his eyes that held her as effectively as a snare around a rabbit's foot…or its neck.

Then Jason winked.

The unexpectedly playful action—and the startling, plainly roguish gleam in his eyes—sent a jolt of surprise screaming through her and she jerked her head, looking away. But she found herself struggling with the uncomfortable sensation of someone swimming through glue. Nothing seemed to be working right. Her tongue felt thick, her mind dazed, and her pulse raced as though she'd just chugged thirty cups of very strong coffee. The emotions rampaging through her were as disturbing and intense as the gaze that had held her captive—surprise, uncertainty, confusion, apprehension…and a definite tingle of excitement.

He'd winked at her? *Winked* at her! What on earth

was *that* about? She lifted a hand to her burning cheeks and was dismayed to see how it trembled.

"Oh, help. What have I gotten myself into?"

The choked, whispered question galvanized her into action. She shoved her hands into her jeans pockets, lifted her chin, and marched toward the lodge, determination in every step.

I'll tell you what that wink meant. Jason Tiber is a man to be avoided at all costs!

And that's exactly what she was going to do. She would simply make a point of staying as far away from him as she could during the week. She wasn't going to waste one more second, one more ounce of emotional energy on the infinitely irksome Jason Tiber.

After all, they would be in a vast mountain wilderness. There was no earthly reason she should have to put up with the man for even a moment.

No earthly reason at all.

🖤 6 🖤

My power works best in your weakness.
2 CORINTHIANS 12:9

Mady settled into the overstuffed chair, enjoying the feel of being engulfed in the soft cushions.

Earl waited until everyone was situated, then gave them a quick, efficient rundown of their schedule.

"Okay. Today we ride to the halfway point. Once there, we'll take care of the horses, set up sleeping sites, and have dinner." His teeth gleamed white in his tanned face. "Believe me, that will be enough. Tomorrow, we ride the rest of the way to base camp. Should hit it around noon or so if we get off in a timely fashion."

"Meaning?"

Earl shifted his attention to Nikos. "Meaning around seven."

"In the morning?"

Lea had almost yelped the question, and Mady worked hard to restrain a smile at the alarm in the other woman's face.

"Not to worry." Earl's tone was soothing. "You'll get to bed plenty early. Believe me, you'll be tired and ready to sleep. Which means you'll be ready to get up nice and early. You'll see." His grin was coaxing. "Trust me."

"I hardly think I have a choice."

At Lea's muttered reply, Earl gave a good-natured shrug. "Anyway, once we reach base camp, we'll set up

sites, and have some lunch. Then you'll familiarize yourselves with your gear and with the area. We'll take a day
hike, practice route finding, forge some creeks, maybe
hunt up some mushrooms for dinner."

"It sounds as though we're together most of the
time."

If Jason's slightly pained expression was any indication, he wasn't exactly thrilled at the prospect.

"You'll spend time together as a group, yes." Earl
took a sip of his coffee. "But you'll also work in three
teams of two. And that's where you'll learn your most
important lessons. Like communication. And listening.
How to understand your environment and each other
better. How to work together to meet a goal. We'll practice some basic outdoor skills, including how to set up a
site, how to find your way in the wilderness, what to do
if you get lost…that kind of thing."

He studied them carefully, and Mady wondered
what he thought of this group as he looked at them. But
his expression was neutral as he went on. "More than
anything else, this is a time for each of you to learn how
to exist in harmony with your surroundings. And all it
will take is a little training—" his grin broadened—"and
a lot of cooperation."

Mady caught herself nodding. Well, why not?
Cooperation was good. She gave Lea a quick glance, taking in the lovely woman's stiff posture and the hesitant
look in her eyes. Mady was hoping Lea would loosen up
some once they headed out. She'd hate to be partnered
with someone who was clearly so unhappy to be there.

Standing from the chair he'd been sitting on, Earl
moved to lean casually against the back of the chair and

take a long sip of coffee. His eyes positively glowed with anticipation. "On the third day you'll break up into three teams and head out for the day. Each team will have a specific route to follow. You'll have maps and compasses, which you'll have learned to use the day before. You'll hit a series of checkpoints, have lunch, then come on back to base camp."

"Teams, eh?" Nikos leaned back in his chair. "Need we guess who is teamed with whom?"

Apparently Earl wasn't ready to share that information yet. He just smiled at Nikos and set his coffee mug on the end table. "Tonight is the easy night. It's your first night together, so take it easy, get to know one another a little. Relax and let us give you the royal treatment. Tomorrow, however, will be a whole new day. Your goal here is to learn all you can, to be open to the lessons all around you, and to face them as a team. So be prepared. No one—" Earl fixed each of them with a firm look— "will receive special treatment."

Special treatment?

Mady frowned. She wasn't expecting it. Neither, she was sure, was anyone else.

Once again her gaze came to rest on Lea.

Well, okay, so almost anyone else.

She turned her attention back to Earl, forcing herself to listen as he went on.

"Now, back to your question about partners, Nikos."

Nikos held up a hand. "I know, I know. You do not need to tell me." He cast a slightly displeased look in his sister's direction. "Lea and I are partners."

Earl nodded. "Yup. But to clue in everyone else,

Nikos and Lea were sent on this little expedition by their grandfather, who happens to be the head of the family business."

"Wanted a break from you, eh?"

Nikos grimaced at Jason's comment. "No more so than we wanted a break from him."

Lea's lips tightened at the conversation, and Mady shifted in her chair. So much for being partnered with Lea.

"Actually, their grandfather told me these two need to learn to work together." Earl's grin was purely self-satisfied. "And believe me, they will."

Mady didn't laugh with the others. She couldn't dredge up the sound. It was strangled somewhere in her throat, thanks to the realization that had just smacked her between the eyes.

If Nikos and Lea were partners…

"As you've probably guessed, Heather and Brian are here to enjoy spending time together, since this is a portion of their honeymoon. So they will be team two—"

And if Heather and Brian were a team, then…

"Which means you, Mady, have the great fortune of being partnered with my buddy, Jason."

She'd blinked. Looked around. Jason? Her partner was…Jason Tiber?

Earl's voice went on, as calm as you please, not even pausing over the bombshell he'd just dropped on Mady's head. "Okay, so Lea and Nikos make up team one, our newlyweds are team two—" he smiled at Brian and Heather—"and Jason and Mady will be…?"

"Team three," everyone responded.

Everyone but Mady. She just sat there, hands gripping the arms of her chair, staring at the rustic, rough-hewn log walls.

Oh no. No, no, no...tell me this is a mistake. Wasn't it enough that she'd sent the man sprawling into the dirt? That she'd treated his back like a landing pad? That she'd given him far too many opportunities to mock her already?

Did she have to be partnered with him? How on earth was she going to avoid him if he was her partner?

She couldn't groan, not with everyone sitting around her. Instead, she clenched her teeth and managed to return Earl's pleased smile. Of course, her own smile was decidedly forced, but at least she wasn't doing what every nerve in her body commanded her to do.

Scream. Loud and long.

As for Jason, his reaction had been...nothing. Not good, not bad. He'd just glanced at her, taking in what she was sure had been her stunned expression with a bland look. Then he turned to offer the dry comment, "Gee, thanks Earl. You're a real pal."

God, are You sure You know what You're doing? Why this man? Why on earth team me with this man?

Jason Tiber was the only person she'd ever met who could confuse her without even trying...who could, with the barest economy of words, get her so frustrated that she was ready to toss her lifelong values to the wind and do the man bodily harm.

And that man was her partner?

I suppose the fact that he's the first man in a very long time to make your knees weak and your head spin has nothing at all to do with your dismay over this, now does it?

Mady grimaced. Well, *of course* it did.

All the more reason to stay as far away from him as

possible. But nooo. Not only was she not going to be able to avoid him, she was teamed with the man! She had to be around him, talk with him on a repeated basis, look into those eyes, endure those dimples—or, more likely, that glare—for the next several days.

A small groan escaped her at that, and she glanced around to see if anyone noticed.

So far so good. Earl just sailed on through the rest of his explanation. Lea and Nikos were listening with half-bored expressions. Brian and Heather were engrossed. And Jason...

Oh, dear.

He was watching her, his eyes gleaming with amusement, a small smile of anticipation on his face.

The wretch looked as though he were enjoying this!

Well, of course he would. She was sure her dismay was evident on her face, and that probably brought him great pleasure.

She barely restrained the urge to make a face at Jason and settled for letting her displeasure shine from her eyes before turning to stare at the potted plant in the corner of the room.

This is a test, isn't it, Lord?

Mady brightened. That had to be it. A test of her patience, her graciousness, her sanity—

She shook that last one away. Okay, so she and Jason were partners. No big deal. She wouldn't let it ruin her week. As a matter of fact, she'd take it for the challenge it was. And she would overcome. All it would take was a little determination and some prayer.

A quick glance back to her erstwhile partner showed he was still watching her, and his smile was broader than ever. She looked away, biting her lip so hard she was surprised she didn't draw blood.

Make that a lot of prayer. As in massive. Huge. More than she'd ever uttered in her life. And she might as well start right now.

Oh, help…

Within an hour after that informative, albeit disconcerting meeting, the horses were saddled up, gear was packed, and the group was ready to go.

Mady and the others had met the wrangler, been assigned horses—Mady was delighted with her spirited buckskin, Dorado—and done several run-throughs on tack, gear, care of the animals, and riding basics. It was obvious everyone had ridden before, even Heather and Brian. Mady breathed a sigh of relief as she watched them handle their horses with confidence. She'd half-expected Heather to need training wheels on hers.

Pulling one last time on the straps securing her gear, Mady found her attention wandering…and landing on Jason. He looked like a cowboy about to go out on a roundup—just a bit rugged, just a bit wild. He swung into the saddle of his coal black mount with athletic grace and ease. Sitting there, tipping his hat back on his head and settling back in the saddle, the man looked as though he'd been born riding.

Stick to the issue, Mady. Look at the heart, remember? The fact that the man just happens to look like every girl's dream doesn't really matter.

Maybe not, but it was a bit hard to ignore.

You just aren't trying hard enough. Or at all, for that

matter. She bit her lip. In all likelihood, the best thing she could do for her concentration—and her peace of mind—was find a way not to think of Jason at all.

She'd no sooner made that decision than she was stealing another quick glance at the man she wasn't going to think about.

He had one hand relaxed on his thigh and the reins casually woven in his fingers. His head was bent as he talked with Lea Panopoulos. She stood beside his horse, her long fingers curled into the animal's mane where it rested near the saddle, her smile warm as she laughed up at him. Jason laughed in response, apparently delighted with whatever Lea was saying.

The annoyance that followed on the heels of this sight was as immediate as it was troubling. Mady turned her attention to the cinch she was supposed to be tightening and gave it a jerk.

With a startled whicker, Dorado tossed his head and stamped a hoof. Biting her lip, Mady reached out to pat the horse's neck. "Sorry, boy. Didn't mean to pull that hard." The horse angled a sideways look at her, and the message in its dark eyes was clear: Well, don't do it again!

She shook her head as she looped the end of the cinch strap and secured it. What did she care if Lea—or *any* other woman, for that matter—stood there, gazing up wide-eyed and clearly admiringly at Jason Tiber?

Actually, she should be glad to see Lea's obvious interest in the man. Maybe he'd shift his irritating attention from Mady, who didn't care for it at all, to the dark-eyed beauty.

Amazing just how disagreeable that thought was.

"What brings such dark storm clouds to such a lovely brow?"

Caught off guard at the low words, Mady spun around. Too abruptly, apparently, for one foot slipped in the loose gravel, and she lurched forward. Strong hands caught and steadied her.

She glanced up to find Nikos's dark eyes laughing down at her. "Now that's what I like to see, a woman unafraid to throw herself into my arms."

Tipping her mouth into a rueful grin, Mady straightened. "Oh, Nikos, I'm sorry. I really need to be more careful before I hurt someone."

Somewhat reluctantly, Nikos let his hands fall away. "I do not mind, Mady. And you are hardly big enough to hurt anyone."

"Hmpf." She brushed at her jeans. "I'll wager the good Jason Tiber would be willing to argue that point."

Nikos tilted his head, a wry smile on his face. His gaze drifted toward Jason and Lea, then back to Mady, and his shoulders lifted in an expressive shrug. "Is that what troubled you when I came up? You seemed somewhat…displeased."

Mady looked down, heat stealing into her face. Displeased? Yes, she was that. But not with Lea. Not really. She was most displeased with herself, her traitorous heart, her weak will.

The last thing she'd had this much trouble resisting was a box of Godiva chocolates she'd gotten for her birthday! And she'd been able to stick those in a drawer and ignore them.

But Jason…well, she didn't think there was a drawer big enough to hold him.

She'd never thought it of herself before, but Mady was starting to think she was an emotional wimp. Bad enough that she couldn't get her mind and spirit settled on issues that really applied to her life, issues like what she wanted to be when she grew up. Like why she could trust God one minute and be filled with anxiety or terror the next.

But to have to deal, on top of all of that, with a man who could confuse her without even trying—A gentle touch on her shoulder drew her attention. Nikos studied her, his dark gaze compelling in its compassion. "Sometimes the best answer is the easiest, yes? If something plagues you to distraction, simply do not allow it further access into the mind." His elegant brows raised a fraction. "Or the heart."

A hot protest jumped to Mady's lips that Tiber had any claim on either, but she fell silent. Once again, as much as she wanted to do so, she couldn't deny it. Jason was on her mind. As for her heart…

Images drifted through her mind…being held in his arms, having her gaze captured by him…that brief, charged moment after she'd knocked him down when their eyes had met and held. Something had passed between them. And despite the fact that it was vaguely disturbing, she was honest enough to admit it drew her.

Yes, indeed. Nikos had hit the proverbial nail smack on the head—and Mady desperately wished she had some aspirin.

Grimacing slightly, Mady brushed a stray wisp of curl away from her face. "You're probably right, Nikos."

His teeth gleamed white in his handsome face. "Of course I am. Now—" he cupped his hands in front of her and waggled his eyebrows—"won't you do me the honor of placing yourself in my hands?"

Mady couldn't help it; she laughed. Nikos was a great guy...compassionate, encouraging, and witty. Why on earth couldn't she obsess over him?

She turned, lifting a foot toward him. Cupping her heel firmly, he gave her a leg up into the saddle.

She shifted slightly, finding the most comfortable position, then looked down. Nikos's eyes watched her thoughtfully, and a small smile played at his lips.

"All right, give over. What are you laughing at?"

At her playful question, his smile grew wider. "I was just thinking how careful one needed to be with you."

"Careful?" She fit her foot into the stirrups, pushing her heel down, loving the feel of being in the saddle again. This was going to be fun.

"Indeed. It's not often one finds a woman strong enough to send a man sailing through the air—"

"Nikos!"

He didn't even hesitate at her laughing chastisement—"*and* light enough to toss into the trees, should one be so inclined."

She reached down to swat at him, and he deftly caught her hand, turned it over, and pressed a light kiss to the back of it.

Mady didn't pull away. Instead, she squeezed his hand gently. "Nikos...thank you."

One dark brow lifted slightly. "For the kiss?"

She gave him a light tap on the head with her free hand. "For everything. Your kindness, your wisdom—" she felt her throat tighten—"for...everything."

She had the distinct impression he wanted to say

something, but he just patted her hand gently and then let her go. "What are friends for?"

"Exactly," Mady said as she straightened in the saddle. Nikos was fast becoming that to her. A much appreciated friend.

He reached up then, laying his hand over hers where it rested on Dorado's neck. "Do you know, my dear Mady, that there are many wonders to be known in this life?"

She started to respond, but he stopped her with a raised hand. "The sad thing is that we're often so busy looking for what we *think* we need that we miss the very answers we long for."

At the unexpected warmth in his voice, Mady was torn between pleasure and a twinge of self-consciousness. She glanced away, wishing she knew what to do or say in response. Fortunately, Lea intervened.

"Nikos, I am not your stable hand. I've been holding your horse for long enough. Either mount up, or I will let the wrangler return him to the stables."

Nikos looked to the heavens, uttered an exaggerated sigh, and then winked at Mady "Ah, my sister's dulcet tones beckon, and I obey." With that, he turned and headed for his horse, leaving Mady caught in a tangle of emotions.

She leaned forward, resting against Dorado's long neck, burying her fingers in his mane. The horse nickered softly, tossed his head, and pawed at the ground. The message was clear: Let's get this show on the road!

"I'm with you, boy." She straightened. "The sooner we get going, the sooner the next four days will be over." With a fortifying breath, she gathered the reins and turned Dorado toward the trail.

Why couldn't men be as easy to read as horses?

❧ 7 ❧

Behold the turtle. He makes progress
only when he sticks his neck out.
JAMES BRYANT CONANT

"Okay, folks, gather round and listen up."

Mady leaned forward in the saddle and patted her mount's sleek, golden neck. The muscles quivered beneath her fingers—a sign he was more than ready to keep going—and she grinned. Apparently Dorado was having as much fun as she was.

They'd been on the trail now for about two hours, and Mady was pleased she wasn't even sore yet. Well—she shifted in the saddle, trying to ease the complaining muscles in her backside—not much.

She drank in the rugged beauty that surrounded her. They'd followed a well-marked albeit primitive trail up the mountainside. The path twisted and turned as it wound its way through woods, over creeks, past towering cliff faces, going ever higher and higher.

The horses had moved forward with confidence. Clearly they'd gone this way plenty of times before.

As for the weather, it couldn't have been more accommodating: a clear, brilliantly blue sky; just enough sun to warm their faces; just enough breeze to keep them from getting overly warm. The ride so far had been beautiful, exhilarating.

And only a tiny bit unnerving.

For the last half hour or so, the trail they were following had been flanked on one side by the mountain and the other by a sheer drop-off, just past the line of trees.

When they'd reached the first sight of the drop-off, Heather had reined in her horse. "You're kidding." She cast Earl a plaintive look. "Tell me you're kidding."

"Hon, Earl knows what he's doing." Brian took her hand in his, and Mady found herself wondering what it would be like to have someone to care about her that way, someone to reassure her, to hold her hand when she was nervous.

Nice. That's what it would be like. Very, very nice.

Earl brought his horse next to Heather's. "Brian's right, Heather. It may look a bit scary here, but there's really nothing to worry about. Just stay on the path. It's solid and plenty wide, see?" His hand pointed to the fact that both their horses fit side-by-side with room to spare. "If you don't trust the path, trust the horses. They're all familiar with it. Just loosen your grip on the reins, and let your horse have her head." He patted Heather's mount fondly. "Buttercup here knows what to do."

"Let the horse have her head?" Heather's eyes all but bugged out of her head. "You mean, just let the horse do what it wants? No way, I'm going to be in control here."

Earl's features grew firm. "Being in control isn't what matters here, Heather. Relaxing and trusting, that's what matters."

"Trust a *horse?*"

Earl's grin was back. "Trust the one who's been here countless times before and knows the way forward and back." He shrugged. "That can apply to the horses, or it can apply to me. Whatever works."

Mady had felt a flash of compassion for the young woman and a bit of respect when she bit her lip and nodded. She could have turned back. But she didn't. And that counted for something.

"Planning to join the circle, Miss Donovan?" Jason's sardonic question surprised her—both because it was spoken so close to her and also because he'd scarcely spoken to her the entire ride.

She looked at him curiously. Why had he broken his seeming vow of silence now? "The circle?"

He inclined his head, and she looked where he indicated. Everyone had gathered their horses in a half circle around Earl. Everyone but her.

And her partner, who'd clearly come to corral her.

"Oh…I'm sorry!"

At her quick apology, Jason opened his mouth. Mady steeled herself for whatever verbal dart he was going to toss, but it never came. Instead, he hesitated, then shrugged. "Don't sweat it. You haven't made us wait too long. Just a few minutes, more or less."

As grudging as the comment sounded, Mady couldn't help but smile. Kind words! As kind as Jason had spoken to her so far, anyway.

"Thanks—"

But Jason had already turned his horse to join the others. She didn't let that dampen her optimism, though. She'd take whatever encouraging signs she could get. And this definitely was one. She and Jason had had a conversation, brief though it may have been, that hadn't ended up in a debate, an out-and-out argument, or with either one of them facedown in the dust.

Hey, it was a start!

Earl welcomed the two of them with a smile, then hooked one knee over his saddle horn and rested his forearms on his leg. "Okay, group. This is where we're stopping for lunch. You were all supplied with sack lunches before we left today, so find a good place to tether your horse and take a break. We've got a half hour until we need to hit the road again."

"How much further is it to the campsite?" Brian's tone was filled with excitement, and Mady grinned at his enthusiasm.

"Another two hours or so. This is the halfway point. Once we're there, we'll get the sites set up. Then you'll have a little free time until dinner."

"What are you fixing?"

Earl answered Lea's question with a cheeky grin. "Me? Nothing."

She stared at him, eyes wide. "Nothing? But—"

"From the time we left the lodge, you folks were on your adventure, remember? The meals are up to you, not to me. I've got the supplies, but the setting up, fixing, and cleanup is all yours."

Lea did not look happy. Nikos, on the other hand, was almost crowing. "Lea? Cook? Did you bring a plentiful supply of antacids?"

She shot her brother a murderous glare, and he held his hands out as though warding her off. "I'm sorry, my sister, but we're supposed to see things we've never seen before, remember? And I've seen *that* lovely look at least a thousand times in my life."

"And deserved every one of them, my brother." Lea tossed her head with a sniff. "What a terrible pity it is,

Nikos, that you are not nearly so amusing to the rest of us as you are to yourself."

Mady wagered, had she been on the receiving end of that glacial comment, she would have frozen solid. Nikos, however, didn't seem the least bit bothered. If anything, he was enjoying himself.

Brian interrupted the exchange. "Heather can cook. She's great at it!" He beamed at his wife, and her cheeks bloomed with color.

"We're *all* going to cook at some point." Earl was clearly doing his best not to laugh. "Each team will be assigned certain duties for each meal time, which will include anything from food preparation to cooking to washing dishes and cleanup."

"Washing dishes?" Now it was Nikos who looked unhappy, and Lea sneered at him as she slid from the saddle.

"Do not worry, Nikos. I'm sure your manicure will survive." She shot a smug look at Mady. *"Not!"*

Laughter escaped Mady at hearing this teen collo-quialism from the oh-so-elegant Lea. Maybe there was more to this woman than Mady had thought.

Reining Dorado toward a nice, sturdy tree, Mady slid from the saddle, tethered her mount securely, then pulled her sack lunch and water bottle from her pack. She pulled out several carrots that she'd added to the sack and offered them to her horse, chuckling as he gob-bled them greedily.

Wiping her hands on her jeans, she gave a happy sigh. She'd spotted the perfect place for a lunch perch: a large boulder that was half in the shade, half in the sun. She reached it just as Jason did.

He looked from her to the boulder. "Dibs."

At his low, amused word, she eyed him, pursing her lips, then stuck her hand in her pocket and pulled out a quarter. "Flip you for it."

His lips twitched. "Heads."

She nodded and sent the coin flipping into the air. It made a graceful arc then landed in the dirt, sending up a tiny cloud of dust. Jason knelt down, gently brushed away the dirt, then looked up at her, tipping his head in concession. "Tails. You win."

Mady clapped her hands, then stuck one out to him. He looked from it to her, then slowly reached out to take it.

She pulled him up with a grin. "Okay, so if I win, I get to say what happens, right?"

"Just with the rock."

Mady planted her hands on her hips. "Yes, just with the rock." She shook her head and muttered under her breath, "Good night. Some people have no trust in their souls whatsoever."

His lazy gaze rested on her. "What was that? You were muttering. I couldn't hear."

"I said we should share the rock." Surprise lit his eyes, and she pointed at the boulder in debate. "There's plenty of room for both of us, don't you think?"

He turned around slowly, his gaze drifting from her to the boulder, then back again. "You sure you want to make that offer?"

There was a gleam in his eyes she didn't quite understand, but she didn't back down. "Yes. I'm sure."

His eyes narrowed slightly. "Sun or shade side?"

She didn't even hesitate. "Sun."

Neither did he. "Done."

He walked toward her, and she thought she saw laughter in his eyes. He stuck a hand out toward her. "Deal?"

"Deal." She slid her fingers into his for a quick shake, noting how his hand engulfed hers. Why that warmed her so much, she didn't care to explore. Any more than she wanted to analyze why what had just transpired between the two of them should make her feel like a kid who'd just received the gift she'd always wanted for Christmas.

Really, when it came down to it, Mady reasoned as she followed Jason to the boulder, there was simply no point in dissecting her every reaction to this man. She already knew most of them didn't make much sense. Why not just relax and enjoy the truce they seemed to have declared?

Besides, who knew how long it would last.

The boulder was huge. The top came up to her shoulders. Fortunately, it had enough bumps and crevasses that she should be able to get a solid foothold. Shifting her bag and canteen to one arm, she gripped at the rough rock with her free hand and sought a foothold. She'd managed to climb about halfway up when one foot slipped, and she fell forward.

"Whoof!"

Her chest landed against the rock, crushing her lunch bag between the canteen and the boulder. Blowing her hair out of her eyes, she started to clamber back up when a pair of strong hands circled her waist from behind and lifted her into place. Warmth stole into her face as she looked back at Jason. "Thanks."

He didn't reply. He just watched her get herself situated, then tilted his head. "You know, you remind me of a song."

She opened her bag and pulled out her flattened sandwich. Her lips twisted. Oh yummy. She peered out from under her bangs to meet Jason's laughing gaze. "Oh? A song, huh? Let me guess. 'Something in the Way She Moves'? Or—" she took a munch of her flat but nonetheless tasty sandwich—"I've got it, 'Shake, Rattle, n' Roll'?"

Amusement danced in his eyes. "Actually, I was thinking more along the lines of 'Amazing Grace.'" He climbed onto his side of the boulder with athletic ease. "Or the lack thereof."

There was no sarcasm in his tone, just fun, and Mady found herself smiling in response. "'Amazing *Lack of* Grace,' eh?" She considered it, then shook her head slowly. "Nope, doesn't work."

"Not for God, perhaps…" At her quick look, he held out a forestalling hand. "Not according to your perspective, anyway."

Fortunately, her orange seemed to have survived the mashing process she'd put her bag through, so she started to peel it. "But?"

"But—" he said around a mouthful of sandwich—"I think it works just fine for…others."

She popped a juicy slice in her mouth, savoring the tart juice as it trickled down her throat. "Others…like me."

He smiled and gave a small nod. "Like you."

She wrinkled her nose but kept her tone light and teasing as she replied. "Yeah, well, shows what you know."

His gaze caught hers and held it. "I think you'd be surprised."

The comment was low and lazy, but there was something burning in his eyes that challenged her in a way she didn't understand. Suddenly uncomfortable, she looked away.

Setting the remnants of her lunch aside, she pulled her knees to her chest and circled them loosely with her arms. The warmth of the sun felt wonderful through her heavy denim shirt. She felt attuned to the fragrances and sounds all around them. Almost as attuned as she was to the man beside her. Though, as she'd pointed out, the boulder was large enough that there was ample distance between them, she was still singularly aware of Jason sitting there, mirroring her motions as he, too, pulled his lunch out of the sack. They sat in a comfortable silence.

Mady forced herself to turn her attention from the man seated near her to the others. They'd scattered to various locations and were now immersed in each other.

Brian and Heather were sharing a fallen log, looking as snug and content as kittens in a basket. They were talking in low voices, and Heather reached up with a giggle to wipe a glob of mustard from Brian's chin. The twinge of envy that shot through Mady took her by surprise. What would it be like to have that connection with someone? To be so clearly for each other, so content in each other's presence?

Someday, Lord?

She stuffed the plea back where it had come from, somewhere deep within her heart. If God wanted that kind of sharing for her, it would come. In His good time.

All she had to do was be patient.

The fact that she'd been supremely patient for thirty-five years now didn't matter. Or it never had before. But now…

Now it still didn't matter. Mady shook off the uncomfortable subject, took another chomp of her sandwich, and stretched her legs out in front of her. Lea and Nikos seemed to have achieved détente as well. They'd spread their lunches out on a large, flat rock between them. For all of their bluster and insults, Mady had a feeling these two were quite close. She watched them as they sat together, engrossed in conversation. From time to time Lea reached out to touch her brother's arm, and he gave her a teasing grin.

Just then Nikos glanced Mady's way and waved at her. "Mady, come join us. You don't need to sit over there all by yourself, you know."

"I'm not alone, you silly man," Mady replied.

Nikos's dark brow creased. "You're not?"

"Of course not, Nikos," Lea joined in. "She's at one with all of nature around her."

Mady laughed and shook her head. "Very funny. But I was talking about—" she glanced over her shoulder— "my unusually mute partner…"

The words died in her throat. She was alone.

She scanned the area, peering into the woods around them, down the path. Jason was nowhere to be seen. She'd been so determined to focus on anything but him that she hadn't even been aware he'd left.

Well!

"You were talking about what?"

At Nikos's question, Mady spun back around. "My…

uh, my part in the scheme of creation." She nodded quickly. "Like Lea said. Sort of. In a little different way, but kind of the same." The two faces studying her were filled with confusion.

Mady made a show of glancing at her wrist, hoping against hope that she was far enough away that neither Nikos or Lea could tell she didn't have a watch on. "Oh gee, look at the time!" She jammed the rest of her sandwich back into the sack and jumped off the boulder. "Better go check on Dorado before we're ready to go." She waved jauntily. "'Bye, you two."

Spinning on her heel she hurried back to Dorado, who thankfully was out of the brother and sister's line of sight. Muttering to herself, Mady shoved the crumpled sack back into her pack and secured it with a jerk.

Perfect. Just perfect. The other two teams were sitting there, bonding, having a good time, laughing and talking…and what does *her* partner do? Disappear into thin air without so much as a "See you later."

Common courtesy, Lord. That's all I ask for. Obviously, it was too much for the good Jason Tiber to handl—

Be still.

She blinked, jerking her head to the side. She could have sworn the words had been whispered in her ear. No one was there…but the words came again.

"Be still…wait patiently…"

They echoed in her mind and rang in her heart, leaving her standing there motionless and silent. All her frustrated thoughts melted away as the source of the words came back to her. Psalm 37. She'd memorized it several years ago. Her heart tightened in her chest when she remembered why. She'd chosen it specifically to combat her tendency to overreact when she felt she'd been mistreated.

As she was doing now.

Closing her eyes, she searched her memory. It had been a long time since she'd recited or even read the psalm, but bits came back, washing over her, bathing her spirit, refreshing her like a drink of sparkling water from a mountain spring.

"Don't fret...or be envious...Trust in the LORD and do good...Take delight in the LORD, and he will give you your heart's desires..."

Her heart's desires. She ached at the thought.

"Commit everything you do to the LORD. Trust him, and he will help you. He will make your innocence as clear as the dawn... Be still in the presence of the LORD, and wait patiently for him. Stop your anger! Turn from your rage! Do not envy others—it only leads to harm....But those who trust in the LORD will possess the land....Those who are gentle and lowly will possess the land; they will live in prosperous security."

Gentle and lowly. Don't fret.

She hugged herself, opening her eyes and looking away. How far she was from meekness, from not fretting. How far she was from peace.

Brushing the tears from her face, Mady looked down the path that had brought them up the mountainside. What had Earl told them? *"Stay on the path.... Control isn't what counts, it's trust that counts."*

Good counsel. If only she'd heeded it with her heart as well as with her horse.

Something hard pushed between her shoulders, and the next thing she knew she was stumbling forward.

Catching her balance, she looked back at Dorado, mouth agape. The crazy beast had planted his muzzle in the middle of her back and shoved! Laughter bubbled up within her, and she held out her hands in surrender. "Okay, okay, I get the message. Walk it off, right?"

The buckskin tossed his head and gave a loud snort. Mady laughed out loud. So *that's* where Jason learned it!

Still grinning, she headed down the path. She figured she had at least another ten minutes or so until they had to head out. Plenty of time to get her head and heart straightened out.

Just as she rounded a bend, a shrill sound pierced the air. Mady halted, turning her head, seeking the source of the sound. It went off again, and she realized it was coming from a tall evergreen at the side of the path. She moved closer, squinting slightly as she scanned the branches through the thick needles…then her mouth opened in a delighted *O*.

There, just above her, a large, chubby squirrel was perched on one of the branches. Its beady black eyes were fixed on Mady, its tail fluffed out like a bottlebrush, and it was scolding her for all it was worth.

Mady clapped her hands, then her breath caught in her throat. Two or three smaller squirrel faces peered from behind the noisy scolder. Youngsters. They had to be.

Holding her breath, moving with slow, calculated steps, Mady eased toward the edge of the trail. She just wanted one closer look at the tiny crew. She inched forward until the toes of her shoes were poised at the brink of the drop-off. A careful glance down told her she'd better not go any further. Curious, she nudged a small rock with her toe and watched as it bounced down the incline and then launched into space.

That next step would be a doozy....

She took firm hold on the thick branch of a tree next to her, then leaned forward, craning her neck to get a better look at the squirrels.

"Are you *nuts?*"

Jason's harsh question came from right behind her. In fact, it was muttered almost in her ear, which was the perfect prescription for making Mady jerk in alarm. As she started to turn to him, horror swept her when she felt one foot slip on the loose dirt and rocks. For a terrifyingly clear, eternal second she felt herself suspended on the edge of infinity, and she opened her mouth in a scream.

It never came out. It didn't have a chance. The air was crushed from her lungs when a steel-banded arm locked itself around her middle and she was jerked backward, off her feet.

Heart pounding at what could have happened, Mady closed her eyes, both hands gripping the arm that held her so tightly. Slowly her breathing returned to normal, and as it did, she became aware of the fact that she was still suspended above the ground, her back pressed against Jason's chest, her feet dangling.

"You...you can put me down now."

Slowly, as though reluctant to comply, she felt him lower her until her feet settled on the hard ground. She waited for him to release his hold on her, but it didn't happen. Turning slightly, she tipped her head back to look up at him.

"Jason..." But whatever she'd intended to say evaporated from her mind as she found herself captive in the intensity of those glittering eyes. Her hands tightened on his arm, and she saw a flicker of emotion in his eyes…awareness? of her? The thought sent her pulse galloping again. She opened her mouth to say something but was once again cut off when he released her without warning. She staggered forward at the unexpected action, catching her balance with difficulty.

One of these days she was going to end up on her nose in the dirt!

"Anyone ever tell you that you need a keeper?"

At the cold, clipped words, Mady spun to face him. When she saw the ice in the gaze he was leveling at her, her chest tightened, feeling as though a semi had just opted to park over her heart.

Why on earth was he looking at her like that? It wasn't *her* fault she'd almost taken flight! She'd been just fine until he startled her. She planted her hands on her hips. "Anyone ever tell *you* it's not wise to sneak up on people?"

A muscle in his jaw jerked. "I didn't *sneak up* on you." He jerked his head toward the edge of the path. "If anything, I saved your bacon."

"My *bacon*, as you so eloquently put it, wouldn't have *needed* saving if you hadn't startled me. I was doing just fine, thank you, until you decided to come *help* me." She moved to push past him, but much to her chagrin, she slipped on the loose dirt and stones. Jason put a quick hand out to steady her, but she slapped it away. "Don't *touch* me!"

A slow smile tipped his lips, but unlike the smile he'd given her on the boulder, there was nothing humorous in it. It looked cold. Even a bit spiteful. "You didn't seem to mind it a few minutes ago."

The words were like a slap, and Mady stepped back, hating that an unwelcome blush surged into her cheeks. "I—you—!" She couldn't *believe* he'd said that! Angry tears pricked at her eyes, and her hands clenched so hard her fingers ached. "Here's a little tidbit to keep in your tiny mind from now on, *Mister* Tiber. The only help I need from you is for you to stay out of my way."

"Of course, your highness. Whatever you say, your highness."

"Your highn—!"

"Everything okay here, team three?"

They both spun at the bland question. Earl stood there, a few feet away, leaning against a tall tree and watching them with a speculative gleam in his eyes.

Mady let her eyes drift shut. Great. Just great. Undoubtedly, Jason would jump at this opportunity to tell Earl how she'd almost done a swan dive off the path and how he'd come in like a knight on a white horse to save her.

Well, Jason Tiber had *plenty* of armor, but the man was no knight. As for the white horse…well, the only relationship he had there was to the critter's backside!

She tensed, waiting for the tirade. But it didn't come. Amazingly, all Jason said was, "Fine. We're fine."

Mady stared at him, mouth agape. Though it was painfully evident he'd answered Earl through gritted teeth, apparently that was all he was going to say. And that only made Mady even *more* frustrated because now she actually felt *grateful* to the man for not sharing her little misadventure with Earl.

How could he do this to her? How could he make

her feel grateful to him? The rat! What was she supposed to do with *that?*

Frustration boiled up in her until she had to vent it. She stomped her foot on the hard ground and glared at Jason.

I hope you're happy now!

Jason's dark brows slanted in a frown, and he lifted his hands slightly, looking at her as though to say, "What? What did I do now?"

"Mady?"

She turned to Earl, whose sharp gaze rested on her, then drifted down to her foot. "Something to add?"

Forcing a smile to her tight lips, Mady managed to keep her tone neutral. "Just peachy."

She tossed a glance at Jason, and he responded with a terse nod. Then he stepped out of Mady's way, bowing slightly and sweeping his hand toward the path. "After you...*partner.*"

Now it was her turn to speak through clenched teeth. "Gee...thanks, partner." She brushed past him, walking as quickly as she could, fighting the overwhelming urge to break into a run and put as much distance as possible between her and her mercurial, confusing, ever-aggravating partner.

Earl stood where he was, hands in his pockets, watching as Mady and Jason stomped their way back up the path toward the group. The tension sparking the air between those two was enough to set the surrounding forest ablaze.

Casting a glance heavenward, he let out a slow, deep

sigh. "Oh, boy." He just hoped this all turned out right—
he glanced after his charges again—and that those two
didn't end up killing each other.

Pushing away from the tree, he followed Mady and
Jason back up the path.

It was going to be a very long four days.

❦ 8 ❦

There are two kinds of people.
Those who say to God, "Thy will be done." And
those to whom God says, "All right, then, have it your way."
C. S. LEWIS

Mady uttered a gasp of delight as they rode into the campsite area. It was a flat, level, grassy area flanked by trees on two sides, a hedge of bushes on the third, and a river on the fourth. Sunlight shone through the branches of the trees, bathing the entire area in a warm glow.

The place looked positively magical.

"The heavens tell of the glory of God. The skies display his marvelous craftsmanship...."

The verse came to life for Mady in a way it never had before as she slid from the saddle, taking in the feel of the cool mountain air and the brisk breeze that blew around her.

How could anyone think all of this had happened by chance?

Earl's voice pulled her from her thoughts. "Okay, gang, the paddock is just down that path over there."

Mady followed his pointing finger and saw a path leading away from the sleeping area, cutting through the neck-high line of bushes.

"It's not far, so go ahead and take care of your horses. When you're done, come on back and pick a spot to set up your sleeping areas. All you need to pull out are your tarps and sleeping bags since we're only here for the night."

Mady was impressed at how quickly they got the horses situated, watered, and fed. The paddock was a large, split-rail enclosure complete with feeding stations and hooks for tack. Shelves had been built onto the top railing for feed and water buckets.

Clearly the horses were used to coming into the paddock. They moved through the gate with confidence, walking to their assigned spots as though it were the most natural process in the world.

Mady took her time unsaddling Dorado, currying him down, and making sure he had plenty of water and feed. With a final pat on the animal's twitching neck, she turned and made her way back up the path to join the others in making dinner.

The meal—which was comprised of vegetables and a hearty stew served in dense, heavy bread bowls—didn't take long to fix. Which was a good thing because the tempting aromas drifting through the camp had everyone standing around and drooling in anticipation.

"That smells amazing!" Mady licked her lips and Earl laughed.

"Nothing like exercise and fresh mountain air to make you ready for food. And for sleep. Food never tastes so good and sleep never feels as good as when you're out here. You'll see." He handed her a rounded loaf of bread, showing her how to tear out the hole for the stew.

Mady filled her bowl with the steaming stew, grabbed a spoon, and went to plant herself on a log. Watching the others follow suit, she nearly laughed out loud at the way the men's eyes lit up when they saw the big chunks of meat in the stew. Heather and Brian played their honeymooner role to the hilt, oohing and aahing over everything, giggling with their heads close together until Mady had to fight the urge to spear a chunk of potato and flip it at them.

A person could only take so much cute.

Happily, Nikos had commandeered the spot next to her. She liked Nikos. He gave her just the right balance of good-humored flirtation and easy camaraderie. When she was with him, she could relax and have fun. He was...comfortable.

Nothing like Jason.

"Oh, darn."

Nikos glanced at her, brows raised in a question.

Mady shrugged. "I just forgot to get something to drink."

"Allow me." Before she could argue, he was up and back, a cup of clear water in his hand. The slow smile that eased across his handsome features as he gave her the cup was purely male, and Mady giggled.

That was something else she had to admit she was enjoying: his old world manners and gallantry. She hadn't been so pampered in...in...okay, ever. And in this setting, with this man, it was downright fun.

She let him spend the meal regaling her with delightful, often funny stories of his family and his childhood in Greece. Lea sat nearby and added a few comments here and there, but Mady couldn't help noticing that her attention drifted from her brother and came to rest with undeniable regularity on one Jason Tiber.

Not that Mady could blame the dark-haired

woman. Jason looked every inch the tall, broad-shoul-
dered outdoorsman tonight. His stone-washed denim
shirt brought out the steel blue of his eyes. And with the
sleeves rolled up to his forearms, it gave him a rugged,
all-male air.

Mady lowered her head, ostensibly to listen to
Nikos, but mostly because it allowed her to keep a sideways watch on Lea and her quarry.

Jason had plopped down on a stump near Lea, and
he was turned toward the lovely woman, a broad smile
on his face. His eyes danced with humor at whatever
she'd just said.

Biting her lip, Mady forced her attention back to
Nikos. But it wasn't more than a few moments before she
was sneaking another peek at Jason. With his eyes lit up
that way and the warmth in his expression, he looked
much more like the charmer she'd thought him to be
when they were at the airport.

His rich laughter drifted on the light breeze. She
shivered slightly. *Must be colder than I thought....*

"Are you all right, Mady?"

She turned her attention back to Nikos, hugging
herself and rubbing her arms. "I think so." She shook her
head. "Never mind. I just had a little chill, that's all."

Immediately he was concerned. "Shall I fetch a jacket
for you? Didn't I see you pull one from your pack before
dinner?"

Mady nodded. "Yes, but I left it laying on my sleeping bag—"

He stood. "I will get it for you."

"Really, it's not necessary," Mady started, but Nikos
was already on his way, stepping over the others' legs

where they were stretched in the middle of the circle.

Mady crossed a leg over her knee, put one elbow on her leg, and rested her chin in her hand. She looked after Nikos...then found her eyes straying back to Jason.

She really liked the way he looked when he smiled. There was something so appealing, so approachable about it. And she liked it that he wasn't too handsome. Oh, he was nice looking, but not so much so that he made a woman nervous just to be around him. She studied his dark brows and firm mouth, both of which seemed to speak to her of strength. His nose might have been almost perfect if not for a bump that indicated it must have been broken at some point. And he had the most intriguing eyes...glacial blue eyes that could look with such intensity, such warmth that you felt like melting when they stared at you, like they were doing now—

Like they were *what?*

Shock screamed across Mady's nerves like hot water hitting a burned skin. She jerked, blood pounding in her ears, feeling hot and cold all at once. Jason had glanced up and caught her staring at him! Well, it was too late to pretend she'd just glanced his way. And she refused to compound her humiliation by turning her head. So she did the only thing she could: She straightened and held his gaze, doing her best to look confident and blasé and not the least bit mortified.

A slow smile crossed the features Mady had just been studying, bringing out those blasted dimples again as Jason reached for the cup of water he had set on the log beside him. He kept his eyes locked on hers...and then he winked.

Well, two could play at that game.

There was something she'd been wanting to do almost from her first encounter with the aggravating Mr. Tiber. Something she knew was utterly childish, absurd, and foolish. A two-year-old's response, to be sure.

And she didn't care a whit.

Not after another one of those darned winks. One was more than enough. Two? Well, let's just say he deserved a little tit-for-tat.

So lifting her chin a fraction, she held Jason's challenging gaze as he sipped his water. Then, wrinkling her nose to let him know she found him about as agreeable as a plate of cold brussels sprouts, she stuck her tongue out at him. She'd done it quickly, darting her tongue in and out like a lizard or snake might do.

She didn't think anyone else had seen the action. In fact, she was sure of it. Jason had quite effectively drawn everyone's attention away from her when he sputtered and choked on his water at her unexpected action.

Mady smiled.

Gotcha.

"Give him room!" Brian yelled.

"Oh, Jason darling, are you breathing?" Lea's tone was slightly panicked.

"If he's coughing, he's breathing," came Earl's calm voice. "Just give him room."

"Somebody hit him on the back!"

Heather's advice apparently sounded right to Nikos, who had just returned to the circle, Mady's jacket draped over his arm. He vaulted the log Jason sat on, then proceeded to pound the wheezing man on the back with emphatic thwacks.

Mady had to smother a giggle against her arm. *Oh,*

my…it might not be right, Lord, but that felt good. She hugged herself and leaned back against the tree behind her. *No, that felt great!*

She forced her smile away, widening her eyes to the appropriately worried level, then watched in silence as the others…*helped* Jason. When he was breathing normally again, Jason settled back on his log and directed a look at Mady that made her pause.

On the surface, it seemed almost…what? surprised? respectful? *admiring?*

She shook her head slightly, tipping her head back to stare up at the ocean of stars starting to twinkle in the darkening sky. No, that couldn't be right. There could be little doubt that Jason had formed certain opinions and ideas about her, but she felt fairly secure that admiration was *not* among them.

Irritation, definitely. Frustration, most likely. Disdain? Probably.

But admiration?

She shook her head. Not in a million years.

And as she pulled her knees against her chest and circled them with her arms, she wondered why on earth that admission should be so utterly and completely depressing.

Mady lay back on her sleeping bag, staring up at the tarp above her.

She was supposed to be sleeping. She *needed* to be sleeping. From the soft sounds of breathing and snores drifting around her in the darkness, everyone else was sleeping.

So why wasn't she?

She rolled over for the umpteenth time and punched her pillow. Yes, the ground was far from feather soft, but that wasn't the problem. Restless. That's what she was. No doubt about it.

Dropping her forehead onto her arms, she squeezed her eyes shut and muttered in a low, weary voice. "Go...to...sleep!"

She held her breath, waiting for the warm, drowsy feeling to drift over her...and flopped over onto her back with a frustrated groan.

It was no use.

"Sleep never feels so good as it does out here...."

Earl's confident words floated through her head, and she sighed. She was sure he was right. If only she could find out for herself. But that was looking less and less likely with each passing minute.

Turning her head toward the paddock, she squinted into the darkness. She could just make out the path leading to the paddock. Maybe a walk to visit the horses would help her relax.

Earl had cautioned them to bring jackets along, and as she reached for hers and pulled it on, she was grateful she'd complied.

"It's warm during the days," he'd said, "even downright hot at times. But you'll be surprised how cold the nights can get."

She could believe it. Already the temperature felt as though it had fallen twenty degrees or more.

She stood, peering out into the darkness. A momentary twinge of apprehension nudged at her, but she pushed it away.

There's no reason to be afraid. I've got a flashlight, so I won't trip on anything. For a change. Her lips twisted at the thought, and she shrugged it away. *It's perfectly safe here. Besides, all I have to do is yelp, and I'd have Nikos and Earl at my side in minutes.*

With that comforting reassurance, she started toward the path, walking as quietly as she could, careful lest she wake the others.

As warm as the day had been—in the low seventies— it was clear and cool tonight. It wasn't frigid, by any means, but cool enough to make her shiver a bit despite the added warmth of her jacket. She slid her hands into her pockets, casting one more look at the others.

They looked dead to the world. She pushed away the jab of envy that they were getting rested up for tomorrow. That's what she should be doing, but she was too keyed up.

There was too much to think about. Too many thoughts and questions whirling around in her head. Better to take a walk and hope the exercise and fresh air would help her loosen up.

She started down the path, glad that the bushes were only three or four feet deep. She stepped out of them, glanced back to be sure they would block the light from bothering the others, then pulled her flashlight from her pocket.

Her thumb moved to the switch, and she hesitated.

Did she really need it? It didn't seem all that dark after all. She lifted her face to study the sky, and her heart caught with wonder at the wash of stars twinkling down at her.

The night was clear and cloudless, and the moon shone so bright it might as well have been daytime.

Mady clapped her hands in the quiet. This place was just amazing. She glanced around, taking it all in as she'd done earlier when they'd arrived.

She couldn't quite believe she was here, in the mountains, surrounded by bushes…and trees…and a cacaphony of sounds…all kinds of sounds.…

What *were* those sounds?

Freezing where she stood, Mady glanced around quickly. If she'd been a dog, she knew her ears would be perking.

Relax, Mady. It's just frogs.

She listened more carefully, nodding slowly.

And crickets. And other insects. The woods are probably full of them. Well, of course they were, hadn't she read that? There were a multitude of birds and frogs and insects out here. It was the wilderness. There was bound to be wildlife.

She willed her tight shoulder muscles to relax and started walking again. Yes, indeed, wildlife most likely abounded in this place. Rabbits, squirrels, owls, bats…and who knew what else was hiding out there, waiting for her.…

"Stop it! Just stop it. Next thing you know, you'll be looking around in terror chanting, 'Lions and tigers and bears, oh my!'"

As soon as the word *bear* left her lips, Mady knew she shouldn't have said it. There were bears in the area. Brown bears. Black bears.

Grizzly bears.

A hint of panic whispered across her nerves as she fumbled for her flashlight and turned it on, shining it from side to side.

"Oh, my…"

The words came out in a sigh, and she paused, contemplating making a run back to the safety of her sleeping bag. But just then the beam of her flashlight caught the end of the path, and beyond that, the railing of the paddock.

With a relieved sigh, Mady moved toward the horses, grateful she wasn't alone any longer.

She stepped into the open area surrounding the paddock, her breath blowing faint puffs of white in the cold night air. A shiver traveled over her as she walked toward the paddock, and she was glad she'd brought warm clothes for nighttime wear and sleeping. Too bad the one-man tents they'd be using didn't come equipped with electric blankets and cappuccino makers!

She grinned at the image, then jumped slightly when her stomach grumbled. In the silence of the night the sound was surprisingly loud. She bit her lip, wishing she'd thought to grab a few of the carrots that had been left over from dinner. If not for herself, then for the horses.

Cupping her hands, she blew on them to warm them and glanced back at the path. She could always go back…but with a shake of her head she dismissed the thought. She wouldn't be out much longer. She could already feel a sweet sense of drowsiness starting to work its way over her.

She started for the paddock again. She'd just give Dorado a scratch or two behind the ears, then head back.

Making her way to the paddock, she called the horse's name softly. A nicker sounded, and she grinned when she heard Dorado paw the ground. She leaned down to step through the split-rail fencing, then moved to lay her hand on Dorado's velvety neck, talking in a soft, low voice.

Dorado nuzzled at her shoulder with his lips, and Mady laughed. She leaned her forehead against the animal's soft neck and breathed in the fragrances of evergreen, wood, leather, and horses.

Her eyes drifted shut. Was it only this morning she'd arrived? It didn't seem possible. Snapshots of the day drifted in and out of her mind: the plane ride, the breakfast, Earl with his cup of coffee and his unrelenting good humor, Nikos looking up at her as she swung into the saddle....

And Jason. Image after image drifted through her mind's eye: Jason's face, his ice blue gaze, his lips tilted in a mocking smile, the glitter in his eyes as he held her at the landing strip...on the path....

"Stop it!"

Dorado jumped at her hissed command, and she reached out a hand to calm the horse. "I'm sorry, boy. It's just that...well, thinking about Jason is about as helpful as thinking about bats and grizzly bears!"

And about as unnerving.

Mady caught her lip between her teeth and moved back through the paddock rails, scuffing her toe in the hard dirt. What was this fascination with Jason Tiber? If she didn't know better, she'd think she was actually starting to *like* the man. Even...

Even feel a little fond of him.

Oh no. No way. Jason might be attractive, he might even have tickled her curiosity a bit, but there was no way her heart was going to get suckered in by a man who seldom even smiled at her.

Hold it. *Seldom?* Try never. She scrunched her face, forcing her mind to scan the day. Had he smiled at her? A real smile? Even once? Not that she could recall. Snorts. Oh, he'd given her plenty of those. Enough to last a lifetime. Which was very possibly what the next four days would feel like.

A lifetime. An eternity. Forever!

Care for the man? Not likely. Truth be told, he bothered her. Even irritated her. And usually that was a hard thing to do! Which went to prove Jason was, plain and simple, a difficult person. She started pacing in front of the paddock with rapid, determined steps. She needed to be moving...needed to think.

How on earth was she supposed to enjoy even one minute of the next few days if she and the esteemed Jason Tiber were—

No. She wasn't going to think of it.

She turned on her heel again and jerked to a halt. She was making herself dizzy. Looking around, she spotted a large boulder nearby and went to settle on it, tucking her hands under her legs. Better to sit and think things through than to roam around in the dark. Last thing she needed was to stick her foot in a gopher hole or have another close encounter with a stump.

For one thing, she might hurt herself. For another, she really didn't want to give Jason anything else to laugh at her about.

She leaned her head back, staring up at the stars, letting her quandary wash over her. She'd been so excited about this trip. Had only felt more so as Earl described all they'd be doing....

And then reality had come in and bitten her right on the nose.

Jason was her partner. Her teammate. The one she was going to have to rely on during the next four days.

Oh, why couldn't things have turned out better?

Because they turned out for the best.

The quiet rejoinder echoed in her mind, but she didn't understand. How could this be for the best?

God,...are You sure You know what You're doing?

Mady stood, suddenly too restless again to sit still. She walked to the paddock, leaning her arms on the top railing, closing her eyes tightly against the thoughts and doubts washing over her.

Why Jason? Why the one person in the group who made her feel stupid and confused and like she had twelve left feet? With a groan of pure frustration, she did the only thing she could think of to stop the troubling thoughts from assaulting her.

She banged her head against the wood rail, making the contact with a bit more force than she'd intended. She blinked away both the stars that were dancing in her head and the smarting tears that sprang to her eyes.

See there? Just thinking about the man made her do stupid things! She rubbed her forehead, kneading the sore spot gently, which helped a little. If only she could do something to ease the numb ache she felt inside.

If someone pressed her, Mady knew she wouldn't be able to give a rational reason for her feelings. But that didn't change the facts. She was rock-solid certain that additional time with her assigned partner would result in one thing: utter calamity.

She straightened her shoulders, casting a glance at

the sky. "Sourpuss, Lord? You teamed me with *Sourpuss?*"

"I'm going to assume you're talking about the horse."

Mady gave a yelp and spun around.

The smile that greeted her in the bright, moonlit night was full of sardonic amusement, as were Jason's eyes and his low, deep voice as he drawled out, "Well, hey there...*partner.*"

9

He who wrestles with us strengthens our nerves
and sharpens our skills. Our antagonist is our helper.
EDMUND BURKE

Partner.

The word—and the mildly challenging tone with which it was spoken—set Mady's already ragged nerves on edge. One more word, one more slight condescension, and she'd do something drastic.

What, she wasn't sure. But she'd come up with something.

Discretion is the better part of valor, wasn't that how the saying went? Well, now was the time to put that to practice before she said or did something she'd regret. That decided, Mady kept her mouth firmly shut.

Besides, it was hard to talk when her teeth were clenched together so hard her jaws ached.

At her silence, a slow smile stole across Jason's features.

Mady's fingers clenched and unclenched at her sides. He was smiling. She didn't trust him when he smiled—especially the way he was smiling right now. He looked like he was up to something.

Not taking his eyes from her, he reached up with one long finger and nudged his ever-present cowboy hat back a fraction, leaned an elbow on the paddock railing, and drawled, "Cat got your tongue?"

The muffled laughter in his voice only served to further confound her. Oh, how she wished she could read this man. Was he being insulting or just having fun? Her narrowed eyes searched his face for a clue. If he were having fun, was it at her expense?

A host of retorts flew to her mind, but before any of them could take shape and slip past her lips, a small, quiet reminder drifted in.

"As much as it is possible, live at peace with all men...."

She bit her lip. *Do you have any idea how hard that is with someone like Jason Tiber?*

Still...

It was a solid principle. She knew that. One she'd tried to follow...one that didn't change just because someone was somewhat—or even *extremely*—irritating. Besides, if she were honest about it, she had to admit there didn't seem to be any mockery in Jason's smile. This time.

Just a kind of considering, curious amusement.

"So—" his eyes scanned her face—"couldn't sleep?"

She leaned against the rough wood of the railing and flicked an imaginary piece of dirt from her jacket sleeve. "I was...restless."

The bright moonlight seemed to give his brown hair a luminescent kind of highlight. Almost like a halo.

Now it was she who was grinning. She turned away, hoping he hadn't noticed. Jason with a halo. Now *there* was an image!

He drew her attention again when he pulled off his hat and ran a hand through his hair. The old woman at the airport was wrong. Jason didn't need a haircut. Mady liked his hair. Long at the front and parted in the middle, it fell in casual, minimum-care waves around his face.

As often as not, he looked like he did right now—as though he'd run a quick hand through it, pushing it out of his way. But there always seemed to be a rebellious bit that fell forward onto his forehead, too stubborn to stay in place.

Kind of like the man himself.

"Understandable. Considering."

Mady blinked. "Excuse me?"

"I just said it was understandable. Considering."

She wrinkled her nose as he leaned down to slip through the fence, clucking his tongue at the horses. *Considering?* What was that supposed to mean?

She watched Jason coax his black horse from where the large animal stood near the back of the paddock. The horse walked up slowly, then leaned his large head forward and blew a soft nicker at Jason. He laughed and held out his hand, palm up. Mady saw he held a couple of small carrots from dinner.

Her irritation was immediate. Oh, fine. He'd thought ahead where she hadn't. Wasn't that just peachy?

She crossed her arms, suddenly even more irritated by that offhanded "considering" Jason had tossed at her.

Forget it, the voice of wisdom whispered to her. *Don't push it. You're overreacting.*

You're right, I know you're right.

She nodded her head, pasted a smile on her face, and turned to tell Jason good-night. But that wasn't what came out. "Considering?"

Okay, so she wasn't in the mood to listen to wisdom.

"What did you mean by that? Considering *what*, exactly?"

Jason didn't even look at her. He just raised his shoulders a fraction, then pulled out a couple more carrots for the happily munching horse.

What had the man done? Brought an entire veggie platter, for heaven's sake?

She tapped her foot. *Considering...* She stared up at him, refusing to let his considerable height advantage intimidate her. So the man all but towered over her. So what? What she lacked in inches she made up for it in...in...

Good sense? Reason? Humility?

She gritted her teeth. *Daring, spunk, self-assurance.*

When Jason didn't respond to her prompting, she filled in the blank herself. It wasn't very hard to do in light of his apparent opinion of her. "*Considering,* I suppose, that I'm not prepared to handle this...this..."

He gave her a sideways glance. "Adventure?" He supplied the word, speaking slowly and distinctly as though tutoring a particularly dim-witted student. He scratched the horse's ears, then wiped his hand on his pants leg. "As for whether or not you can handle whatever we're getting into, dunno." The somewhat pained tolerance she saw in his eyes brought a swift heat into her cheeks. "But the fact that you can't even think what to call it doesn't exactly build my confidence."

"Well, forgive me for not being little Johnny on the spot—"

He shrugged. "Didn't expect it of you."

Mady planted her feet, crossed her arms over her chest again, and fixed him with a glare. She searched her mind for a fitting comeback. "You are the most infuriating—"

She cut off the *words, holding up her hand. *Infuriating* just wasn't vile enough. "No, make that the most *despicable*..."

No, that didn't do it, either. "You...you..." It was no use. The words just weren't there. She couldn't think of anything rotten enough to let him know how maddening, how detestable he was being. Words alone just couldn't convey the depth and breadth of her emotions. *A heavy object, on the other hand, would do quite nicely.* She didn't even blink at the thought. Rather, she found herself glancing around, her eyes searching the ground, the surrounding area, the tack hanging here and there...

Surely there was something nearby? A piece of wood? A horseshoe, even. She spotted a half-full water bucket sitting near the fence. Now *that* could be promising—

Before she could take a step, Jason was there, leaning down to grab the bucket by the handle and set it up on the shelf atop the railing. Apparently Mady's eyes had fully adjusted to the night because she had no trouble at all with seeing the twinkle in Jason's eyes as he met her glare.

If she didn't know better, she'd think he actually knew what she'd been contemplating. His next comment confirmed the fact.

"Hate to have it get dumped by someone." He sounded about to burst into laughter. "Or *on* someone."

She held back her gasp of dismay. Barely. Blast the man for being so perceptive! Her attention flew from the water bucket to his face, and she opened her mouth, ready to deny the charge. But try as she might, she couldn't make the words come out. Bad enough she'd been ready to do bodily harm to someone. She wouldn't compound her transgression by lying.

At her silence, he stepped back, bringing a hand to his chest and placing it over his heart. "What's this? No heated denial?"

To her intense chagrin she felt an unwelcome heat flooding her cheeks. *Please, Lord, please…give me a break here. Let the darkness hide the fact that I'm blushing!*

No such luck. Jason's face split in a full-blown grin. "Hmm. Unless I miss my guess, those red cheeks amount to a confession." He crossed his arms and leaned against the railing. "So you were considering dumping that bucket over my head, were you? Not a very partnerish thing to do, Miss Donovan."

She was amazed to find herself having to fight the almost irresistible urge to snicker. The more she pictured herself grabbing that bucket and dumping its contents over Jason's head, the harder it was to muffle the hilarity— or was it hysteria?—clamoring to get out.

"No…" She cleared her slightly strangled throat and managed to continue in a stronger voice. "No, it wasn't."

The surprise that sparked in his eyes at her agreement gave her a definite sense of satisfaction. She tipped her head to the side and studied the enigma that was Jason Tiber, and after a few moments, the amusement in his expression faded. He didn't flinch at her scrutiny. Rather, he bore it in an admirable silence. The only sign that he was feeling even the least bit self-conscious was the way his hand kept flexing at his side.

Though she hated to admit it, Mady knew what she needed to do. "Jason, I'd like to apologize."

From the way his mouth dropped open, he hadn't

been expecting that. She laced her fingers together and tipped her head. "Do you want to know something interesting?"

He gave a slight nod, and she went on. "I have never in my life—well, not that I can recall, at any rate—wanted to do someone bodily harm."

A flash of outright humor crossed his face at that. "So...the remarkably efficient job you did this morning with your commando flying backpack was...?"

She cleared her throat. "Purely unintentional, I assure you."

He rolled his shoulders. "Well, here's hoping I never encounter intentional."

Mady choked out a laugh, then shook her head. "You know, I couldn't sleep tonight. I thought it was because I was excited about being here."

"It's not?"

She shook her head. "No, it's not." Slipping her hands into her jacket pockets, she lifted her shoulders in a shrug. "It's you."

His brows arched at that. "Me?"

"It's true. I've been walking around for a while now, going over it in my head, trying to figure it out."

One dimple peeked out at her as he leaned against the wall, slipping his hands in his jeans pockets. "Figure what out? Maybe I can help."

She bit her lip at the offer. Well, why not? Who better to help her understand her partner than the man himself? She moved to finger a halter hanging from a hook. "First, there's something I want you to know about me."

"I can hardly wait."

Ignoring the muffled laughter in the remark, she went on. "It might surprise you to hear this—" she shot him a glance and grinned—"Okay, it might *stun* you to know this, but I'm looked on by my friends and those who've known me for a long time as a fun and encouraging person. I've been called—" dare she say it?—"easy going."

To his credit, the snicker that escaped him was a small one. Undaunted, she went on. "As a matter of fact, until today I've always thought most people I've encountered would say I'm generally gracious, kind, and optimistic."

"I take it you haven't landed on top of any of these people? Stomped on their hands? Nearly taken them off the edge of a clif—"

"No." She restrained the urge to kick him, but just barely. Drawing a calming breath, she pushed forward. "I've even been told that one of my gifts, so to speak, is finding the good in everyone."

His chuckle was a bit more pronounced this time. "Meaning if someone rubs you wrong, he must not have any good in him?"

She ignored the comment. Rife as it was with strangled laughter, she didn't think it was sincere. "So you see, it's a real puzzle to me."

"What is?"

"Well, why we seem to irritate each other so easily when we've only just met. Why we can't go five minutes in each other's company without ending up..."

He completed the thought for her. "Locking horns? Butting heads? Drawing blood—"

She held up a hand, halting the too-ready flow of

words, giving him a warning glare. He held his hands up as though to say, "I was only trying to help."

With a sigh, she dropped her hand. He'd been right on target, and she knew it. "Yes, well, all of the above, I suppose."

His expression at this was unreadable, and Mady fought a wave of sudden panic. She was going out on a limb here, and she didn't care much for the way it felt. *The truth will set you free.* Hadn't she heard that all her life? So why, then, did telling the truth feel as though a vice were around her chest—and it was getting tighter with each second?

Still…she'd gone this far. She shifted from one foot to the other, then pushed forward. "Anyway, I just wish I understood why it is that you seem so adept at getting to me."

Still no real reaction from him.

Mady pressed her hands together to keep them from trembling. "It seems ridiculous, and I sure don't understand it, but there you have it." She held her hands out in front of her. "You bring out the worst in me, and I'm sorry I let that happen."

There. She'd said it. Confessed the embarrassing, ridiculous truth.

She hadn't really expected an answer, so she wasn't terribly surprised when none was forthcoming. But a little whisper of hope drifted up inside of her, like a ribbon of smoke from a tiny fire. Maybe now she and Jason could get past the way they seemed to irritate one another and find some kind of common ground. Surely they could do that, couldn't they?

The look on his face wasn't exactly encouraging, but

she was ready to try. Hadn't they almost reached a kind of truce at lunch today? Shared a boulder? Talked without fighting?

Yeah, and it lasted all of fifteen minutes. That's how long it took for you two to be blazing at one another again.

Shoving the discouraging thought away, she offered him an encouraging smile. "'If it is possible, as far as it depends on you, live at peace with everyone.' Considering I memorized that as a kid in Sunday school, you'd think I would have learned to apply it by now, huh?"

Silence. She cleared her throat. This was getting downright awkward. "So…anyway…I'm—uh, I'm sorry for not doing my part." Her voice was starting to shake a little now. "You know, with the living at peace thing."

Not a word, not a budge, not a flicker of an eyelash. Had the man fallen asleep on his feet, with his eyes open?

She let out a frustrated huff and stuck her hand out. "What say we just call a truce?"

He just stood there, his eyes searching her face—and what she saw in those blue depths when his eyes met hers made her blink, then look again in disbelief.

Resistance. A haunted fear…even, though she could scarcely believe it, a bit of alarm. But the most confusing emotion shining out at her was a longing so intense, so raw that it reached out and took hold of her heart with an iron grip.

What happened to this man?

If the expression in his eyes was any indication, it was something that had cut him deeply, lacerating his heart and spirit.

She shook her head slowly, trying to make sense of it. The raw ache she saw in his features had little or nothing to do with her, that much she knew. Unless she was totally off the mark, this was no recent, sudden pain.

This was a long-term anguish…and somehow something she'd said had resurrected it, brought it back to blazing, burning life.

Instinctively, she moved toward him, reaching out to lay a hand on his arm. "Jason, can I help?"

He stared down at her hand, then looked at her face again. With a slow, deliberate motion, he laid his hand over hers. Warmth and hope surged through Mady— until he took hold of the sleeve of her jacket with his forefinger and thumb as though it were an offending piece of garbage, lifted her hand, and removed it from his arm.

She stared at her hand, then looked up, startled and confused. The eyes that met her gaze were solid ice, as cold and bitter as the winter storms that blew through the mountains every year, leaving everything in their path frozen and desolate.

"Save your Bible talk for the kiddies at vacation Bible school, Miss Donovan."

Mady jerked back at the bitter words Jason all but spat at her.

"I—excuse me?"

"You heard me, save it for the infants. They don't mind pabulum." He took a step toward her, and she found herself retreating from him. He gave a hoarse laugh. "Relax, woman. I won't hurt you."

She jutted her chin at his disdainful tone. "And I should believe that…why, exactly? Because you're so rational? Because you're such a gentleman?" Her chin lifted a fraction, and she gave him a half-lidded stare of dismissal. "Forgive me if I don't buy it."

His eyes raked her from head to toe, and he let out a disdainful snort. "Then how about this? I'd have to care a whole lot more than I do about anything you say or do to get worked up enough to come after you."

The cold words struck hard, and Mady found herself blinking back unexpected tears. She shut her eyes, biting her lip and shaking her head.

She wasn't equipped for this kind of verbal swordplay. She wasn't adept enough to avoid getting wounded....

Lord, You still perform miracles. Every day. I know You do. Please, could You perform one now and make me disappear? She allowed herself a grim smile.

Either that, or make Jason disappear?

But when she opened her eyes, they were both still there.

Jason's smile was grim. "Sorry, the magic wish didn't come true."

Again Mady blinked, her mouth falling open. "W-what?"

His chuckle was low and filled with arrogance. "I know your type. You're fine in a fight until you get cornered, then you just want it all to go away." His eyes dared her to deny it, but she clenched her teeth and held her silence.

"No comment?" He crossed his arms across that broad chest...had it been just this morning that he'd held her there, cradling her with that protective air? How could that man—who had looked down at her with such intensity in his eyes—and this man—whose entire stance told her how deeply he disliked her—be the same?

"It doesn't make sense."

Mady's eyes widened when she realized she'd said the words out loud. Jason stared at her, frowning.

"What doesn't? That I don't buy your little Christian platitudes? Give it a rest, Mady. Not everyone is that gullible. And since we're going to have the *pleasure*—" he drew the word out in a way that made it clear he thought it was anything but—"of each other's company for the next four days, do us both a favor and stuff the sermons, okay?"

He waved his hand at her. "I've heard it all, and then some. And I got over my taste for that particular brand of bunkum a long time ago."

Mady might have been offended at the words if it hadn't been for the raw edge to Jason's voice…an edge that tore at her heart with the way it spoke of aching and despair and sorrow.

An edge that told Mady the cold and distant Jason Tiber was neither. No, what Jason Tiber was—and Mady would bank her life on this—plain and simple, was afraid.

Now if she could just figure out why.

❧ 10 ❧

Do not remove a fly from your friend's head with a hatchet.
CHINESE PROVERB

Mady's mind was spinning its wheels, stuck in a muck of confusion. *What's going on, Lord?*

Jason stepped away from her with an abrupt shake of his head. "What's wrong, partner? Surprised I knew you were quoting the Bible?"

His words were clearly intended as an insult, and she took them accordingly, going stiff.

He gave a harsh laugh. "Oh yes, right on cue. Play the offended miss." He stuffed his hands into his pockets, his stance casual. "Do you realize how predictable you are? Quote a handy little Bible verse to cover your Christian behind, thereby excusing your less than model behavior. Wrap up those ugly, *un*-Christian little tidbits like anger and sarcasm in a few pithy quotes from Proverbs or Psalms. They're always good for a panacea. Then, having dispensed your words of life, you're free to go on your merry way."

His gaze was pitying. "Well, it won't work for me, Miss Donovan. You see, I probably know the good book better than you could ever hope to."

"What a pity knowing it hasn't done you any good, *Mister* Tiber." Mady could have bitten off her tongue when a look of pure triumph glittered in Jason's eyes.

"*Much* better. There's the Mady I've come to know

and endure. And you're absolutely right. Knowing the Bible, even believing what it had to say before I knew better, did me no good whatsoever." He flipped his hand into the air, as though shooing a mosquito. "Forget the Bible verses, Mady, they're just a bunch of empty promises and one-liners that don't do anyone any good."

Something happened then that Mady had experienced only once before. It had been a year ago, in the dead of winter, and her car had hit a patch of black ice. She'd felt the tires losing traction, knew she was going into a spin, knew nothing she could do was going to stop it...and as the car began whirling like a caffeine-crazed top, Mady's awareness had focused and sharpened.

It was as though every sense was heightened, and she could see and hear more clearly than ever before.

In thirty seconds the spin-out had been over, and Mady's car had come to rest on the side of the road, miraculously undamaged. But every detail, every second of that horrifying experience was clearly etched on her memory. And her every thought and prayer had been calm and confident, rooted in the rock-solid awareness that she was in hands far greater than her own.

It was like that now.

She saw, with startling clarity, the dizzying twists and turns her conversation with Jason had taken, the unconscious—for she couldn't believe he'd ever willingly expose that in himself—fear and sadness that tinged his words and expression. And as though a heavenly hand reached down to pull back the curtain hiding a magician's tricks, she understood.

"You're *trying* to be obnoxious."

Her only response was a crease between those expressive brows and the slightest flicker of emotion deep in his eyes, but that was enough. Triumph filled her with near elation, so that she had to force her words to come out calm and even.

"What's wrong, Jason? Something hit too close to home?" She didn't wait for an answer, she just nodded. "And what better way to throw the conversation off track than to start acting nasty to make me back off."

Now it was her turn to cross her arms, her stance deliberately casual, and lean back against the paddock railing. "I must say—" she nodded slowly, brows arched in mock appreciation—"you're quite good at it. Being nasty, I mean. Apparently you've had a good deal of practice at it."

"What I had—" he shot back—"were good teachers. Each and every one in the church."

He hadn't meant to say that. She was sure of it. It was evident in the way he stiffened suddenly, the way he clenched his jaw and stepped back from her.

As she watched him, it was as though a heavy veil cloaked him, effectively creating a concealing barrier between the two of them.

It didn't matter. In fact, it was all Mady could do not to break into a grin and let loose a "Yee haw!" that would do the cowboy in Jason proud.

Fine. Let him try to hide. It was simply too late. She'd seen inside him, and that brief glimpse had accomplished something remarkable. It had finally, after days of wondering, explained to her why she was here. She'd thought this crazy trip, this culmination of twists and unexpected events, was for her, to help her sort through something, to understand something about her-self…her life.

But now? Now she knew her purpose as clearly as if she were a foot soldier and a five-star general had marched up and handed her a set of orders.

She was here for Jason.

"Wrong."

Her eyes flew to meet his cold gaze. "W-what?" Could the man read her mind, for heaven's sake?

"You didn't hit close to home at all."

Relief coursed through her, and she dismissed the niggling of doubt that had jabbed at her a moment before. No, Jason couldn't read her mind. And she was right in her assessment.

It only made sense. Why else would she be here, without Eva? Why else would Mady find herself part-nered with a man who ran her emotions through the grinder? Besides, hadn't something about him drawn her almost from the moment she'd set eyes on him?

His looks.

No, not that. Well, okay, yes that, she admitted grudgingly. But it was more. It was something com-pelling in his eyes, in the tone of his voice….

"Hello? Anyone home?"

That tone? The condescending one?

"No!"

Her hand flew to cover her mouth as Jason studied her with a mixture of puzzlement and drollness.

"Nobody's home? Well, I confess I never expected you to admit that."

Mady lifted a hand to rub at her aching temples and wished the frustrating back and forth going on in her mind would pipe down and stop confusing her.

"Conversation giving you a headache, Miss Donovan?"

Once again her mouth got ahead of her gray matter. "Yes, but not the one with you."

"Excuse me?"

Mady waved her hand at him, shooing the conversation away and clamping a lid on the internal debate. She knew what she was supposed to do, and she'd do it with her whole heart.

And when she was done, Jason Tiber was going to bless the day he'd met her.

Not, of course, that he'd believe her if she told him so right now. In fact, the half-lidded look on his face communicated the exact opposite. "Are you always this peculiar, Miss Donovan?"

Go ahead. Be insulting. It won't work. I'm on your side, whether you like it or not.

"No, as a matter of fact, I'm not. Usually I'd be *much* more normal. And like any normal person who's being insulted, I'd pick right up on your cues." She snapped her fingers. "I'd dance to your little tune and hop on the resentment and anger train, and we'd go racing down the track."

She met his dubious stare without blinking. "But this time? Well, this time I'm not interested. Besides, I'm tired of fighting with you."

"Hey, I understand."

He couldn't have surprised her more if he'd reached out to poke her in the eye. "You…you do?"

His shoulders lifted in a blasé shrug. "Sure. It's got to grow tiring to have someone always proving you wrong."

Her mouth opened to argue, but she snapped it shut. What was the point? He wasn't going to admit she was right. And she sure wasn't going to admit she was wrong.

Doubt poked at her again, and she hesitated. *I'm not wrong, am I, Lord?*

Silence.

Well, okay…so she didn't feel some resounding sense of confirmation, no heavenly chorus belting out the "Hallelujah" chorus to let her know she was on the right track.

So what? No need to feel concerned. Confirmation would come later, when she wasn't so distracted. It was evident Jason wasn't ready to see the truth of what she said, and that was fine. No point in pushing. Just as well to call it a night.

"Fine. Okay. If you say so. You're not trying to distract me." She gave him the most serene smile she could muster and reached out to pat him on the arm—and was suddenly assaulted by the image of the little old ladies at church who so often patted her as they croaked, "Don't worry, honey, it's never too late for love."

Oh, dear, if she was even half as irritating to Jason as they were to her…

She looked at his face and broke into a grin. His expression was priceless! He was staring at her like she'd gone around the bend. So much the better. Keep him guessing.

"So how about if I leave you alone to bask in the glory of showing me that I'm all wet. Good night, Jason. Here's to pleasant dreams."

She swept her arm out, fully intending to give him a

gracious, graceful wave. Unfortunately, her hand smacked right into the bucket still balanced on the shelf on top of the paddock railing and sent it, water and all, flying.

Right toward Jason.

With a yelp he moved to sidestep the impending baptism, but he didn't make it. The bucket hit him in the midsection, and the water sloshed out, drenching him thoroughly.

They both stood there, too stunned to speak. Mady tried, several times, but slightly hysterical, utterly mortified laughter kept choking off her words.

"Oh…oh my!…well, now we're…we're *both* all wet, I guess."

Jason's head shot up from staring at his now soaking self, and he pinned her with a glare.

The laughter that had been bubbling up from deep within died in her throat as Jason stood there, dripping. And scowling. Mady dropped her gaze…only to find herself biting her lip at the growing puddle at Jason's feet.

Galvanized into action by the sight, she grabbed a rag hanging on a nearby hook and started dabbing at his soggy clothes. But the rag was too small and the water too plentiful.

Jason reached out to snatch the rag from her hands. "Do you *mind?*"

"I was just trying to help."

"I think—" the words were ground out—"you've done enough."

Dropping her hands to her sides, she gave a small shrug and glanced toward the path back to the campsite. "Maybe I'd better just go…."

The pointed look she got was confirmation enough. She stepped back, hesitated, then reached out an impulsive hand to lightly touch his arm. His piercing eyes fixed on her, and she bit her lip. "I'm…sorry, Jason. It was an accident."

She thought she detected a slight softening of the hard edge to his glare, but she couldn't be sure.

"Go to bed, Mady. Tomorrow's a new day."

Nodding, she moved away from the paddock rails and started for the path. But before she was out of earshot, she head Jason's wry mutter.

"Here's hoping I survive it."

Jason stood there, dripping on the ground, staring after Mady Donovan as she strolled down the path into the trees.

He continued standing there, staring, until he grew aware of the ache in his jaw from the way his teeth were clenched. His throat was sore from his ragged breathing, and his fingernails had left impressions on his palms from pressing into them so hard….

Okay, so she'd gotten to him.

Heaving a sigh, he forced himself to relax, flexing his fingers and rolling his shoulders to work some of the tension from his muscles. He tried wringing some of the water from his jeans, but it was a lost cause.

With a muttered oath, he hurled the soggy rag into the darkness, gaining some sense of satisfaction at the loud splat it made when it hit a tree.

What was wrong with him? Why was he letting one tiny woman push his buttons this way? Heaven knew he'd dealt with people like this before—irritants, people who rubbed him wrong from the get-go. People who expected him to watch over them, to take care of them, to be their protector...

People who spouted principles that they didn't bother to live by.

Don't think you're being entirely fair, old buddy....

His lips thinned and he leaned down to pick up the now empty bucket. He walked over to set it outside the paddock, doing his best to ignore the way his boots squished with every step.

Not being fair, eh? Oh yes he was. Mady Donovan was as predictable as they came. He knew her type; had dealt with them more times than he cared to admit. And he'd always had to keep his tone conciliatory, his attitude respectful and obliging. He'd had to make sure he was ever the perfect leader and caregiver; ever cautious and sheltering, no matter how moronic people's behavior became. All so his reactions wouldn't reflect badly on...

The ache in his jaw was back, and again he flexed the muscles.

Relax, Jas. She's not worth it. None of them are.

There was no point in letting it frustrate him any longer. He was free from all that now. He'd made his decision, and it was the right one. He didn't have to ignore stupid behavior any longer. He could call a spade a spade and not worry about the truth coming back to bite him. *Or those you love and respect.*

He looked away. Whatever. It didn't matter. What mattered was that those days were over, thank God.

He couldn't stop the wry smile that came to him then. Ah, well...old habits die hard.

Ignoring the ache deep in his gut—and pushing away the sudden, piercing image of eyes, whose blue depths were a mirror of his own...eyes filled with sorrow and disappointment—he forced his mind to other things. Things more deserving of his attention.

Mady Donovan, for example.

She was a pain in the neck, no doubt about it. If only she didn't come in such an appealing package. There was something about her that stirred feelings in him that would be better left unstirred. Protective feelings that surged to the foreground whether he wanted them to or not, urging him to do the most ridiculous things....

Like bury his fingers in that tangle of blond curls. They'd almost distracted him twice, danced around her face as she bandied words with him. Then, when she stood there staring down at the results of her close encounter with the water bucket, those crazy curls had tumbled forward to frame her face like some kind of off kilter halo.

He gave a muffled snort. If Mady Donovan were an angel, heaven was in trouble.

Still, he couldn't deny she was appealing, in an insane, take-your-life-in-own-your-hands kind of way. For one thing, there were those dark, sweeping lashes... those wide, changeable eyes. The woman had eyes that turned a man's resolve to pudding.

Almost made provoking her worth the risks.

Almost. But Jason knew better. Sure, those eyes almost convinced him to give in to her soft words and outreached hand. And yes, when her fingers had come to rest on his arm, he'd felt a definite weakness in his knees.

But she'd saved him from making a fool of himself by spouting her handy-dandy Bible verses....

He gave a quick shake of his head. She'd sounded like a good little Sunday schooler, which, he supposed, had been a favor to him. It had quite effectively brought him up short, reminding him of something he'd almost forgotten: Never trust wide, hypnotic eyes and sincere words. Nine times out of ten, they both lead to disaster. Pure, in-your-face, rip-your-guts-out disaster.

Oh no. No thank you. He wasn't interested, no matter how appealing it might be on the surface. Not a chance. Sliding his hands into his jacket pockets, he moved toward his horse, resolve growing within him.

He'd be wise to keep the delectable Miss Donovan at a nice, safe distance.

Tough to do when she's your assigned partner for the next four days.

His fingers found one last carrot in his pocket, and he drew it out, moving to offer it to the coal black horse who'd been watching him with such anticipation. He held it out, scratching the animal's chin and neck absently. No...it wouldn't be easy. But he'd find a way to do it.

He had to.

To do otherwise would only bring him—and, in all probability, Mady—more pain than either of them was prepared to face.

❧ 11 ❧

The best preacher is the human heart; the best teacher is time; the best friend is God.
JEWISH SAYING

When Mady's travel alarm, which she'd buried beneath her pillow so it wouldn't disturb anyone else, went off the next morning, she moaned and pulled her sleeping bag up over her head.

Just a few more minutes...please.

Apparently the alarm couldn't hear her pleading. Either that or it just didn't care. It kept emitting three sharp beeps, over and over, until she pushed out of her cocoon and reached beneath her pillow to punch the off button. Sitting up slowly, groaning a bit as she did so, Mady squinted at the digital display on her watch.

Five-thirty

"This is inhuman."

"No, it's an adventure."

She started and looked up to find Earl standing over her, a cup of steaming coffee in hand. Running a hand through what she was sure was a tangle of hair, she blinked up at him, half tempted to throw something at his beaming grin.

"Up and at 'em, Mady."

She mumbled a response and he laughed. "Not a morning person, eh?"

"Not since I was four." She frowned, then shook her head. "Nope. Take it back. Not even then."

"Well, breakfast will help you wake up, I guarantee it. It'll be ready in about a half hour."

"Then can I go back to bed?" She gave him her most pathetic puppy dog look.

Earl chuckled. "Then you can roll up your bed and get ready for another glorious day!" With that he turned and practically bounced toward another sleeping form buried in a sleeping bag.

Mady watched him go, grimacing. Obviously the man was a morning person. And there was nothing more irritating to a nonmorning person. She gave another groan and fell, face first, into her pillow.

"Then the adventure begins." She muttered around a mouthful of pillow case. "Goody goody gumdrops." She reached out to pull the sleeping bag over her head. "Why couldn't I have picked an adventure that started each day at the crack of noon?"

Pushing herself up, stretching the kinks and aches from her muscles as she stood, she went to dig her toiletry kit out of her pack.

If she had to be awake this early, at least she was going to get rid of the sweaters on her teeth.

She slipped her feet into her shoes and started toward the river, then paused. Trotting back to her pack, she pulled out her compact Bible. First she'd brush her teeth. Then she'd splash water on her face to wake herself up. If that didn't work, she'd dunk her head.

Thank God for cold water.

A scant ten minutes later, Mady stood combing her hair, staring at her reflection in the mirror she'd finally balanced on a face-high tree branch. But she didn't really see her reflection. What she saw was Jason's face...the way he had looked last night at the paddock.

"What happened, Jason?" She tapped the brush against her hand, wondering...then tossed it to land near her kit where she'd set it on a large, flat rock. She had four days to find out, to figure out how she could help.

Four days.

She drew in a determined breath. Four days to help Jason see that God was still there, very real and very set on loving him. And to draw the man out of whatever it was that had put that haunted look in his eyes.

Four days? How on earth was she supposed to do that in four days?

Clamping a lid on the panic that threatened to strangle her, Mady glanced at her watch, then went to grab her Bible. She dropped to the grass, sitting Indian style, and breathed a quick reminder to herself: "'I can do all things through Christ, who strengthens me.'"

So why did she feel about as ready for this task as a toddler taking the SAT?

Plain and simple, she knew the verse was true. Knew it was more than some holy cliché. And yet the uneasiness pricking at her heart refused to budge.

Four days. What on earth could she possibly say or do in that short amount of time to change a man's heart? She pictured Jason's expression again...the tight lips, the hard glitter in his eyes...the biting sarcasm in his words....

The wall he had around his heart was not going to come down easily.

Neither did the wall around Jericho.

"Yeah, but there were a bunch of people in that battle. And they had *trumpets,* Lord!" Biting her lip, she closed her eyes. It didn't matter. What you used, how many people were involved…it was all moot. What mattered was who called you into the fight. If it was God, then the battle was already won.

If it was God…

She frowned, opening her eyes. Well, of *course* it was God. Good grief, she wouldn't go waltzing into something like this on her own. It wasn't like she *wanted* to get involved in Jason's life. She had enough struggles of her own, thank you very much. She didn't need to get mixed up in whatever turmoil he was facing.

But the man was angry with God, that much was clear. And that…bothered her. No, more than that. It made her ache inside, someplace deep within. She lifted her hand to press at the pain. So what if Jason was a virtual stranger? His reaction last night, the look of pain and longing in his eyes…it had hurt her heart.

With an impatient sigh she dropped her hand from her chest to the smooth leather cover of her Bible. She was an empathetic sort, she knew that. But the impact this man's struggle had on her just didn't make sense.

Not unless she was supposed to do something about it.

She moved her fingers over her Bible. "Show me, Lord. Show me what you want from me."

Yes, it was a silly way to seek guidance. If she'd had more time she never would have done it. But four days! Well, desperate times—or, more appropriate, desperate *time lines*—called for desperate measures. Well, didn't they? God had called her to this task, so surely it was reasonable to ask him to give her the guidance she needed.

She flipped open the Bible, planted her finger on the page, and looked down. Proverbs. A smile eased over her face. Of course. There was so much practical wisdom in Proverbs, so much encouragement.

She read the verse her finger had pinpointed: "'If you keep your mouth shut, you will stay out of trouble.'"

Her mouth fell open. *What?* This was her grand, insightful guidance from God? She read it again. Surely it hadn't said what she'd thought it said.

But there it was again, clear as day: "'If you keep your mouth shut, you will stay out of trouble.'"

Mady uttered a short laugh. Well, maybe this was direct guidance from God and maybe it wasn't…but it was still good counsel. No matter what Jason threw at her, no matter how provoked she felt, she'd keep her mouth shut. It wouldn't be easy, but she'd do it. Nothing would prompt her to speak out against him.

"Behold, Mady Donovan—" she gave a graceful flip of her hand—"the very epitome of restraint and serenity."

Oh, brother. And if anyone bought that, she should see what else she could sell them!

Swallowing hard, Mady squared her shoulders. It wouldn't be so bad. Besides, hadn't she wanted to go on a silent retreat? It had sounded so refreshing when she'd first heard about it a few years ago…to go someplace quiet, someplace where you didn't talk, where you focused on the Lord and the Word and listening….

So—this would be her time of silence. Her time to focus on Jason and listen beyond the words to hear his heart—

She stopped, her mouth dropping open at the realization that hit her then. She really did want to do that. To listen to Jason, to help him, to somehow ease the pain she'd seen in his eyes last night.

This time her prayer was simple and sincere: "Help him, Father. You're the only One who can."

Peace settled over her, and she breathed it in. Hope kindled within her, and she settled back, circling her knees with her arms.

Four days. It would be enough. God never set an impossible task before those who sought to follow Him. He'd do whatever work He needed to do on her....

Mady's eyes flew open. No, not on *her*. The work needed to be done on Jason, not on her. She was fine.

Shaking her head at the unconscious slip, she rose and gathered her things, heading back toward where she saw the others already starting in on breakfast preparations. But with each step, she felt a gnawing uneasiness.

Relax, Mady. It was just a mistake. Just a sign that she needed to get more sleep. That was all.

Nothing more.

As with dinner last night, breakfast was made, devoured, and cleaned up with surprising speed and ease. Though the powdered eggs had been far from appetizing, Mady had enjoyed the work and the growing camaraderie.

Heather and Brian had the rest of them in stitches as they told stories of all that had gone wrong on their wedding day, from a Frisbee landing in the middle of their wedding cake to a minister who dozed off during the service.

"He'd taken allergy medication that morning," Brian exclaimed amid the disbelieving laughter. "I think he'll be changing his prescription now."

The stories and laughter followed them as they went through the process of packing everything up. So it seemed like no time at all before the horses were saddled, and they all were ready to go.

"How far do we ride today, O Great Leader?"

Earl swung into the saddle and tossed a grin at Nikos. "All the way to the campsite."

Nikos's mouth twisted wryly. "Ha ha. How many hours?"

Nudging his horse with his heels, Earl started out. "About five hours, all total. We should get there right around lunchtime." He cast a smile back over his shoulder as the group fell in line. "Just in time to unpack, set up sleeping sites, take care of the horses, and start in on the meal preparation."

A collective groan met this pronouncement, and Earl's only response was the laughter that drifted back to them on the mountain breeze.

Grinning at the exchange, Mady settled onto Dorado's saddle and started up the path when a cry of alarm split the air.

She spun just in time to see Lea's wide-eyed terror as her horse reared, pawing at the air. Suddenly, Jason was at Lea's side, taking the reins from her and speaking in a low, soothing voice to the startled animal.

It was over in seconds, and Lea turned to bury her face in Jason's chest, clutching his shirt like it was a lifeline. As Jason bent his head low, speaking to Lea in the same, soothing tone he'd used on the horse, Mady felt a clear stab of a very unpleasant emotion.

Jealousy.

"How odd…"

Mady jumped at the comment, then sought out its source. Nikos, seated on his horse, was beside her.

"Odd?" Had her emotions been that obvious? "Why odd?" True, she hadn't known Jason long. But you didn't have to know someone a long time to be drawn to him, to find your heart leaning toward him.

Nikos nudged her with an elbow, his dark eyes twinkling with amusement. "Odd because Lea is a consummate horsewoman. She's competed in many events, including steeplechase, for years."

Mady shot a glance back at Lea, who was still clinging to Jason. "Is that so?" The little fake!

"Indeed. But isn't it fortuitous that your most accommodating partner was at hand to…assist her."

"Fortuitous. Yeah…sure." She should ride right over there and tell both Lea and Jason what she thought of them: Lea, for her deception, and Jason for falling for it!

Nothing will provoke you, remember? The epitome of restraint and serenity, remember?

No, not at the moment. She was too busy leveling a glare at Jason. He had the nerve to call her gullible? *Well, that was a bit of the pot calling the kettle black, wouldn't you say, Mister Tiber?*

With a sniff, Mady willed him to look up and look her way. Then they'd see who was gullible!

She almost fell off her horse when the man did exactly that. As though sensing her scrutiny, he looked up from handing Lea the reins and met Mady's steaming glower. Never one to let a perfect opportunity go by, she maintained the contact for just a moment, letting her contempt show as clearly as she could. Then, when a slight frown creased her so-called partner's brow, she gave a sniff and a toss of her head.

Turning her attention to Nikos, she flashed him a bright smile. "How fortuitous, indeed. And how fortuitous for *me* that *her* partner is here to keep me company on the long ride ahead of us."

The chuckle that escaped Nikos's chest was low and resonating. "And does the fire in your eyes burn for me, fair Mady—" there was a tinge of melancholy in the smile he gave her—"or for one who has yet to realize the direction and inestimable blessing of your heart?"

Swift regret filled her and she reached out, wanting to soothe any hurt she might have caused him. "Nikos, I'm sorry. What a horrid thing to do."

His eyes were gentle. "What? Ask me to ride with you?"

She shook her head, though she was grateful for his kindness in letting her off the hook so easily. "You know what I'm talking about." She looked down, feeling suddenly too sheepish to meet those dark, gracious eyes. "I was going to use you to…to…"

Mady frowned. To what? Make Jason jealous? But why on earth would it matter one way or the other to him if she were with Nikos. Or with any man, for that matter?

She was the one fighting a battle in her heart, not Jason. She was the one torn between irritation and fascination, disdain and desire.

Gentle fingers lifted her chin, and Nikos smiled into her eyes, then leaned forward to place a soft kiss on her cheek. When he released her, she put a hand over the place his lips had brushed.

Farl's call broke in on them. "Get a move on, gang. We've got a ways to go and work to do once we get there."

Nikos took her hand and tugged at it. "Come, let's ride together as friends. The sunshine is just peeking over the mountains, and soon it will shine bright and warm. There is much in this day for us to enjoy together."

Grateful tears stung Mady's eyes. "Nikos, you're far too nice to me, you know that, don't you?"

His teeth gleamed white against his tanned face. "My dear Mady, do not worry yourself so. Don't you think I understand?" He lifted his shoulders in an easy shrug. "Don't you think I realize you'd far rather have your heart focused on one so very deserving as I?" The laughter glittering in his eyes did her heart good. "Alas, we have little control in such matters. The heart goes where it is drawn, does it not?"

She nodded, biting her lip lest the tears escape her eyes and stream down her cheeks. "I'm an idiot, aren't I?"

"But a most appealing one, I assure you."

With a laugh, she reached out to deliver a light punch to his arm. "Oh, Nikos, you're good for me." She sat straighter in the saddle, lifting her face to the sunshine. "Let's make a deal. Let's talk about completely unimportant things. Let's laugh and tell stories. Tell me about your childhood and those wonderful beaches of white sand where you used to swim. Talk about yourself—" she infused the words with enthusiasm—"so I can get to know my friend better. Let's not even mention you-know-who for the rest of this ride."

He inclined his head. "Your wish, as they say, is my

command. Besides—" his eyes twinkled with mischief—
"I cannot think of a better way to pass the morning."

❧ 12 ❧

Men occasionally stumble over the truth,
but most of them pick themselves up and hurry off
as if nothing happened.
WINSTON CHURCHILL

It was around one in the afternoon when they finally reached base camp. Jason took in the clearing, situated in the center of a circle of towering evergreens.

He gave Earl a sideways glance. "Well, I'll say this much for you, buddy. You know how to pick a camp-site."

Earl's pleasure was evident in his expression. "Thanks, Jas."

Jason nodded. "It's a perfect spot. Even better than the site last night."

"That's just an overnight stopping place. This—" his gaze swept the area—"this is pure base camp. People love spending as long as they can here."

Jason could certainly see why. The grassy area before them was level and spacious with plenty of room for a number of sleeping sites. They'd be close enough to feel like a group, but far enough apart to have a sense of privacy if they wanted it.

The corral was also large and well laid out, situated far enough from the campsite to draw the horseflies away but not so far that they couldn't keep an eye on the animals.

Two large tents already stood at the far end of the clearing.

Must be Earl's tent and the supply tent.

Knowing Earl, the supply tent was well stocked with everything from fishing gear to emergency equipment like strobe lights, mirrors for signaling, short-range radios, first aid kits, and so on. He figured Earl would hand everything out just before their hike.

Just then a man stepped out of one of the tents and strolled toward them.

"Ho, Ben!" Earl called out, and Jason realized it was the wrangler from the lodge. He'd left early yesterday morning, shortly after they'd all arrived and met him. Earl had said he'd be out here during their four days to keep an eye on the horses while they hiked.

Ben waved, and Earl turned his horse so that he faced the group as they gathered. "Okay, gang. Good ride out here. You all did great."

"So of course we all deserve a nice nap and room service for lunch."

Everyone chuckled at Nikos's wry question, and Earl hooked his thumbs in his belt. "Considering that the horses have done most of the work, I figure they're the ones who deserve room service. Which you all are going to provide."

He nodded toward the corral. "Just like yesterday, folks. First order of events is getting your horses situated. Unsaddle 'em and give 'em a good rubdown. You'll find curry combs and feed and water in the supply tent, along with assigned spots for keeping your tack." He nodded toward the wrangler. "Ol' Ben here will keep an eye out in case you need help. Once the horses are set, we'll talk through setting up your tents."

Heather gave a little groan. "We have to do all that now? I'm tired."

Jason shook his head at the girl's comment, but Earl's expression stayed as relaxed as his words. "Well, until you get your horses taken care of, you can't set up your tents. And until you get your tents up, there's not exactly anyplace around here for resting." He shrugged. "Unless, of course, you're fond of lying on the ground. Something I'm sure the chiggers would welcome."

Jason restrained a grin at Heather's quick scan of the ground around them. Her husband leaned over to pat her arm. "Come on, hon. It'll be fun, you'll see."

To her credit, the young woman managed a game smile and headed her horse for the pen.

The others followed suit, and it wasn't long before the horses were brushed down, watered, and fed. Jason had finished first and now sat on a nearby fallen log, watching the rest work with their animals.

"Taking a break?"

He glanced behind him and found Earl walking up. With a happy sigh, the older man leaned casually against a broad tree trunk.

"Ah, work...I could watch it for hours."

Jason chuckled. He knew it was a crock. Earl loved working hard and playing hard.

"Good to see how comfortable this group is with the horses."

Jason followed to where Earl was looking. Nikos and Lea were making short work of removing the saddles and tack. In fact, they performed the tasks quickly and skillfully. Evidence that Jason had been right earlier on.

Lea's fright when her horse had reared had been an act.

"Our Lea seems to have recovered well from her…terror earlier, wouldn't you say?"

At Earl's grinning, sideways look, Jason shook his head. "She was pretty obvious, wasn't she?"

"Not necessarily. But I'd been watching her pretty close when we started out. Wanted to be sure she'd be okay with the horse." He shrugged. "Pretty evident she knew what she was doing."

"With the horse or with me?"

Earl laughed quietly. "Both."

Jason had been fairly sure the whole episode had been for his benefit. He'd caught Lea watching him more than once since they got off the plane, a speculative gleam in those lovely, dark eyes. He'd made a point of not paying much attention to her, which had only seemed to increase her fascination.

When he heard her scream and turned to see her horse rear, he'd almost turned back to Ebony, his own horse, and swung up into the saddle, leaving her to handle the situation on her own. Like Earl, he'd seen enough at that point to be fairly sure Lea could handle the animal without any trouble. And yet…

His upbringing had won out. He could almost see his sweet mother standing there, shaking a finger at him. "Now Jason William, I raised you to treat women with respect and consideration. Get going and help that gal!"

Sure enough, though, the moment he'd grabbed the struggling horse's reins, Lea had turned to him, burying her face in his chest and grabbing hold of his shirt.

Earl pushed away from the tree, grinning down at

him. "She sure seemed grateful to have a big, brave fella come to her aid. Fair hung off your shirt when you stepped in."

It was true. She'd clung to him like a baby chimp on its mama. What's more, her voice had cracked just so, and when she lifted her eyes to him, he'd even seen a sheen of tears glistening on her lashes.

"'Course, I'm sure you didn't mind all that much."

Jason looked up, a grin easing across his face. "Well, it was a trial, having a beautiful woman throw herself into my arms and all, but I suffered through it."

Earl swatted at him. "The day you suffer for a woman, Jas, is the day I eat my hat."

He let the teasing statement slide. Earl knew him too well.

As for Lea, well, the whole encounter had been just a bit too convenient, a bit too...practiced.

"Well, I'm glad to see she's doing better," Earl remarked as he moved away. "Hate to think that pretty little thing was traumatized on the first day."

"Somehow I think it would take a good deal more than a fussing horse to traumatize that one."

Earl paused at the muttered comment and glanced back at Jason. "Hmm..." He let his glance swing from Jason to the others at the corral, then back to Jason again. "Just watch your step, pal. Methinks the woman has her sights set on you."

Narrowing his eyes, Jason watched as Lea moved with confidence, watering and feeding her horse.

"And I'm gonna need you focused on the task at hand." Earl looked toward the corral again. "And the woman at hand, too."

Jason gave his friend a quick look. "Meaning?"

There was no grin on Earl's face now; he was the serious, forthright expedition leader. "Meaning I need you focused on your partner, buddy. There's a reason you two are teamed up—"

"Yeah." Jason let the word drip with sarcasm. "You hate me."

Earl's grin was quick to return. "Actually, I don't. But like I told you earlier, this hasn't been my doing. All I'm saying is stick to the task at hand. Don't let yourself be distracted."

With that, Earl sauntered toward the supply tent, whistling a carefree tune as he walked.

Disgruntled, though not completely sure why, Jason went back to watching Lea. She moved to inspect her horse's legs and hooves, running her hand down a rear hock. The animal gave a snort and stamped its leg fitfully. Lea didn't even flinch. She held firmly to the leg, inspecting it before she let it go.

She started to turn in his direction so Jason averted his head. Last thing he wanted was to get caught staring at the woman and have her read the action as interest on his part. But as he shifted his gaze, he locked eyes with Lea's brother, whose tanned face was creased in a knowing grin.

Jason smiled back at him, inclining his head and giving a shrug of his shoulders.

Even from this distance, he saw the flicker of realization on Nikos's face, and the man's smile broadened. He lifted his hand and gave Jason a quick salute, as though to say, "Congratulations on not being taken in."

Jason chuckled. Lea's manipulations might have

been skillful, but they certainly weren't good enough to fool him. Even as he'd played the role, letting her cling to his shirt, he'd known what she was up to. And he had half a mind to let her know what he thought of her....

Then he realized there was a much more satisfying way to respond. Ignore her. Odds were good that would have a good deal more impact than anything he could say.

His smile turned into low laughter.

Impact? Shoot, it'd drive her crazy. Yup, that was the way to go. From now on, the luscious Lea was invisible.

So you've got two people to ignore now? Lea and your partner?

At the thought of Mady, Earl's words drifted back to him. "Just stay focused on the task at hand. Don't get distracted."

Distracted, eh? With Mady as his partner, how could he avoid it?

He shook away the cynical thought. From what he could tell, his accident-prone partner was in the process of finishing with her horse. He'd expected her to look weary and worn out by now, but what he saw lighting her face as she ran the curry brush over the horse's back was pure delight.

Quite a contrast to the nasty glare she'd shot at him when he was calming Lea.

Well, let her glare all she wanted. What did he care what Mady Donovan thought of him or his discernment. He didn't...not one little bit.

No more than he cared about that smarmy little kiss Nikos had planted on Mady's cheek.

The stick in his hand gave way with a sharp snap,

and he glanced down in surprise. He tossed it away, brushing his hands clean. If only he could brush away the effect Mady was having on him as easily.

He leaned his elbows on his knees, glancing from Mady to Nikos, who was just leaving the corral. What exactly was going on between those two?

Why do you care?

Good question. Especially since he was supposed to be avoiding the woman. But every time he turned around, there she was...drawing his attention even when she didn't know it.

He directed a glare of his own at Mady, then paused. She was scratching the horse's smooth neck, and he caught the timbre of her voice as she spoke to the animal in low, affectionate tones. Watching her, Jason found himself running a gamut of emotions.

She drove him crazy.

Take their little encounter that first day out on the path, when she almost took a header off the cliff. Speaking of which, why had he followed her?

"Who knows?"

He tossed out the question, irritation burning inside. He sure didn't know. It certainly wasn't because of the appreciation she showered on him for his effort on her behalf. More often than not, those color-shifting eyes of hers blazed at him for some imagined affront.

Sneak up on her. Yeah, right. Like he had nothing better to do.

Well, you didn't exactly announce your presence.

So? He'd been curious. He'd seen her by her horse, standing there, eyes closed, with a dismayed expression on her face that had torn at his heart, twisting inside of him as effectively as a switchblade.

Darned if he hadn't taken two steps toward her before he realized what he was doing.

"Idiot!"

But even as he hissed the accusation at himself, he could see again the curious transformation that had come over Mady's features. Anguish had given way to a small, wistful smile. And then pure joy had shone in her face.

He'd nearly gone to her then, asked what had happened…but her horse—who seemed almost as quirky as Mady sometimes—had chosen that precise moment to give her a shove toward the path. And she'd waltzed off, happy as a lark, as though it were the most natural thing in the world to have a horse nudge you into action.

As though someone had slipped him the answer key to a quiz he'd been agonizing over, understanding dawned. That was it. That was what drew him to Mady with such force.

She was constantly taking him by surprise.

Mady Donovan was a petite bundle of contradictions and curiosities, and he couldn't get her out of his mind. Nearly every time he'd expected her to back down, she stood firm. When he anticipated a battle, she lowered those long lashes of hers and conceded.

She barely came up to his chest, but she wasn't the least bit hesitant to stand up to him if she thought he was wrong.

He straightened, watching Mady as she checked the horse's feed and water.

The first time she'd turned those wide eyes on him and apologized…well, he'd been speechless.

"I'd like to apologize to you."

The words were as stunning now as they'd been when she offered them to him, with that oh-so-sincere tone and those oh-so-wide eyes. He still couldn't quite believe she'd said them.

When was the last time someone had surprised him that way? He frowned, tilting his head, searching his memory. He'd always had a knack for reading people, for being able to dissect their issues and predict how they'd act or react. He'd seen through Lea as easily as looking through a piece of crystal.

In fact, the only people who had proven him wrong—really wrong—in the last several years had been Mady and—

He jerked away from the realization. But it came anyway, against his will, against his concentration to block it out.

His father.

The only people over the last few years who had gone against what he'd been sure they would do were Mady Donovan...and his father.

He closed his eyes as his chest constricted. *Don't. Don't go there. You weren't thinking about him. You were thinking about Mady.*

Right. A Mady who had quite neatly pulled the rug of preconceived notions right out from under him. He saw again her expression when she stared at him...and he'd stared back. Couldn't have taken his eyes from hers if his feet had caught on fire. There had been a shift in her expression, her stance...and then she reached out to him—

Reaction jolted through him now as it had at that

soft touch. He felt his breathing grow ragged, his pulse race....

"Might as well admit it, Tiber." He shook his head in disgust. "Mady Donovan scares you." His lip curled. "Spitless."

He stood and walked toward his sleeping area. With abrupt movements, he rearranged stuff unnecessarily.

It was true. She scared him. Which explained the way he'd reacted last night....

Save it for the kiddies at Vacation Bible School, Miss Donovan.

Oh yeah, definitely offensive. But even in that she'd taken his expectations and ground them into the dirt with her small heel. He'd expected anger, frustration, verbal retaliation...and for one glorious moment, he'd been sure he'd get it.

Fire had blazed in her eyes, and she'd drawn a breath. She looked ready for battle, and he'd tensed, eager for the derailment. Then...

He frowned. What *had* happened then? He was still trying to sort through it. Still trying to understand where she'd come up with that disarming, too-close- and too-calm-for-comfort statement: *You're trying to be obnoxious.*

Well, sure, but she wasn't supposed to know that.

He shook away the disturbing emotions he'd felt then...felt again as he recalled the encounter. But as quickly as he erased them, other feelings, other memories took their place.

Once again he saw Mady, perched on the edge of the path, face intent as she craned her neck to look at the squirrels in the tree. He'd stood there, staring at her, utter disbelief blending with the panic inside. He still didn't think she had any idea how close she came to taking a swan dive into the wild blue yonder. But he'd seen it...seen the way her feet were inching ever closer to infinity.

Okay, so maybe he'd overreacted. Even been kind of harsh. So sue him. It had made his heart do weird things to see her standing there, oblivious to the danger she'd put herself in.

Why?

He paused. Why, what? Why had she risked her neck? Who knew? The woman was a veritable well-spring of borderline lunacy—

No, why did you react that way? Why the panic?

Ah. That.

He strolled toward the horse pen, watching as Mady gave Dorado a gentle pat, then bent down to retrieve her saddle and tack.

Why, indeed? Good question. One to which he simply didn't have an answer. She got to him. He didn't know why, but she did. His gaze traveled to her again, and he bit the inside of his lip.

There was only one thing to do. He had no choice but to make a change in his plans. Rather than avoid the woman, which clearly wasn't working, he would do what he could to understand her.

He'd find out, come hell or high water, what it was about this one, small, ridiculous woman that grabbed him deep inside and twisted his gut in knots.

Somehow, over the next few days, he was going to solve the puzzle that was Mady Donovan.

And then he was going to forget he'd met her.

❦ 13 ❦

All rising to great places is by a winding stair.
FRANCIS BACON

"Need help?"

At the deep voice, Mady turned from Dorado to find Jason leaning on the top rail of the horse pen, studying her.

"Help?" She wasn't sure she'd understood.

A small smile played at the corners of his mouth. He inclined his head toward Dorado. "With the horse."

She quickly shook her head. How lame did he think she was? She could handle her horse on her own, thank you. Her chin tipped. "Nope. I'm fine. In fact—" she brushed her hands together with a quick, decisive action—"I'm all done."

He stiffened slightly and stepped back as she ducked through the rails and moved to pass him, walking back up the path toward their tent sites.

"So, what did I do wrong this time?"

Mady's determined steps faltered. She glanced over her shoulder, fully expecting to see the mocking light she'd come to know so well in Jason's eyes. But to her surprise, all she saw in those blue depths as he walked behind her was a spark of humor.

And something else. Something that made very little sense.

Compassion.

She stopped cold. Just like that. And Jason promptly plowed into her.

"Oof!"

"Watch—!"

Thrown off balance, Mady grabbed at whatever she could get ahold of to keep from falling. Both hands seized the fabric of Jason's shirt just as his fingers closed around her arms and pulled her forward. The combined actions smacked her up against a very firm, very broad chest.

"Oh...my..."

It was all she could think of to say, held there as she was, Jason's arms snug around her, her nose pressed against the buttons of his shirt.

"Nice to see you getting along, team three."

They jumped apart, and Jason raked a hand through his hair as he met Earl's amused look. The two of them spoke in chorus.

"Mady tripped."

"Jason was just keeping me from falling."

Earl's smile was as noncommittal as his "Ah. Of course." He jerked a thumb over his shoulder. "We're ready to set up the campsites. Unless, of course—" he eyed them—"you're not finished here?"

Mady and Jason looked at each other.

"Done? Yeah, we're done."

Mady gave a quick nod. "Sure. Of course. All finished."

"Completely," Jason added.

"Totally." Mady gave another nod, feeling like one of those goofy tipping wooden birds that sat on the edge of a glass and bobbed up and down uncontrollably. "Yes."

"Well, then, by all means…"

Mady could tell, as Earl stepped aside and indicated they should go ahead of him, that he wanted to laugh. Badly. But he restrained himself.

Shoving her hands in her pockets, Mady stepped out quickly—at just the same time as Jason. They didn't even look at each other when they collided. Just bounced away like bumper cars. Jason backed out of Mady's path, and, chin held high, she quickstepped her way toward the others, doing her best to ignore Earl's chuckle as it drifted along after her.

From his spot on a log near the fire—and near the pot of strong, black coffee—Earl watched his group with growing fascination.

And only a twinge or two of misgivings.

Team two, Heather and Brian, were doing fairly well. It had been obvious early on that this whole thing was more primitive than Heather had anticipated. But for all of that, she'd done a good job of putting aside her apprehension to enter into the adventure.

Though far from proficient, she and Brian had managed to get their two-man site set up. Their tent was in pretty good shape, despite a definite tendency to list to the right. He'd help them fix that in a minute. They'd pulled small camp chairs from the supply tent and were now sitting close together, engrossed in studying the wilderness survival manual they'd borrowed from Mady.

All things considered, they were doing pretty well. The few conflicts they had were settled quickly and with good humor. And, of course, a hug and a kiss. With each activity they tried, they improved in both communication and cooperation.

A regular group leader's dream, those two.

He sipped at his steaming mug, letting the fragrance and taste of the coffee calm him. Contrary to most folks, coffee soothed Earl's nerves. He loved coffee. Everything about it. He knew it wasn't the best thing in the world for him, so he generally restricted himself to one cup at morning, noon, and evening. Unless, of course, things got tense.

Coffee helped keep him calm when he needed it most. Stick a cup of hot, steaming black brew in his hands, and he could face anything.

Even team one.

Lea and Nikos fluctuated between affectionate camaraderie and out-and-out warfare. One minute they were talking, helping each other, working together with an ease that gave clear evidence of how well they knew each other…then she'd let out a screech, or he'd give her one of those condescending glares, and they'd be off.

Those two had bickering down to an art form.

Nikos had tried to help Lea get her tube tent set up, but she'd thrown one verbal barb too many and he turned his back on her, set up his own equipment, then walked back toward the horses.

Earl pressed his lips together. He was going to have to do something about Nikos's tendency to bail when his sister got too ornery. And he would—his eyes narrowed—just as soon as he dealt with Jason's tendency to step in and fill the gap Nikos left.

Lips twitching, Earl remembered how surprised he'd been to find Jason and Mady clutching each other on the path. They'd jumped apart like guilty teenagers. Though he couldn't be sure, Earl thought it was the first time he'd ever seen Jason blush. He'd almost had to bite his tongue off not to say something about it, to milk his buddy's uncharacteristic chagrin for all it was worth. But the looks on Jason's and Mady's faces made it clear that wasn't exactly a great idea.

He had the feeling they were more surprised than he to find themselves in such close proximity. *Very* close.

They'd walked double-time to join the others, and both had been immersed in setting up their tents and arranging their packs. Jason, of course, was done with his sleeping site almost before Mady even had her bivy sack rolled out. His tarp was expertly tied off to a tree at one end and anchored to the ground at the other, forming an efficient shelter from the rain. His sleeping bag and pad were in place in the bivy sack, ready to go.

Earl had held his breath, waiting for what would happen next.

Mady stared at Jason as he sat on the ground, leaning his back against the tree where he'd tied his tarp support. Everything, from the crossed arms over his chest to the small, blatantly superior smile on his face, was smug.

"Done yet?"

Earl leaned his elbows on his knees, shaking his head. *Way to encourage teamwork, Jas.* Since when had Jason become a jerk? It wasn't like him to rub someone's face in his or her lack of knowledge.

Understandably, Mady reacted poorly—though whether to the question itself or to Jason's attitude it was hard to tell. She glared from him to the tarp and bivy sack she was wrestling with. She'd made no secret of the fact that she was a novice at all of this. She was sharp, no doubt about that. She caught on quickly. But even the simplest set up could be a bit daunting until you knew what you were doing.

Come on, buddy, offer to give her a hand.

No such luck. Instead, Jason eyed Mady's tarp dubiously, raising his brows at the way she was bunching one end of it in her hand and wrapping the tie-off cord around it over and over. When a smirk crossed Jason's face, Earl wanted to throw something at him.

"I take it you need some help...*partner.*"

If Jason's undue and obviously sarcastic emphasis on the word made Earl grit his teeth, it was nothing compared to Mady's reaction. She bristled like a cat facing down a pit bull.

"Not...in...a...million...years."

Each word overflowed with loathing. Earl would have considered this clear warning that it was time to tone the attitude and sarcasm down. Jason, on the other hand, treated it like a red flag to a bull.

"It'll take you that long to get your tent set up."

Earl slapped a hand to his forehead. What was *wrong* with Jason? If Earl didn't know better, he'd swear the man was doing everything he could to make Mady detest him.

And a fine job he was doing.

Mady's features reddened, and she turned her back on him with a jerk. Her actions as she stood to tie the tarp cord to the tree were abrupt and angry. Jason walked over to take hold of the tie-off cord, and Mady tried to pull it away from him.

"I can do this myself, thank you!"

"You are the most stubborn, uncooperative—"

Time for a referee. Earl started to rise, but the sound of more arguing—this time from another direction—stopped him. He glanced toward the Panapoulos's site. Nikos had returned. And he and Lea were in each other's faces, their tones giving evidence of their escalating anger.

With a deep sigh, Earl leaned forward to fill his coffee mug again. This was definitely going to be a two—maybe even *three*-cup afternoon.

"I think it's time we declared a truce."

Mady looked up at this suggestion and eyed Jason dubiously. "Oh? And why is that, exactly?"

The wide-eyed attempt at innocence made her want to throw something at him. "No reason. Just seems like a good idea."

"Uh-huh." She glanced pointedly at his hands, which he was holding behind his back. "Bringing me a surprise?"

"Well…"

"Oh, let me guess. A spider. No, that would be too juvenile, even for you. A bouquet of poison oak?"

"Not even close. Now, about that truce…"

Crossing her arms over her chest, Mady stared up at him, not responding.

Seeing her resistance, he gave a sigh and brought his hands out from behind his back. "You want a knife?"

She couldn't help the wicked smile that crossed her face. "Depends on whom…I mean, *what* I get to use it on."

"The veggies. Nothing else," came the controlled response.

"Oh." She held out her hand and he set one of the knives, handle first, in her outstretched palm. "What a pity."

She was surprised to hear Jason chuckle as he lowered himself into a crouch beside her. They'd been assigned chopping duty for dinner preparations, and Mady had found the perfect flat-topped rock to use for a cutting surface.

"Vicious little soul, aren't you?" he muttered as he set a carrot on the rock and started cutting it into chunks.

"Only when provoked." She eyed him. "*Very* provoked."

He chuckled again and nodded. "Too true. I admit it, I was a bit—"

She couldn't resist. "Rude?" She chopped slices off the mushroom she held with each suggestion, her knife making a satisfying little click on the rock with each cut. "Obnoxious? Repellant? Odious?"

"Oh, now wait just one minute!" His aggrieved objection would have been quite effective if not for the glint of laughter in his eyes. "That's going too far. I'm *not* odorous! I bathe on a regular basis."

Mady surprised herself by laughing.

"Well, if I'd known chopping vegetables would be this much fun, I would have volunteered."

Jason and Mady turned to find Lea watching them, her arms crossed, her head tilted as she studied them with interest. "Earl sent me to see if you're finished yet."

With a sweep of her hand, Mady scooped the rest of

the diced and chopped vegetables into the large bowl Earl had given then. "Yeah, we're done."

Jason's quick glance at her stopped her in midsweep. As did his grin when he said, "Yup. All finished."

Now her lips were twitching. "Completely."

"Totally."

With that they burst into laughter, which only increased when Mady saw Lea's look of utter astonishment. She was gaping at them like they were totally looney.

And when it came right down to it, Mady couldn't argue the point. Not one little bit.

When they finished dinner and after everyone had remarked on how delicious the food tasted, Earl took them on a walk around the base camp. He showed them the different paths they could take, explaining where they led and what there was to see.

The last path he showed them was little more than a narrow, trampled-down lane through tall, dense bushes and trees.

"That's a path? Doesn't look very well traveled." Mady didn't mean to be critical, but there was hardly room for one person to walk. And the ground, covered as it was with bent and pressed down vegetation, looked custom-made for catching and summarily tripping unsuspecting feet.

"Oh, it's quite well traveled, actually." Mady saw both humor and patience in Earl's smile. "It's a game trail that leads to the river. I know it's a bit imposing at first glance, but it's really a nice, easy walk. And the river's worth it."

"There's no such thing as a nice, easy walk for some people."

Mady glared at Jason. So much for their truce. He was obviously making a point of not looking at her, staring down the path as though it were the most interesting thing he'd seen in days. Well, he didn't fool her. She knew as well as he did about whom he was talking. What had he called her? *"Amazing Luck of Grace"*? Hmpf!

Earl was going on as they all moved back to their seats around the fire. "The riverbank is a nice place to sit and think."

Lea paused in midsit. "Is it safe after dark?"

Earl pursed his lips, considering the question. "Depends on what you're asking about."

Lea lifted one elegant, perfectly manicured hand to her throat. "Animals. Specifically, bears."

The temperature had just started to drop a bit, and Mady blamed her shiver on that. Pulling her jacket around her shoulders, she peered down the path, taking in the thick brush on either side of the narrow trail.

It did look like the wilderness equivalent of a dark alley.

"Make enough noise and you shouldn't have to worry about any unnerving encounters." Earl's tone and smile were easy, reassuring. "Trust me, they're no more eager to have a meeting than you are."

"Surely there isn't anything around here that's actually dangerous?"

Earl had grinned at Heather's wide-eyed plea. "We're

in a wilderness setting here. This region is home to all kinds and sizes of wildlife. Some are plenty harmless—" he pushed his hat back a bit on his head—"some aren't."

"I read there are mountain lions *and* bears in the North Cascades."

Mady turned a frown toward Brian at this supposedly helpful comment. Didn't he know better than to say something like that when Lea and Heather were already nervous?

How about you?

She wrinkled her nose. *I'm not nervous. I'm just…cautious.*

Heather's eyes grew a fraction wider, her face a bit whiter. "Lions? Bears?"

She sounded like the scarecrow from *Wizard of Oz,* for heaven's sake. Any minute the flying monkeys would be coming.

Damage control. That's what Earl needed right now. And from the look on his face, he knew it. "Yes, but you really don't need to—"

"Small bears, yes?"

Earl gave Lea a slow shake of his head. "Not always."

She cast an alarmed glance at her brother, and Earl held out a restraining hand. "Relax, Lea. All of you. Like I said, there's a fairly simple way to handle your concerns. Just make enough noise to let any resident animals know you're visiting, and they most likely won't come around. The likelihood of seeing a bear is very small. We've made sure everything, especially the food, is stored carefully so it doesn't draw them. Bears generally won't come close without some kind of temptation. As for seeing a cougar, the odds of that are pretty much nil."

Now it was Heather who frowned. Scooting closer to Brian, she shivered. "'Most likely'? 'Generally'? 'Pretty much'?"

Leaning forward to pull the metal coffeepot away from the flames of the fire, Earl poured himself another cup. With slow ease, he sat back in his camp chair, sipping the steaming liquid.

Mady cringed. From the coal black color of what he'd poured, that stuff had to be bitter. And how on earth could he drink coffee that hot? Maybe all of Earl's outdoor experiences had left his tongue as calloused as his hands.

He fixed Heather with a small smile. "If you're asking me to be more definite, to give you guarantees, I can't." He lifted his cup, using it to direct their attention to the woods around them. "These woods, the river, the valleys, and glaciers…this is the wilderness, Heather. It's unpredictable. We have a good bit of knowledge about visiting it with safety, and I've told you what you need to know about that."

"Make noise? That's your advice for dealing with bears and cougars?" Lea didn't look convinced.

Earl drew his cup back to his lips, watching her over the rim as he drank. "Usually that's enough. I told you, the animals out here aren't any more eager to meet than you are. But there are never any guarantees when you're dealing with the wilderness. This is the animals' home. You're the visitor. Or, if you're not careful, the intruder." His smile was mild. "So be careful."

Lea gave a huff. "Sounds like we haven't got much choice."

"Oh, there's always a choice." Earl stood and

stretched, then gave her a sideways grin. "You just might not like the consequences if you don't do things the right way."

"Your way, you mean?"

Mady imagined many a man had been cowed or at least taken aback by that haughty, condescending tone. But Earl just gave Lea an approving pat on the back as he strolled past her.

"Glad to see we understand one another."

With that, he sauntered away, and Mady had to bite her lip to hold back her laughter at the open-mouthed shock on Lea's face.

Mady checked her flashlight again, turning it off and on, satisfied the batteries were still strong.

She studied the sky. The sun was dropping closer to the horizon, but she guessed she had at least a half hour or more of daylight left. Plenty of time to take a quick walk to check out the river.

And if she didn't head back until after dark, well, no problem. She had her trusty flashlight, and between its bright beam and whatever noise she could make—stomping and whistling were definite possibilities—well, there would be ample warning to whatever nocturnal wildlife might be roaming the bushes around her.

Of course, one thing might help...

She walked around slowly, eyes scanning the ground as she nudged at the undergrowth with her toe. With a triumphant grin she leaned down and picked up a nice, sturdy stick. It was about an inch thick and close to three feet long. Perfect. She could smack the bushes around her as she walked. If that didn't warn off the animals, they simply weren't in a mood to be warned.

Frowning at the unpleasant thought, she turned back to the path. Tomorrow she'd have to hunt up a real walking stick, but this would do for now. Ready at last, she started down the trail.

"You sure you want to do that?"

Mady paused, closed her eyes for a beat, then turned back to face Jason. He was standing at the head of the trail, thumbs hooked in his belt loops, watching her.

"Do what, exactly?"

He indicated the path with a nod. "Heading for the river?"

"Just can't escape your finely honed sense of the obvious, can I?"

At her dry comment, his mouth pulled into a lazy smile. "Hey, just trying to make sure my partner thinks things through." His gaze swept the sky, then came back to rest on her. "Not a whole lot of daylight left."

"Enough."

"Whatever you say. You obviously know what you're doing...."

Mady caught his unspoken ending loud and clear: *not!* Without another word, she turned and stomped down the trail—but there was only one animal she wanted to warn off, and he didn't seem to be listening.

Earl was right, the river was worth the walk.

The sight of the rushing water cutting its way between walls of towering trees all but took her breath away. The water was so blue it had green casts to it, and so clear she could see to the rocky bottom in several spots.

Mady trailed her hand in the water, shivering at how cold it was, even this time of year. She walked awhile on the rocky bank, looking upriver and down, taking in the rugged beauty, how everything seemed in harmony, balanced.

If only she felt that way inside. But the last thing she felt was harmonious. Or balanced.

She lowered herself to the ground. Picking up small rocks and tossing them into the water, she watched as the ripples expanded then disappeared. It would be the same if she tossed one of the huge boulders in. No matter how big the initial disturbance, the effect would vanish eventually. And the water would flow on.

"Fret not…" She listened as her low whisper drifted around her. She wanted to remind herself. "Fret not."

Wrapping her arms around her knees, she hugged them to her chest and watched the reflection of the fading sun in the clear water. As the last remnants of daylight faded, she leaned her head back and closed her eyes, glad for the enveloping darkness all around. There was something comforting about it, something serene.

A light breeze rustled the bushes behind her and lifted her hair gently. It was like a light caress, and Mady smiled. Out here, with the night sounds and the wind blowing, with the darkness embracing her and the stars winking from light years away…here it was easy to feel at peace. Here she could breathe in the presence of the One who owned her, she could rest in the sure knowledge that her time was held in tender, almighty hands.

How quickly that peace could be dissolved by a glittering pair of blue eyes.

Mady shifted restlessly and rested her chin on her knees. She watched the river flow by, watched the water as it rushed and danced in the growing moonlight. Not unlike her emotions whenever Jason was around. One glimpse of that rugged, dimpled smile shining on her, and it was as though she'd opened the door to a summer day, complete with flowers and songbirds and children's laughter.

One smile, and she was a laundry commercial, for crying out loud!

But let the man direct his oh-so-glacial glare her way, and she was caught in a rushing current of tumbled emotions: confusion and anger, frustration and loss, regret and resentment. In either circumstance, she had about as much control where Jason was concerned as a stick that had been tossed into the rapids. Never before had she felt grabbed emotionally, picked up and swept along as she crashed into and bounced off of her intentions and her awareness of what was right.

If only...If only she could hold on to her certainties. If only she could remember, no matter what Jason said or did or how he looked at her, that she was here to help him.

Her fingers closed around her flashlight, and she turned it on, letting the beam slice into the darkness. She watched how the small circle of light danced as she moved the flashlight from the trees across the river, to a boulder in the middle of the water, to a fallen tree upriver.

That was what she was supposed to be. A light. Maybe not a bold spotlight, but you'd think she could at least manage to provide a tiny beam cutting through the darkness, helping Jason find his way back.

Instead, she felt like a candle that kept sputtering out. Or catching the house on fire.

Lord, I know You can use us in our weakness, but do I have to be so usable all the time?

Pushing herself up from the ground, Mady turned to start back down the path. She was too weary to sort through all this tonight. What she needed was a good night's sleep.

She walked with careful steps, her eyes trained on what she could see of the trail in the flashlight's beam. But she hadn't gone more than a few steps when she paused and glanced around. On the walk to the river, the bushes and trees lining the path had seemed sheltering, even comforting.

Now...

Mady felt the hair on the back of her neck stand on end. Now those same trees were looming shadows, pressing in on her from all sides until she could scarcely breathe.

She rubbed her arms, then shot her beam of light along the trees. "See?" Her voice sounded small and frightened in the still night. "N-nothing to be afraid of."

But that uneasy sense of being a tiny tot lost in a maze of long legs and unrecognizable knees wouldn't go away. As evidenced by the way the flashlight beam was shaking.

Her ears pricked then, attuned to the slightest sound...and her heart constricted when she realized there was a symphony of sounds. Chirps and rustles, haunting howls and moaning calls, crashes and snaps...they were all around her. She was surrounded.

And she had the terrifying feeling she was being watched.

She scanned the suffocating woods around her, sure she would find yellow, malicious eyes following her every move, just waiting for the opportunity to strike....

A twig snapped right behind her and Mady spun with a scream, swinging madly with her stick. Nothing was there. Not that she could see. But she wasn't going to give whatever was out there another chance at her.

She spun around and pounded down the trail, her breath coming in gasps, pains shooting up her side. If she made it back to camp alive, she was *never* going out at night agai—

Something grabbed her foot, and she catapulted forward with a screech. Her stick went flying, and her flashlight somersaulted into the bushes, the light swallowed up in the dense foliage.

Mady lay on the ground, still as death, waiting for the feel of teeth tearing at her....

Instead, gentle hands slid beneath her arms and lifted her to her feet. "Hey, are you okay?"

Even in the darkness she recognized Jason's face, and with a muffled sob she threw her arms around him, pressing her nose into his jacket. His arms closed around her, and his voice enveloped her as he soothed her in low, gentle tones.

She knew she should step away. Knew she should laugh off her panic and head back to camp. But she couldn't move. Or, more accurately, didn't want to. It felt so safe, so sheltered to just stand there in the circle of those solid arms.

So when she felt Jason shift, slip a hand behind her

back and under her knees, she didn't resist. He lifted her into his arms, cradling her against his chest, and started walking.

Neither of them said anything, and for that she was glad. She just leaned her head against him and looked up at the stars through the trees. From the safety of Jason's arms, what had seemed ominous moments ago now looked…serene. Even beautiful.

And the man she had considered so hazardous to her heart and peace of mind was a haven.

Amazing how quickly one's perspective could change. How very different things were from how they seemed. Maybe…

She gazed at the heavens and felt tears roll down her face.

Maybe she'd been wrong about other things, too. Maybe she needed to look again, with new eyes…eyes tuned to the heart and not outward appearances.

Open my eyes to see Your wonderful truths, Lord.

Jason slowed and then stopped, and Mady saw they were at the end of the trail. He stepped from the path out into the open and gently set her on the ground.

She stood there in front of him, gazing up, wanting to thank him, but unable to speak. A small sob caught in her throat, and she wiped at her tears.

He tipped her head back, studying her face in the glow of the moon. He wiped a tear from her face with his thumb, and what she could see of his expression in the darkness seemed troubled.

Without thinking, she reached up to smooth away the frown between his eyes, then lowered her hand to rest it briefly on his chest. She felt his heart beating beneath her fingers—a steady, strong pulse—and she ached to erase its pain, to bring it a sense of the peace that went beyond human understanding.

Touch him, Father. Free him. He came, this man You've put in my path, and lifted me from fear...no, from terror to comfort, security. Tears filled her eyes again. *Please, Father God, won't You do the same for him?*

Mady wasn't sure how long they stood there, but suddenly it was as though a cloak of fatigue settled over her. Stepping back slowly, she finally found her voice. "Thank you."

His eyes roamed her face, and he nodded. "You're welcome."

She turned then, and he followed her as she walked past the paddock, past the silent tents, and to her sleep site. She lowered herself to the ground, pulled off her shoes, slid into her sleeping bag, and zipped the screen shut.

With a deep sigh, she lay there, staring up at the stars, her mind and heart filled with one thing only: prayers for Jason. She whispered them to the heavens, not caring that her tears soaked her pillow.

Finally her eyes drifted shut. But they opened again when the sound of a deep, gentle voice drifted to her on the night breeze.

"Sleep well, Mady."

With a smile, she rolled over, snuggled into her pillow, and did exactly that.

❦ 14 ❦

Character cannot be developed in ease and quiet.
HELEN KELLER

Early the next morning, Jason stepped carefully and quietly past his sleeping companions. It was a perfect morning for some time alone at the river, with just him and the fish.

He walked along, enjoying the feel of the pole and tackle box in his hand. He'd found everything he needed in the supply tent, and then some. Then he frowned as another image drifted into his mind: Mady as she'd been last night, in his arms, cradled against his chest.

Why on earth had he followed her? Why had he waited there, near the path, watching and listening for her return? He didn't know. But he couldn't honestly say he was sorry he'd done it.

She'd been terrified. Plain and simple. And no one should have to face that kind of fear alone.

Thought you were the one who wanted to be removed from it all, distant from people and their problems?

Usually, yeah. But the situation with Mady was different. He reached the river then and plunked his tackle box down with more force than necessary. So he wasn't quite sure why it was different. So what? It just was.

Pushing all thoughts of Mady—and all the others—from his mind, he focused on his reason for coming out here. Quiet. Solitude. Peac—

"Drat!"

He looked up quickly, his eyes seeking the source of the sound. There, not fifty feet up the bank, was Mady. Fishing pole in hand, she was playing tug of war with a tree that had snagged her line.

Disappointment nudged Jason, but he pushed it aside. Okay, so he wasn't entirely alone. That was okay. She could do her thing, and he would do his. He might even move a little further down—

"Oooo, this is *so* exciting!"

Jason closed his eyes, letting out a small groan. Oh no...

"Shhh! Hon, come on. You'll scare the fish away before we even get there."

With a soul-deep sigh, Jason looked to the path just in time to see Brian and Heather step out onto the rocks.

Brian's expression when he spotted Jason was about as thrilled as Jason knew he looked. "Oh. I see we weren't the only ones with this idea."

"Not hardly."

At Jason's low comment, Brian glanced around, frowning when he saw Mady. "Well, crud. Might as well not even fish!"

Jason frowned at Brian's petulant comment, especially when he saw the disappointment on Heather's face.

"But you said you'd teach me your favorite sport, sweetie. I was really looking—"

"It's no fun with a crowd." Brian sounded like a muttering four-year-old. Couldn't he see his bride was looking more crushed with each second?

So what? It's not your business? No concern of yours at all, right?

Right. Which made Jason wonder why he was standing slowly, catching Brian's attention. He held the younger man's eyes for a moment, then nodded upstream. "Plenty of room up there. No one around for miles from what I can see." He glanced at the sky. "And it's a nice mornin' for a walk with the woman you love."

Brian had the grace to look shamefaced at Jason's pointed words and look. He turned back to Heather, all thoughtfulness.

"Here, sweetheart. Let me carry your pole."

Jason let him go without a snort. The kid had been embarrassed enough for one morning. He kept an eye on the two as they made their way upstream. They stopped about forty feet away. Not as far as Jason might like, but far enough.

He turned to walk to the water's edge, glancing Mady's way as he did so. The look he saw on her face surprised him. Approval. Respect. She inclined her head to him, and he returned the gesture, then turned to cast his line.

Well, what had he done to deserve that kind of reaction from the oh-so-critical Mady? *Don't know and don't care. All I wanna do is fish.*

He listened with satisfaction to the plop of his lure in the water. He focused on the action of reeling in while tugging the lure. For all of two or three minutes. Then his attention wandered, in spite of himself, upstream.

Brian was gesturing wildy, pointing and coaching, as Heather whipped back her pole and made a wild cast into the air. She wasn't going to catch any fish that way. Some poor bird, maybe. But no fish.

As Brian stomped around, Jason groaned softly. This

wasn't what he had in mind! All he wanted was a quiet morning with the fish. How had he ended up baby-sitting the newlyweds?

Heather's piteous voice drifted back to Jason on the breeze. "I'm sorry I'm so stupid about all of this!"

She was about to cry. That much was clear. *Stay out of it. They're not your concern!*

True enough. He turned back to the river, making another well-aimed cast. *Heeeere, fishy, fishy, fishy...*

His pulse jumped when he felt the distinctive tapping on his line. His muscles tensed, and he waited for the fish to take the bait.

Snap! Whap! Stomp!

Jason jumped at the loud sounds, turning with a snarl just in time to see Brian thrashing his way back downstream and then up the path, pole and tackle firmly in hand. A quick look upstream told the tale. Heather stood there, pole in hand, fishing line tangled in the rat's nest to end all rat's nests, tears running down her young face.

Oh, man!

Not your problem. Not your problem.

The mantra was clearly true. So why did Jason find himself gathering up his stuff and walking in Heather's direction?

"I-I'm so s-stupid!" she wailed as Jason drew close.

He took the pole from her hand. "It's not a case of stupid, Heather. Just being familiar with what you're doing."

In short order, he had the line cut, a new hook in place, and the pole ready to cast. Heather stood staring at the pole like it was some kind of enemy. Jason chuckled. "Look, it's really not that hard. How about I show you a few simple pointers. Then tomorrow morning you can woo Brian back down here and show him your stuff."

Heather's protruding lip eased a bit at that, and she reached out for the pole. Jason was surprised to find she was actually a quick learner. After her third good cast, she gave him a shy, sideways look.

"It's much nicer when someone's not yelling at you."

"I can imagine. But you're doing great, Heather. You'll be a prize fisherma—uh, woman in no time."

"I hope so. All I want to do is make Brian happy. And he loves fishing so much." She stared at her line in the water. "I just thought it would be fun to do this together sometimes. Not all the time. He needs time alone. But once in a while…."

Jason shook his head. Brian was an idiot. But he didn't say so. "Brian's a lucky guy. He's married to a woman who knows one of the most important ingredients in a good marriage is kindness and consideration." He smiled at her. "Give him a little time. He'll respond."

"Oh, he already does. He's not usually like this. He was just so excited about teaching me to fi—"

Just then her line jerked, and Heather gave a mighty yelp. Jason coached her calmly, not stepping in to take over. She'd made the cast and hooked the fish. She could bring it in.

Which she did. Like a pro. Pulled the flailing trout out of the cold river and flipped it on the rocks. Of course, Jason had to dive for cover, but the girl had caught her first fish. And she was thrilled. Screaming at the top of her lungs.

"IdiditIdiditIdidit!"

Jason grinned at her. "You sure did."

The sound of running feet drew his attention, and he looked to see Mady rounding the bushes. She took them both in and promptly set down her pole and started clapping.

"Way to go, Heather!"

The younger woman blushed, then jumped when the still-flopping fish slapped up against her ankle. Mady laughed and went to help Heather with her catch.

Jason gathered up his gear. So much for a quiet morning of fishing. But he wasn't nearly as disappointed as he'd thought he would be. Between Heather's excitement at having a fish to show Brian and the warm look of approval from Mady, he was actually feeling pretty good.

Go figure.

Mady had just stowed her fishing gear when she heard Brian's whoop. She went toward the group, smiling as they all gathered around Heather and Brian.

"Is that a beaut or what? And my wife caught it!"

Earl's laughter was wholehearted. "Well, how about if you share your beauty with the rest of us for breakfast?"

Heather nodded shyly, her cheeks tinged with pleasure at the suggestion. "I'd like that."

"Brian, what say you and I go clean that catch of your wife's?"

Mady turned to watch in surprise as Jason, hand on Brian's shoulder, led the younger man away.

What was that all about?

"Mady, you up to chopping some chives for the fish?"

She looked at Earl and nodded. "Sure, just let me go get my knife."

Running to her sleep site, Mady knelt next to her pack and opened it up. She found her knife and started to stand but stopped at the sound of voices drawing near.

Jason and Brian had apparently come to a halt just on the other side of the bushes from her. She waited, not wanting to interrupt or embarrass either of them.

"You were wrong, Brian."

Jason's tone was firm, brooking no argument. But Brian didn't seem to catch that.

"You saw what she was like—"

"No, I saw what you were like. Impatient. Overbearing. Basically stupid."

"Now, wait just a—"

"Look, she's your wife, and it's up to you how you treat her. But take it from someone who's seen a lot of marriages dissolve, the best way to have a great wife is to be a great husband. And that means treating her with respect and consideration. And apologizing when you don't."

"But she—"

Mady couldn't stop herself. She leaned forward to peek through the bushes, then pursed her lips at the look on Jason's face. No wonder Brian broke off.

"You were wrong, Brian."

The younger man turned red, and Mady thought he might start arguing again, then he just deflated. "Oh, I know it. You're right. I was an idiot." He actually looked like he was about to cry! "I was just embarrassed. I mean, you were standing there, and she flat *stunk*—"

Jason inclined his head. "Next time, do yourself a favor and think twice about that, pal. You've got a beautiful, sweet-hearted woman who thinks you can do anything. I'd treat that pretty special, if I were you. A lot more special than some stranger's opinion of her fishing skills." He arched a brow. "Or yours."

Mady stepped back. *Well, well, the antagonist becomes the counselor.* And he was actually pretty good at it. She crossed her arms, waiting until the sound of their footsteps faded.

Obviously, there was a whole lot more to one Jason Tiber than Mady had imagined. And the Jason she'd just seen and heard was a man she found herself liking. And respecting.

Would wonders never cease?

"Jason, you seen your partner?"

Jason directed a look at Earl that spoke volumes. "It's not my day to watch her."

Earl smiled. "Actually, it is. She's your *partner*, remember?"

At Jason's snort, Earl gave a weary shake of his head.

"So," Jason said, glancing around, "where'd you see her last?"

"I asked her to chop some stuff for breakfast. She ran back to her sleep site to get her knife."

To her sleep site…

A quick look was all Jason needed. He'd thought he and Brian would have some privacy behind the wall of bushes. Apparently, he'd been wrong. Mady's sleep site was on the other side of where they'd been, and he was willing to bet the bushes had had ears. Ears topped with golden curls and an overactive curiosity.

"All set, Earl!"

Jason looked up with a jerk at Mady's bubbly voice. She gave him a sugar-wouldn't-melt-in-my-mouth look, and Jason just leaned back, crossing his arms.

"Been out birdwatching? Or listening?"

The dull red that crept up her neck told the tale clearly enough for Jason.

"Jason, I—"

"Save it, partner. But tell you what, next time I plan to have a little talk with someone I'll just invite you along. Save us both a hassle."

With that, he stood and walked away, fuming. To think he'd felt good about the way she'd looked at him, about her approval. Why? Why should her opinion matter one bit? She was just like all the others, talk a good game of faith and integrity, and live something very, very different.

Well, this was one time when he wasn't getting caught up in it. Partner or not.

❧ 15 ❧

We are restored to wholeness as we surrender in defeat.
ROBIN NORWOOD

"Watch your step here, gang. These things aren't as easy as they look."

At Earl's warning, Jason took in the knee-high, moss-covered fallen log in their path. With his long legs, it wasn't much of an obstacle. But for someone small like Mady...

She'll be fine. She's not your responsibility.

He pressed his lips together tightly and stepped up onto the log, planting his feet carefully on the slick surface, then hopped down, landing on the other side in the loamy soil with a soft thud. No sweat.

He looked up to lock gazes with Earl, who was standing there about ten feet in front of him. Earl's look spoke volumes, and Jason heard it loud and clear.

She's your partner.

Jason couldn't stop the wave of embarrassed discomfort that washed over him. He turned to check Mady's progress. She'd just reached the log and was studying it quietly.

"Need a hand?"

At his clipped question, those emerald eyes turned to study him—and he found himself shifting uncomfortably beneath that considering gaze. So his offer hadn't been enthusiastic. So what? At least he'd made it. She should be gratefu—

"No, thanks."

No anger or resentment in the words. Just…resignation. Like she didn't expect—or need—anything from him.

That should have made him happy. It was what he wanted, wasn't it? But what it did was bug him. Big time. She was his partner. If she needed help she should just say so. He opened his mouth to tell her that just as she planted those small hands on the top of the log and vaulted over it in a surprisingly graceful motion.

Almost.

One foot didn't quite clear the obstacle. Instead, it grazed the slick surface of the log, throwing Mady off balance, sending her into a head-first tumble.

Jason dove, catching her like a wide receiver snagging a yards-long throw just before it hit the ground. They landed hard—Mady cocooned in his arms, his shoulder digging a rut in the decaying leaves and loam covering the ground.

They lay there for a heartbeat, then he chanced a look down—and found his nose buried in a mass of sweet-smelling curls. He couldn't stop himself. He drew in the fragrance that was purely Mady—a mixture of vanilla and something he couldn't identify…something intoxicating and fresh…something that went straight to his head.

His eyes drifted shut and his arms around her tightened.

"I…"

"Hmm?" he mumbled into her hair.

"I…can't…"

His heart ached. *I know. Me neither. I can't take this—*

"…breathe!"

His eyes flew open at the gasped exclamation and he sat up quickly, loosening his grip. But that resulted in her sitting in his lap, cradled against his chest. And that definitely was not acceptable. Not with her looking up at him like that, confusion and questions floating around in those wide, hypnotic eyes.

Like a man jumping away from the weakening edge of a cliff, Jason vaulted to his feet, pulling Mady to her feet as he rose. He held on to her long enough to be sure she was steady, then dropped his hands and backed away.

She stared at him for a moment, then her lips tipped slightly. "It's okay, Jason. I'm not going to attack you."

He followed her gaze down to where his hands were held out in front of him, like a barrier against her. He dropped them, shoving one into his jeans pocket and clearing his too tight throat.

"Right. Well. You okay?"

She gave him a slow nod. "Fine. Thanks for the assist."

"Sure. That's what partners are for."

Her only reply was a slight arch of her brows. At least, that was the only reply he stuck around to see. Spinning on his heel he moved quickly through the brush to join the others, not even looking to see if Mady was following.

Jason noted with a small groan that the rest of the group had been close enough to observe the whole event.

"Nice catch."

Jason didn't miss the double meaning in Nikos's laconic comment. Nor did he miss the spark of jealousy in Lea's eyes as she watched him and Mady approach. Or the small, oddly approving smile on Earl's face.

"Ooooh, that was *so* amazing the way you caught her!"

This from Heather, who was hugging her groom's arm with a sigh.

"Amazing," Nikos echoed dryly.

"The way you dove for her, like all that mattered was saving Mady...." Heather sighed again, and Jason clenched his fists.

"I didn't sav—"

"It was just like watching a hero in a romantic movie!"

"Oh yes—" Nikos nodded, wide-eyed—"My heart was all aflutter."

Jason bit his tongue so hard he brought tears to his eyes.

"You okay, Mady?"

Jason could have hugged Earl for shifting the focus off of him. He glanced down at Mady, who was standing beside him—and he could have *kissed* her for her reply.

"Fine. Ready to push on."

With a nod, Earl turned and started walking. Pushing away the too potent image of kissing Mady, Jason fell into step with the rest.

As Jason shifted his pack, he sighed. He should have stuck with the plan he'd made on his way back from the river that morning: to ignore Mady completely.

It had been fairly easy at first, despite working side

by side as they helped fix breakfast—and the way she kept glancing at him, confusion creasing her forehead. Obviously she wasn't sure what she'd done to irritate him. Well, tough. He hadn't been in the mood to explain himself.

Which was good since he wasn't sure he could.

It's simple. She was eavesdropping. Proves she can't be trusted.

But that wasn't it—not entirely. And Jason knew it. But he wasn't in the mood to examine his feelings too deeply. Not right now.

The silence between them had continued as they got ready for the morning hike. He'd moved to his sleep site, grabbing up his gear with quick, stiff movements. It felt good to jam each item in as firmly and forcefully as he could.

His extra socks, waterproof jacket, and gloves went first in a waterproof bag; they fit nicely in the bottom corner of his pack. The small first-aid kit, miniflashlight, and map of the area went into another bag.

Whoosh!

There. They fit just fine in one of the outside pockets.

Next came the compass, waterproof matches, water purification tablets, a pocket-sized two-way radio.

Just as Jason had thought, Earl passed everything out that morning after breakfast. Jason forced himself to be more careful with the strobe light and signal mirror as he packed them.

Smaller items he slipped into baggies for waterproofing, being sure to leave a little air inside as he sealed them.

When Earl had suggested doing so this morning, Nikos had spoken up. "I suppose it lightens the load?"

Everyone laughed.

Good natured, as always, Earl just shrugged. "Only if you go into the water, but it helps you pack things without smashing anything. Oh, and one more thing. If any of you do, by some twist of fate, get separated from the rest of us and get lost, once you signal, stay where you are until we reach you. Wandering around is the worst thing you can do. Stay where you're safe and dry and in the open."

Stay where you're safe....

Why hadn't he followed that sage advice and just stayed home?

Because you wanted to get away.

Yeah, but not like this. Not with Mad—

He grimaced. *Not with these people.*

Muttering darkly, he grabbed the rest of his supplies, giving the duct tape, tarp, nylon rope, aluminum drinking cup, canteen, and some power bars a solid shove into his pack. Amazing how therapeutic smashing something into a small, wadded mass could feel—

He looked up when a hand came to rest on his shoulder.

"Doing your trash compactor imitation, Jas?"

He scowled. How did Earl *do* that? How did he show up just when Jason was really getting a good temper worked up?

A grin played at the man's mouth, but to Earl's credit he managed to restrain it. "Ah, I see. Not a trash compactor. This is your grizzly imitation."

"Ha. Ha." Jason made his words clipped and distinct.

With a shoulder-lifting sigh, Earl removed his hand from Jason's stiff shoulder. "Well, you're entitled to a mood here and there." His eyes narrowed a bit and he fixed Jason with a firm gaze. "Just so you're over it by the time we start our hike. Because today is the day you and your partner start working as a team."

Great.

Earl made a show of checking his watch. "So you've got plenty of time to snap out of it. At least sixty seconds or so."

Jason arched his brows. "Gee, that much time?"

Earl inclined his head. "Hey, you know me. Always willing to go the extra mile for a buddy."

The snort Jason let loose didn't even faze his friend as he strolled away. Jason's eyes drifted from Earl's back to Mady, and he felt himself tense all over again.

He clenched his teeth. This was *not* going to be fun. He was sure of it.

And, as evidenced by what had just happened with the log, he'd been right. He should have ignored Earl's slightly condemning look earlier and stuck to Plan A: Pretend Mady Donovan doesn't exist.

He allowed himself a small laugh. Obviously, if he was going to make it out of this little adventure with his sanity intact, that's exactly what he'd better do for the rest of the day. The rest of the trip.

The rest of his life.

Considering the way the day had begun, Mady was pleasantly surprised to find she was having a good time.

Earl was a veritable fount of information, and he

stopped here and there along their hike, pointing out flowers, trees, and plants. He even showed them several things that were edible.

"You'd be amazed how much there is out here that you can eat." Earl spread his hands out, indicating the ground around them.

Lea grimaced. "That *you* could eat, perhaps...."

Earl shook his head. "I'll bet I could even please a discerning palate like yours, Lea."

"Surely you jest." Nikos swept a gaze around them. "Are you hiding china, silver, and crystal goblets out here?"

"No...but there's something better."

That caught everyone's interest. Heather peered from behind Brian. "Better?"

Earl waggled his eyebrows. "Much better. There's something out here that is not only delicious, it's priceless."

Lea crossed her arms. "You're teasing us."

"Not at all. As a matter of fact, you stepped on one of them not ten feet back."

They all turned to glance behind them, and Mady couldn't hold back a giggle. "What? Moldy leaves?"

"Close."

At this cryptic response, they followed Earl as he walked to the spot he'd indicated, right at the base of a tree that looked more dead than alive; then he knelt and carefully brushed ways some leaves.

There, poking up out of the ground, was what looked like a huddled mass of tiny haystacks.

Nikos peered down, then his face broke out in a grin. "Mushrooms!"

"And that's not all." Earl pointed to a grouping of yellow flowers scattered around them.

"Weeds?" Lea's brow arched delicately. "You expect us to eat weeds?"

Nikos peered at the flowers, then tossed a shrug at his sister. "Looks like the salads you eat at those fancy restaurants of yours."

Her straight nose lifted. "Hardly."

"Actually—" Earl stood, brushing dirt from his knees— "Nikos is probably right. Dandelion leaves make great salads. As do many other things that grow out here."

Earl started walking again, and the group fell in behind him.

"So, what you're saying is there's plenty to eat out here if you ever get lost, eh?"

He cast a pensive look at Brian. "Well…yes and no. You need to know what's safe and what isn't. As far as mushrooms are concerned, unless you know for a fact they're okay, I'd avoid 'em."

Heather punched Brian lightly. "I *told* you they were poisonous."

"Some are, but it's hard to tell which are which."

"But if you get lost…" Nikos studied the trees towering over them. "Well, you could survive without food for a while."

"Sure." Earl stepped over another fallen log. "Most folks could go without food for a month or two under favorable conditions."

"Meaning if there is a McDonald's nearby?"

"*Please*, Nikos!" Lea glared at her brother. "We're talking about food. And your penchant for grease and salt is hardly helpful."

Earl just went on. "But if you're fairly lean…well, for some, the body becomes auto-cannibalistic after a few hours without food."

Heather wrinkled her nose. "Auto…what?"

"It feeds on itself." They all stopped abruptly and turned to stare at Jason. The silent one had spoken! Mady fought back a grin at the look of embarrassed irritation that crossed his rugged features.

Earl chuckled, drawing attention back his way. "Best thing to keep in mind, if you get lost, which you won't on our little trek because I won't let that happen—" there were nods and grins all around at that—"is that you need a diet high in fat. And that you should never pass up any reasonable source of nourishment when you're in need." Earl's expression was somber. "Way too many people have done so out of fashion or fastidiousness—and died."

"Care to tell them what the best source of nourishment is, Earl ol' buddy?"

At Jason's amused question, Earl paused, then inspected the area around them carefully. Heather frowned as she watched him.

"What are you looking for?"

"McDonald's…" he muttered, then his eyes lit up. "Follow me."

Nikos cast Mady a curious look. "Do you see any golden arches around here?"

She giggled, then halted next to the others.

But Jason had heard Nikos's question, and he'd fixed Mady with a hard look. "Nothing out here like that. Nothing to help you but yourself. Your smarts. Your knowledge. Your determination. Just you."

Mady held her silence until she was standing next to Jason, watching as Earl knelt down next to a fallen, decaying log.

"You. And God."

Mady's quiet words hung in the air, which was suddenly alive with a crackling tension. Jason turned his head slowly to look down at her as she waited for what was sure to be his sarcastic reply....

But Earl chose that moment to pull apart the log, and with a screech, Lea jumped back, scrambling to get behind her brother.

Mady looked down, then stepped back herself. The log was full of creeping, crawling creatures, all of which scattered as their shelter gave way to Earl's tugs. She stared at the writhing display, then looked up at Jason. He was actually grinning, their debate of a few moments ago forgotten.

Or, more likely, postponed.

Shaking her head at him, Mady shuddered. "*This* is a source of nourishment?" She shuddered again. "You've got to be kidding."

Jason's grin widened. "Nope." He moved to reach down and snag a particularly big bug, holding it up for their inspection.

"Eeeeewww." Heather squealed, and Mady had to agree.

"Hey, insects are a great source of food." Jason's comment was met with a disbelieving silence. He shrugged and tossed the wriggling bug to the side.

"Hate to say it, but he's right, folks." Earl stood. "Insects are mostly fat, which is exactly what you need if you've gone without food for too long." He looked to

Nikos and Lea. "I'm surprised to see you two look so shocked. I thought it was mostly Americans who turned their noses up at eating insects. They eat ants in many countries, and in Japan, dragonflies are a delicacy." He smacked his lips in an exaggerated motion. "They're delicious."

By now, Heather and Brian both looked a bit green, and Brian's grimace was eloquent. "Suddenly a fat-free diet sounds positively delicious."

They moved on, coming to a small creek. The water looked clear and cool, sparkling in the rays of sun that broke through the tree branches. Mady could hardly believe Earl's caution before they'd left base camp: "The safest rule is to assume all water is impure."

He'd showed them how to use their purification tablets, grinning at Lea's grimace when she tasted the treated water.

"May not be Perrier, but at least it won't kill you."

"How delightful," Lea muttered. "Like everything else in this godforsaken place."

When they reached their destination, a small meadow surrounded by woods, Earl instructed them all to pull their compasses and maps from their packs.

"One of the things you wanted to learn was how to find your way in the wilderness. Well, today we'll learn the basics, and tomorrow you'll get to test what you've learned."

"What happens tomorrow?"

"Another day hike. But this one you take on your own, with your partner."

"Oh, how fun!"

Mady wrinkled her nose. Easy for Heather to say. She was probably thrilled with the idea of spending time alone with Brian in the woods.

She peeked at Jason and found him watching her, an unreadable expression on his face. Groaning inwardly, Mady pulled her map and compass from her pack, pushing with determination against the sense of dread that nudged at her.

So she was going to have to wander around in the woods with Jason. So what? They'd be fine. Certainly they could get along for a day together.

Of course you can. You've done such a wonderful job of it so far today....

Mady cast her eyes heavenward. She'd thought this morning while they were fishing that she'd seen a whole new, more likable Jason. Then she'd blown it by listening in, albeit inadvertently, to his conversation with Brian. The rest of the day she'd had the painfully clear impression Jason would rather be partnered with a grizzly with diaper rash than with her.

Except...

There was the way he'd jumped to catch her when she slipped on that slimy log. She could still feel his arms close around her, pulling her against his chest, holding her securely as they fell. And after they'd landed...

She could swear he'd leaned his face into her hair...held her longer—and tighter—than necessary.

Don't be an idiot! He was probably trying to catch his breath after having you land on top of him.

Lord knew she'd found it hard to breathe...though not because of Jason's grip on her. No, what had taken her breath away was the simple warmth of the man...the sheltering feel of his arms around her.

"Any idea where you're going with this?"

Mady choked and looked up with a start. Earl stood there, holding the map in one hand and the compass in the other. With a quick sigh of relief that he hadn't been referring to the direction of her thoughts, she tuned in as he gave clear, concise instructions, showing them the basics of getting one's bearings in the woods.

Concentrating so hard her head started to ache, Mady did her best to track and then follow his instructions. But the compass just didn't want to cooperate.

Either that, or due north kept jumping around.

Whatever the cause, she kept heading off in a direction other than where she was supposed to. Surprisingly, Jason didn't comment. He just indicated the correct direction with a flick of his head.

Finally, Earl sent them out in teams to practice together. "Decide who's going to start out in the lead, then the second person will bring your team back. Got it?"

Everyone nodded, even Mady, though she didn't feel as though she *had* anything. Except maybe a headache.

You're just being a coward again! You're supposed to face challenges with confidence, with trust that God will help you! Where's that faith you keep telling Jason he needs?

Pressing her lips tightly together, she looked down at the compass and map in her hands. She was on solid ground, surrounded by people who knew what they were doing. So why was her heart pounding as forcefully as it had that first day when their plane was being bounced around in the turbulence?

"It's all about trust."

Mady started as Earl's voice broke in on her thoughts. Had he known what she was thinking? No, he was watching the others, hands crossed casually across his chest.

"You need to learn to trust yourselves and each other out here." He eyed each of them. "So here's what I want you to do. The person who's not using the compass can't say a word, not unless the leader specifically asks for help. But what that means is if you're using the compass and you need help, you've got to be willing to ask." He regarded the woods around them. "I don't want any of you getting lost out there, okay?"

He grinned, but Mady couldn't muster a responding smile. Instead, she just gave a little nod. *I get it, Lord. I need to trust You....*

Jason had offered to go first, which Mady had accepted with relief. Surely coming back to a known, recognizable location would be easier than heading out into the unknown. She carefully watched everything Jason did, not the least surprised that he moved with confidence and ease.

Why does everything come to him so easily, Lord? How's he ever going to realize he needs You when he can handle everything on his ow—

"Your turn."

Mady froze and stared up at Jason. He gave her a curious look. "Hello? Did you hear me?" He held out the compass and map. "Your turn. Lead us back."

Taking the tools in her hands, Mady stared down at them intently. *Okay, relax...set the compass on the map...*

She peeked at Jason from under her bangs. His expression was dubious—clear evidence that he knew she wasn't exactly confident in what she was doing. At least he was following Earl's instructions not to say anything unless she asked for help. But Mady could tell it was taking all his restraint not to let go of those two little words he so often asked her: "Need help?"

A quick refusal sprang to her lips, but on the heels of that urge came an echo of a phrase that held her lips closed.

"With many counselors, there is safety."

She sighed and gave a nod, then held the map and compass out to Jason. "Can you just show me how to set this up again?"

Surprise flickered in his eyes, and then was replaced by a grudging respect. Score one point for Mady! He obviously had figured she wouldn't ask. Well, maybe now he'd realize he didn't know her as well as he thought he did.

He stepped toward her to take the map and compass. "Sure." He lined them up and showed her how to pencil in the line from one destination to the other, how to mark points of reference as she went.

Following his guidance, it made sense. Mady felt a thrill of excitement at the sight of the meadow in front of them through the trees.

We did it, Lord! We did it.

Relieved and thrilled, she turned to Jason, the action abrupt enough that he nearly ran into her. She grabbed at his arms and grinned up at him.

"We did it!"

A smile tugged at his lips. "We did, indeed." Then

something flickered in his expression, and he gave a small shrug. "Like I said, as long as we rely on ourselves, we do just fine."

Mady felt as though he'd dumped a bucket of ice water over her. In a heartbeat she swung from near-elation to disappointment, then irritation.

Jason stood there, poised, awaiting her response. Well, he could just go on waiting. She wasn't in the mood to spar.

Spinning on her heel, she walked away from him, stepping out into the sunshine, into the ocean of wildflowers dancing in the breeze. Slightly dazed at the beauty surrounding them, Mady paused, and her heart tightened.

If all of this can't prove to him You're real, Lord, then what chance do I have?

None. But it's not up to you....

Walking toward Earl and the others who were waiting, Mady paused, taking in that truth.

Not up to her? But God had called her to help Jason. She looked over her shoulder and watched as he followed her to join Earl and the others.

He walked with easy, long strides, his hands loosely holding the straps of his backpack. Everything about him said this was a man who was confident, in charge— a man who didn't need anyone.

But Mady knew that wasn't true. Knew it with a certainty that wouldn't let her go. Jason lacked the One he needed most—and that One had called Mady to open Jason's eyes and heart to that need.

Just how she was supposed to do that in the few days they had left, she didn't know.

It's not up to you....

The words drifted through her again, and she hugged herself as she came to stand beside Earl.

He looked from Jason to her, a quizzical expression in his eyes. "Everything okay?"

Mady bit her lip, fighting the sudden urge to cry. Swallowing hard, she gave Earl a half-hearted nod. "It will be." She looked away. "Somehow…"

Lord, just show me.

She knew He was listening. Knew He would answer. but she couldn't shake the odd feeling that she wasn't going to like what she saw.

❧ 16 ❧

It is very easy to forgive others their mistakes.
It takes more guts and gumption to forgive them
for having witnessed your own.

JESSAMYN WEST

The forest was alive with sound.

Mady lay there, snuggled in her sleeping bag, and listened as the day awoke. Birds chattered and sang, the wind rustled the sides of her tent and whispered through the trees around them, water rippled in the distance…and it all seemed to be saying the same thing:

You're in trouble…You're in trouble…You're in tr—

"Oooohhh! Shut up!" Mady pushed out of her bag and tossed open the flap on her tent. Stepping out into the cool morning air, she glanced around. Daylight was just touching the sky. She could hear the various sounds of breathing and snoring drifting toward her, combining with the muted sounds of Earl rustling around as he fixed his ever-present coffee over the fire.

The man had to have the stuff running in his veins.

Lifting her face to the rays of sun just peeking through the thick foliage, Mady let the gentle warmth bathe her eyelids and cheeks.

It was a glorious morning. And from the looks of it, a perfect day for a hike. She should be excited and filled with anticipation at what God was going to do today. Not pressed down by dread and apprehension.

Why can't I just trust You?

With a shake of her head, Mady headed for the creek. Walking down the path, she listened to the sound of her footsteps in the silence. *You're with me every step of the way...You're before and behind me...why do I fear?*

She knelt beside the tumbling river and dipped her hands in, splashing the frigid water over her face. It took her breath away for a moment, and a small laugh of delight escaped her. She could live in a place like th—

"Do me a favor and don't fall in."

She spun around, then sat back abruptly when she found herself staring at a pair of jeans-clad knees. Looking up, her gaze landed on Jason, who was standing over her, a small smile playing at his lips.

As casually as possible, Mady pulled her knees to her chest and circled them with her arms. "Nice to know you're worried about me, partner."

He chuckled. "I'm more worried about having to go in after you. My only other change of clothes are still damp from the dousing you gave me at the corral."

Kneeling beside her, he dipped his hands in the water and splashed it on his face, just as she'd done. He scooped another handful and doused his head, then shook like a dog, sending drops of water flying.

Mady yelped and jumped away. Jason peered up at her from under his dripping hair. They smiled at each other, laughing. Carried away by the sudden elation that filled her, Mady didn't notice right away when Jason stopped laughing. Not until she met his eyes and saw that the light of humor had shifted, changed to something different...something deeper.

All at once the sounds around them seemed to dim.

Her focus honed in on Jason, and her heart turned over in response to what she saw glittering in his eyes. His steady gaze bore into her with a silent kind of expectation.

Her breath caught in her throat at the awareness skittering along her nerves. This man was so disturbing to her in every way. He moved her, challenged her, pushed her beyond her neat, little boxes until she was forced to stretch emotionally, even spiritually. He radiated a confidence and vitality that drew her more powerfully every day.

And in the midst of it all, she'd found herself captured on a level she didn't even understand by the longing that looked out at her every time their eyes met.

Her heart ached in her chest, and she struggled to breathe. How could she feel this way about a man with whom she disagreed on everything that really mattered—even the very nature and meaning of love?

And that reality pierced her with a sorrow that was almost too deep to bear.

For as long as she could remember, Mady had longed to fall in love. Longed for the day her heart would surrender to one man, the man with whom she would spend her life. Well, that day was here.

She knew now why it mattered so much that she help Jason, why she wanted so desperately to see him freed from the struggle that troubled him so, why his smiles and approval warmed and moved her, why his frowns and barbs could hurt so much....

She was falling in love with him.

Her heart had somehow decided to surrender itself to him. And Mady knew she'd have to steel herself so he never guessed she'd been so foolish. What was the point? Why tell Jason how she felt when it was obvious they couldn't be together, when he didn't share the part of her life that mattered above all others. Loving Jason could mean only one thing: walking away from God. And that was something Mady could never—would never—do.

God...O Father, help me....

A small sound escaped her, part sob, part gasp.

"Mady?"

Alarm shot through her at the hoarse sound of his voice, and when he rose to his feet, one hand reaching toward her, that alarm ground the gears and shifted into pure panic.

She meant to back up. She was sure that had been her intention. Knew it was the only sane thing to do. But instead, she found herself glued to the spot, watching as though mesmerized while Jason came toward her.

When his fingers touched her cheek, traced her jaw, Mady let out a muffled sound and closed her eyes. The feel of his hand as it cupped her face was heady.

"Mady, look at me."

The soft plea wrapped around her like a warm blanket, and she eased her eyes open. He watched her intently, the blue of his eyes deep and fathomless now. He hesitated a heartbeat, as though giving her the opportunity to step away, to stop him....

She didn't do either.

And when he lowered his head, she simply lifted her face to his, the action the most natural thing she'd ever done.

As his lips covered hers, she felt as though she were

floating, carried to a place she'd never even known existed, a place of crystal clarity and unbearable beauty. Her hand must have come to rest against his chest, for she grew aware of the movement of his breathing, of the rapid beating of his heart.

She didn't know how long the kiss lasted, she only knew it seemed an instant and an eternity all at once. He lifted his head slowly, staring down at her, eyes filled with the same desperate confusion Mady felt swirling within her.

God... God... what are we going to do?

After a moment, Jason's hand moved from her face, and Mady almost cried out at the pain of the separation. He stepped back, licking his lips, and looked away.

"I-I'm sorry."

Mady held up her hand. "I should have stopped you, Jason." His gaze came back to hers, and she gave him the only thing she could. The truth. "But I didn't want to."

"Mady, I..."

When his words trailed off, she bit her lip, fighting the hot tears that stung at her eyes now. They were lost. Together. Lost in the chaos of their feelings and all that they wanted to be...all that could never be.

She lifted her hand, touched her fingers to her still tingling lips, and caught back a sob. She couldn't bear it any longer. Spinning quickly, she ran. Back down the path to the camp. Back to where the others—and, please God, some semblance of sanity—were waiting.

After their turbulent episode by the creek, Mady avoided being alone with Jason. When he'd come to go over the equipment checklist with her, she grabbed Nikos as he was strolling by.

"Why don't you and Lea go over the list with us?"

Nikos had glanced from Mady to Jason, curiosity brimming in his eyes. She'd been sure he was going to ask what was going on, so when he just nodded his head, she almost grabbed him and kissed him.

But seeing as kissing had gotten her into this mess, she restrained herself. She settled for patting him on the arm.

"Great." Mady hoped the word didn't sound as utterly relieved as she was afraid it did. "Great. Good."

Nikos eased his hands into the pockets of his shorts. "I'll go get Lea."

"No!"

He jumped at Mady's cry, and this time he did start to question her. "Mady, please, what—?"

She cut him off, forcing a calm, even cheery note into her voice. "It's just that there's no need. I mean, I saw her walk down the path toward the creek. I'll just run and get her." She was already in motion. "Won't take a minute. I promise. We'll be right back."

She'd raced down the path, spurred on by the need to escape the concern in Nikos's eyes—and the speculative glitter in Jason's.

Jason stood watching Mady as she fled down the path to the river, fighting the anger growing within him.

Yes, he'd given in to feelings he shouldn't have this morning. Yes, he'd let himself reach for her and kiss her. The impact of that contact still rocked him.

But did she have to treat him like a two-headed rattlesnake, for Pete's sake?

"Our Mady seems a bit...distraught."

Jason fixed Nikos with a glare. *Let it go. It's not worth fighting over.* Sound advice. Pity he wasn't going to listen. *"Our* Mady?"

Nikos's eyes grew speculative. "Would you rather I call her *your* Mady?"

Jason gritted his teeth. "Call her what you want."

Cocking his head, Nikos studied Jason. "It does make one wonder..."

I'm going to kill him. Right here. Right now. "About?"

The other man's shoulders lifted in a careless shrug. "Simply what you could have done to disturb Mady so."

Okay. That was it. Jason crossed his arms, squaring off with Nikos. "Anyone ever tell you not to stick your nose where it doesn't belong—" he hardened his expression—"and isn't welcome?"

To his credit, Nikos didn't look the least bit intimidated. In fact, he broke into what looked like a genuine smile. "Relax, Jason. I do not seek to come between you and your Mady."

"She's not *my* Mady." No matter how much he wished she were.

"I simply believe in looking out for my friends. Especially when they seem troubled."

Jason digested this, then dropped his arms with a sigh. "We...had words. That's all."

Nikos's nod was considering.

"And I may have done something that...disturbed her."

Another nod.

"But we talked it out and we're fine." He leveled a firm look at Nikos. "Okay?"

"Of course. If you say so. Okay."

But as Jason turned away, he had the distinct impression this conversation wasn't over. Not by a long shot.

Mady's morning had developed a definite downhill slope.

After going over the equipment check with Nikos and Lea, she'd gone to sit on her sleeping bag, her head in her hands.

A gentle touch on her shoulder brought her head up. Nikos crouched beside her. He lifted his hands to point at his ears.

"I find these are not being used at the moment, so thought I might offer them to you."

With a muffled sob, Mady went into his kind embrace, crying against his shoulder while he patted her on the back, uttering soothing words in Greek.

After a while, she leaned away from him, sniffling. "I'm sorry. It's just been a hard morning."

"Jason said you two had words?"

Surprise lifted her brows, and she nodded. "In a manner of speaking. I guess what we had was a revelation, more than anything else."

"Of your feelings for each other."

Pulling her knees close, Mady hugged them to her chest. "I've never felt this way about a man before. Being close to him makes me dizzy, like I can't breathe. And yet he can make me so angry...."

"Deep emotions stir deep responses, Mady. It's ever been so between male and female."

She saw compassion and understanding in his eyes and reached out to take his hand. "You're a good friend, Nikos."

"Ah, sometimes we must settle for what we are given."

Mady laughed and swatted at his arm playfully.

"Tell me, I can see how deeply this man affects you. And it is evident in his every glance in your direction that he is drawn to you. Why do you struggle so with your feelings?"

Would he understand? Probably not, but maybe getting it into words would help her sort through the confusion. So Mady told him…explained her faith, her beliefs, and Jason's response to them. "It's as though he's angry with God."

"So that anger splashes onto you when you speak of Him?"

That made sense. "Yes, I think so."

"And for you, this difference, it means what?"

"Everything." Even as Mady said it, she knew it was true. "It means everything. I can't give my heart to a man who doesn't believe in God, doesn't share the faith that is my very foundation."

A frown creased Nikos's brow. "Surely that is too harsh…."

Mady shook her head. "When I give myself to a man, it will be heart, body, and spirit. The man I love will be second only to God in my life, but he cannot be more. And if I married a man who did not love God, who was not submitted to Him, then I would be torn between the two. And ultimately my love for Jason would draw me away from my love for God. I've seen it happen, over and over."

"Then perhaps you do not need your love for God at that point?"

Mady's heart constricted painfully. "I will never stop needing God, Nikos. I can't fathom life without Him. I owe Him everything. My very life, my breath, all that I am. I belong to Him. It would tear me in two to walk away from Him." She shook her head again. "I just couldn't."

"And so, you are left with nothing."

The smile that tipped her lips surprised her. "Oh no, I'm left with everything. I can't live without God, Nikos. But I can live without Jason." She bit her lip as she said it. "I don't want to, but I can. And I will."

With God's help…because that's the only way she'd be able to do it without falling apart.

"I can't live without God, but I can live without Jason."

The words echoed over and over in Jason's head. He hadn't meant to overhear. He'd been coming to check on Mady, make sure she was all right, only to stop in his tracks at the sight of her in Nikos's arms.

Rage, white-hot and all-consuming had flowed over him, and he'd had to turn and walk away quickly before he grabbed one or both of them by the throat.

He wasn't sure how, but he'd ended up on the other side of the bushes, where he'd talked with Brian earlier. And there he'd stood, craning his ears, calling himself every kind of fool for eavesdropping.

Well, he'd found out what he wanted to know. Nikos had only been comforting her. But his relief had been short-lived—and his anger had grown, bit by bit, as he listened to Mady share her struggle—and then simply dismiss him.

Just like that.

She could live without him, she said. Well, fine. He didn't recall having asked her to do otherwise. He kicked at the hard ground with a force that was totally uncalled for.

He felt his teeth grinding and forced himself to draw in slow, deep breaths, to relax. As the tension eased from his shoulders, he turned his face toward the bushes…toward Mady's area.

Maybe he should just help Mady in her new conviction. Help her see she could get along just fine and dandy without him. Well, wasn't that what he was supposed to be doing anyway? Ignoring her. Avoiding her. Not getting tangled up in any way…with anyone?

He nodded. Right. This morning had just been a…a lapse In judgment. In sanity. From this point on, the lines were drawn, and Mady had drawn them herself.

Live without him? You'd better believe it. A slow smile stretched his mouth. He'd do everything he could to help her see that was the smartest thing she'd said all week.

This day couldn't be over soon enough for Mady.

She'd headed to the horse pen to check on Dorado, then spun on her heel when she saw Jason there, leaning his arms on the top rail as he fed Ebony a carrot. Her heart racing, she hoped against hope he hadn't seen her coming. She ventured a glance over her shoulder only to find his hard gaze following her.

From that point on, Jason went above and beyond the call of duty as a critic. Everything she did—from the way she packed her gear to the way she adjusted her pack—had earned her yet another verbal jab. Of course, the comments were never direct, but then they didn't have to be.

There was the shot he took when Lea strolled over to watch Jason fasten his pack into place. She'd uttered an admiring sigh. "You look so prepared. Like you can handle anything."

Mady cast her eyes heavenward. Puh-*lease*...

"Hey, *somebody's* got to be prepared."

Though said with a chuckle, the glittering gaze Jason had sent Mady's way as he spoke made his meaning abundantly clear: Jason was prepared; Mady was not.

Not long after that, Earl had stopped by to see if they had any last-minute questions. Mady stood beside Jason, her stance as stiff as his.

"So"—Earl glanced from Jason to her, then back again—"just relax and have fun. Don't worry about a thing."

Jason's shrug spoke volumes. "I haven't got any reason to worry."

Slight emphasis on the *I*. Mady got the message. Again.

"Uh-huh." Earl didn't sound convinced. "What do you think, Mady? You ready for this?"

Jason answered for her. "You don't need to worry

about our little Mady, Earl." Then, before she knew what he was doing, he threw an arm around her shoulders and hugged her close to his side. "Mady can take care of herself. After all, she's got God on her side." His hard eyes glittered down at her. "Isn't that right...*partner?*"

For the first time on the trip, Mady saw anger flash in Earl's eyes. The older man looked about to jump in, but Mady cut him off—though how she spoke around the lump of tears almost choking her, she wasn't sure. But she did it. "Sure." The word came out in a croak, and she cleared her throat and tried again. "Sure, no worries. None at all."

"That's my girl!" Jason gave her another hug, then let her go so abruptly she had to do some fancy footwork to avoid doing a nosedive onto the ground.

"Uh-huh," Earl said again, looking even less convinced than before. "If you both say so...." He started to leave, then paused and turned back to them. "Do me a favor?"

Mady looked at him.

"Don't kill each other."

Before either of them could reply, Earl walked away, shaking his head. Mady forced herself to look at Jason, and his grim expression was enough to let her know he wasn't making any guarantees.

"You all ready for this?"

Nikos gave a deep chuckle. "Isn't it a bit late to be asking us that?"

Earl shrugged, the customary grin lighting his features, making him seem almost boyish. "Yup, I s'pose so." He studied them all. "Now remember, this is the big event. Your day trek into the wilderness." He let his gaze rest on each of them as he went on. "Don't worry about anything. You've been great in training, and you're going to be even better today. You know what you're doing." His gaze met Mady's, and he gave her a fortifying nod. "You *know* what you're doing."

She hoped so. Oh, how she hoped so. But the foreboding that had been gnawing at her since their last venture into the woods was only growing stronger. She'd gotten out of that one by the skin of her teeth.

No, by God's grace....

The reminder should have encouraged her, yet she had to swallow hard to still the nausea that was trying to build. *Breathe, Mady, in and out, slow and rhythmic....* She willed herself to focus on Earl's calm voice.

"Each team is to work together. Your goal is to follow these maps—" he handed each team a map. "They've been clearly marked with landmarks, points of reference, and notations to help you find your way along your specific trail. Stop every fifteen minutes or so to check your bearings. There will be four checkpoints along the way, and those are marked as well."

Mady glanced down to see the bright red marks indicating a checkpoint.

"When you reach a checkpoint, you'll find a small box with paper and pencil. Record the time you arrived, the time you depart, and the direction you're headed." His tone grew more serious. "That's not an option, folks. God forbid anything should happen—"

The band around Mady's heart tightened.

"—but if it does, we'll have a good idea where to

look for you. Remember, if something does go wrong, just stay calm. You won't be alone, and each of you has an emergency strobe. Just stay where you are, set up your beacons like we discussed yesterday, and wait for us. We'll find you." He sounded so confident, so sure.

There's nothing to fear but fear itself.

She grimaced at the cliché that drifted through her mind with almost mocking ease. Who came up with these things, anyway?

"Each of you will lead for an hour. After four hours you should arrive at your assigned site. You'll take a break for a nice lunch, maybe even take a bit of a rest, then head on back for dinner and a congratulatory celebration." He fixed Mady and Jason with a firm look. "And you will work *together,* got it? Teamwork. That's what you're here for."

"And if one of us isn't sure what we're doing?"

Mady refused to react to Jason's dry question.

Earl sighed deeply. "Ask for help. That's what being a team is all about." He went on, but Mady wasn't listening any longer.

She was a liability. She didn't know what she was doing.

"Work as a team." That's what Earl had said, right? Well, if there was one thing she and Jason were not, it was a team. They had to at least trust each other for that.

Quick tears stung her eyes, and Mady bit the side of her cheek, forcing them away.

"So, we all clear?"

Earl's question startled her, bringing her attention back to the matter at hand. His gaze was on her, and he was looking oddly concerned. She stiffened her spine and nodded quickly, putting on her most confident front.

She might not be completely sure what she was doing, but she had Someone on her side who would work everything out. God would help her when she needed it, and together they would show Mr. High and Mighty Jason Tiber that with God, nothing is impossible.

And the fact that the whole venture terrified her would only make the victory that much sweeter.

It was time.

Mady stood there at the starting point, shifting her pack into a more comfortable position as she peered into the woods in front of her.

"Ready to give up?"

She shot Jason a glare. "No, of course not. We haven't even started."

He shrugged. "Just thought I'd try to save you some humiliation—"

She turned on her heel and started into the forest.

"Mady."

She kept walking.

"Oh, Mady."

She turned back to him, hands on her hips. "What?"

He met her glare calmly, holding up the map and compass. "I just thought it might be a good idea to actually know where we're going."

Heat filled her cheeks, and she bit back a retort. As usual, he was right. Charging into a virtual wilderness, especially without the proper equipment, was not a good idea. Not unless she wanted to get lost right off the bat. And she wouldn't give Jason the satisfaction.

He held the map and compass out to her, but she shook her head. "You go first."

"Of course, your highness. Your wish is my command."

Gritting her teeth, she stepped aside as he took the lead. Falling into step behind him, she tried to relax, to focus on the beauty of the wilderness around them rather than on how very much she was hoping Jason would step into a hole. Or, better yet, walk off a cliff.

A slight smile quirked her lips at the thought, and suddenly her mood improved. She shifted her pack and matched her steps as best she could to Jason's long, even strides.

He moved branches aside, and she noted that he was careful not to let them snap back at her. So there was still a spark of the considerate, even gentlemanly Jason in there today. She'd been convinced he was determined to be his most disagreeable.

With a small sigh of relief, she studied his back, the broad expanse of his shoulders, the way the sun pulled gold highlights from his thick, brown hair.

Images floated through her mind then...snapshots of Jason, of their interactions...sound bites of their conversations, their heated debates...the almost euphoric feeling she had whenever she bested him at anything....

She'd never met a man who stirred her anger more. Or her heart.

Quickly, she banished the thought. It wasn't right. Love couldn't come into play, no matter how much she wanted it to. She couldn't allow herself to think of him as the man she loved. That wasn't what God had brought her here for. But try as she might, she couldn't halt one memory that filled her mind…the two of them at the river this morning. As though she were watching a video, she saw the way Jason's blue eyes had darkened, the expression on his face as he watched her so intently, the cautious entreaty as his hand reached out to her—

"Oooff!"

She'd smacked right into him, her face making rough contact with his pack. She grabbed the fabric of his shirt to steady herself.

"Hey—!" Jason looked at her over his shoulder.

Letting go of his shirt as though it had burned her, she cut him off. "What's the big idea of stopping like that?"

His eyes narrowed and he turned slowly, speaking carefully and distinctly. "Stop every fifteen minutes or so to check our bearings, remember?"

Once again she felt her cheeks warm. Why did he have to be right all the time? She knew she should apologize for not paying attention or at the very least for smacking into him. But she couldn't force the words out. Instead, she gave a curt nod. "Fine. So go ahead and check. Who's stopping you?"

Shaking his head, muttering to himself the whole time, he spread out the map on a boulder and laid the compass in place. After a moment he straightened, rolled the map up, and tucked it and the compass into his shirt. Then he looked at her.

Mady met his gaze for a moment, then deliberately turned her face to study the trees, the bushes, the flowers…anything but him. She was being childish, but at this point she didn't particularly care. Darned if *she* was going to say anything.

The silence stretched out until she thought she would scream. *Say something,* her mind yelled at him, but he just went on staring at her, that piercing look in his eyes. *Why don't you just say*—"Oh, for heaven's sake, what?"

His brows arched a fraction. "I was just waiting until you were ready."

She shooed him ahead. "I'm fine. I'm ready. Let's go. Time's a'wastin'."

"Suppose you can pay attention this time?"

God, give me strength! "Of course."

She was startled when his expression softened a fraction. "Is there anything you'd like to talk about?"

Her misgivings increased. "Like—like what?"

"How about like whatever you were so immersed in that you didn't see me stop?"

Her mouth went dry, and she said the first thing she could think of. "You'd be the *last* person I'd want to talk to about *that!*" The second she spoke the words she realized how they sounded, and she bit her lip, wanting with all her heart to take them back, at least to explain. But the damage was done.

Jason jerked back, his expression hardening.

Oh, Father, I'm sorry! Regret, sharp and deep, pierced her. Why couldn't she just keep quiet? *Be still.* Hadn't God told her that time and time again? Why didn't she listen? *I just keep pushing him further away. Saying things that are stupid and hurtful.* "Jason, I—"

He held up his hand, and when she saw the expression on his face, she felt the nauseating sinking of despair in her stomach.

She'd hurt him.

He'd made an effort, opened himself to her just a bit, and she'd all but slapped him with her rejection. She felt sick.

Without another word he turned and started walking, his strides long and furious. Mady followed as best she could, fighting her way though the dense brush that he was no longer holding out of her way. But what made it so difficult to keep up wasn't Jason's speed or the brush.

It was the bitter tears that she couldn't seem to keep from flowing down her cheeks.

❧ 17 ❧

A given: life will guarantee you adversity.
The only question is how to deal with it.
CHRISTIAN HAGASETH III

God, God, please…

Mady looked down at the compass, positioned it again on the map, then glanced up at the dense forest surrounding them.

Jason had remained silent for the remainder of his hour in the lead. They'd reached the first checkpoint—a tree marked with bright red construction tape—without any trouble. Jason had marked it down in their trip log, found the small box with paper and recorded the information Earl had requested, then turned and handed her the map.

"Your turn."

The words had been low and distant, and she'd had to fight hard to prevent her tears from starting to flow again.

I'm so sorry.…

She'd said the words over and over in her mind, but even now she couldn't get them to come out. So she'd taken the map, pulled her compass from her pack, and, steeling herself for the task at hand, sent up an urgent prayer for guidance.

Now Mady stared at the map again. Apparently those prayers had been short circuited. Nothing was making any sense. Once, as she'd pushed ahead, hoping against hope that she was going the right direction, she'd felt a nudge deep within to stop, to tell Jason what was happening, to ask for his help.

The impulse had been so strong that it had seemed a physical force. And she'd almost listened, almost given in. Then another voice came.

Admit your failure and you admit God's as well. He's sufficient, remember? He's all you need. Isn't that what you've been telling Jason all this time. Imagine how he'll gloat to know God can't even keep you from getting lost.

A wretchedness of mind and spirit that Mady had never known before washed over her. Why had she thought she could do this? She'd lied to Jason, to herself, to God. There were good reasons she played life safe: She couldn't handle it otherwise!

Look at me! Look at what I've gotten us into.

A terrible sense of bitterness assailed her. *See, God? See what happens when I step out, when I think trust is enough? And You want me to try starting my own business? To risk everything on the chance that anyone will care what I can do? That it will make a difference to anyone?*

Only two words came to her in response. Two simple words that made Mady close her eyes, feeling utterly miserable: *Follow me.*

I have followed you! And it got me lost!

Quick shame came on the heels of that thought, and she was actually trembling now. It wasn't God's fault she was lost. It was hers. She'd marched into the fray, blithely expecting some miracle to float down and show her the way.

Well, why not? Wasn't that how it worked yesterday? Hadn't God cleared her confusion and helped the compass make sense?

With Jason's help, yes.

She swallowed hard and lifted her chin. No, she didn't need Jason. She needed more trust. More faith. Less terror clawing at her heart as she looked around.

I was afraid yesterday, too, but it worked out just fine.

That was true. But now…now she wasn't sure anything was going to work out.

She and Jason were deep in the forest, surrounded by trees, waist-high ferns, and dense bushes…and now, when she needed it most, it was as though everything she'd learned about getting her bearings out here had drained away.

And the longer she stared at her compass and the map, the more confusing it got.

"Many advisers make victory sure."

The very words that had spoken peace and reason to her heart yesterday now only made her angry. *I don't need his help. God won't let us get lost…He wouldn't…*

But they were. She had no idea where they were, how far off the trail they were, which way to go to reach the check-in point. Her fear rose a notch, bringing frustration burning through her chest and into her throat. She tightened her already tense grip on the compass and the map.

"We're lost, aren't we?"

Mady bit her lip at the low question and forced nonchalance to her tone. "Of course not." She took her time placing the compass on the map, peering down at it, willing it to make sense.

Please, don't let this happen—

Jason gave a snort. "Yeah, you look like you know where we are."

She felt the heat flood her face at his biting sarcasm. Jutting her chin out, she started walking. "Of course I do."

Jason grabbed the back of her shirt and jerked her to a halt with such force that she fell back against his broad chest. With an angry gasp, Mady jumped away then spun to face him. "What are you doing?"

"Stopping the insanity." His tone was cold and lashing.

Mady's throat burned as she tried to swallow the blinding sense of failure. *I'm not going to cry. I absolutely am not going to cry.*

If only her eyes would cooperate. They seemed determined to let the tears flow down her hot cheeks. She swiped at them with the back of her hand.

She was stunned to see compassion touch Jason's face—even more stunned when he reached out to her. The unexpected tenderness in his eyes took her breath away and was almost her undoing. A sob caught in her throat as he closed his hand around hers. "Mady, come on. All you have to do is ask for help. I'm here."

She swallowed around the lump that had lodged in her throat. *"I'm here…"* The gentle, reassuring words washed over her, stirring such a sense of relief that all she wanted to do was walk into his arms and weep.

He rubbed his thumb across the back of her hand, and the soft, soothing motion was almost hypnotic. She looked up at him, searching his face. *What are you doing to me?*

Watching her carefully, he spoke, his voice low and

comforting. "Just admit you're lost, that you need help—"

She felt as though he'd slapped her. She jerked away from him, her face flooding with heat. "From you, you mean? After all, there's no one else out here, is there?"

"Mady, be reasonable. We should have arrived at the checkpoint a half hour ago." He waved his hands at the dense woods and undergrowth surrounding them. "You see a clearing around here anywhere? Because I sure don't!"

"I know what I'm doing!"

With a muttered oath, he walked up and grabbed the map from her. "So show me where we are, Miz Daniel Boone!"

"Nowhere!" This time she didn't try to stop the tears. "We're exactly where we've been from the moment we met. Nowhere!"

Some indefinable emotion flickered in his hard, blue eyes. "That's not how it has to be, though, is it?"

She threw up her hands. "Isn't it? Where else can we be, Jason, when you're so sure I'm a blind fool following a powerless fantasy?"

His eyes burned. "Aren't you? What good has *God* done you? Take a look around you, Mady! We're lost in the middle of the woods, and night is coming, and *nobody* is going to get us out of this but us."

"Don't you mean nobody but *you?* The great, all-knowing, all-powerful Jason Tiber?" She poured as much contempt into her words as she could. "No wonder you don't need God, Jason. You *are* God. At least, in your own warped mind."

He moved so fast she didn't have time to react. Her

arms were grasped in steel bands, and he gave her one hard shake.

"Shut *up.*"

There was violence in the quiet words, and a tingle of fear danced along her nerves. "You—you're hurting me—"

Without warning, he let her go, and she staggered back, so shaken she thought her knees might buckle. She leaned against the rugged bark of a tree, trying to get her pulse and breathing under control.

"I'm...sorry." His voice was hoarse, raw with emotion, his breathing ragged. "God...holy God..."

Mady started and looked at him, scanning his face. He sounded as though he were praying. Was it possible?

He met her stunned gaze, and his eyes hardened. "Mady, I don't want to hurt you. But you make me crazy! You are the most infuriating, exasperating—" He broke off with a harsh laugh. "You're not the idiot here, *I* am. I thought I could help you, thought I could reach you—"

"You help *me?"* She stared at him, not sure if she wanted to laugh or cry.

Ice filled his glare at her words, like fingers of frost inexorably smothering a windshield in subzero weather. "You just can't do it, can you? You can't admit you were wrong. God forbid you should be human enough to make a mistake, to need someone's help."

She pushed away from the tree. "I have *God's* help—"

"Stop it!" He took a step toward her, and she backed up, slamming into the tree so hard her teeth ached. He halted his advance, his hands clenching into fists at his sides. "Stop hiding behind God." His eyes were dark and filled with an emotion that she recognized but didn't understand: desperation.

He looked as desperate as she felt.

His words were ground out through clenched teeth. "Do you think God *approves* of what you're doing here? That he condones you lying about knowing where we are? The foolhardy way you've put us both at risk?"

She opened her mouth to spit a retort at him, to defend herself and her God…but nothing came out. An awful awareness washed over her and she was struck mute. Jason's biting words echoed in her mind, sweeping through her and filling her with a realization that she couldn't ignore.

He was right.

God forgive her, he was right.

She'd been so determined to prove herself right— to prove *God* right—that she'd closed her heart and spirit to the voice calling her to truth, to reach out and ask for help. She'd convinced herself that was the voice of doubt, but in reality she'd been too proud, too ashamed of her weaknesses and fear to admit she couldn't do it.

My God, my God… Grief washed over her, and her face went hot and then cold and clammy. Shame wrenched her heart and she closed her eyes. How had this happened? How had she let her fear and pride bring her to this frightening place? Why hadn't God reached her, stopped her, shown her somehow what she was doing to herself…to Jason…

"Why…where *are* you, God?"

Her eyes flew open. Had she said that aloud? Alarm pounded in her veins, making her head ache, making her knees weak. She'd only whispered it; maybe Jason hadn't heard....

But one look at his shocked face told her he had. Dear heaven, wasn't it bad enough that he'd seen her make a fool of herself? Why had he been the one to hear her words of doubt?

She bowed her head as despair pressed in on her.

Jesus, what are you doing to me?

Jesus, what are you doing?

Jason stared at the broken woman before him, and his heart constricted sharply. He couldn't breathe past the stabbing pain. He couldn't move. And yet everything inside him urged him to step forward, to take Mady in his arms, draw her close and shield her from the anguish that was so evident on her face. When she'd whispered that broken question, asking where God was it had struck him with such force that he'd almost cried out.

So this was what it was like to dismantle someone's faith.

He should be happy. Should be rejoicing that he'd shown her how foolish her trust in God was...but all he felt was shame. It was so acute that it was a physical pain assaulting him, tearing at him.

"Mady—"

At the sound of his voice, she lifted her head. Her eyes were glazed with despair, and he reached a hand out to her, wanting to touch her, to comfort her. She jerked away, the action desperate.

"No!"

At that one, tortured cry, he halted. He held a hand out toward her, carefully, cautiously, as though she were a deer poised to flee for her life. "Mady, listen to me—"

She shook her head again and pushed away from the tree, looking around frantically. "No." It came out in a hoarse whisper. "I don't want—I can't…" She rubbed a hand at her eyes, and he saw how badly she was shaking.

God…help me. Don't let her run—

But even as the prayer was forming in his mind, even as shock jolted him that he was talking to the One he'd thought he no longer believed in, begging for help, Mady took a quick step back. She gave him one, awful, agonized look. "I'm sorry. I'm so sorry."

And then she was gone.

Mady ran.

She didn't know where she was going, nor did she care. All she knew was that she had to get away. Away from Jason, away from herself…away from the growing certainty that they would never get out of this, that she'd led them both into trouble too deep to escape.

Branches slapped at her, scratching her face and arms as she pushed her way through the foliage.

"Mady!"

At Jason's angry call, her feet flew faster over the rough ground. She stumbled several times as her feet caught on roots or rocks, but she managed to regain her balance and keep going. Then a branch caught her across the eyes, bringing stinging pain. Before she could recover, her foot hooked on something, and she went down.

Branches swiped and scratched at her as she fell, and she hit the ground hard on her hands and knees. The jolt shot through her entire body, and she cried out.

"Mady, please! Where are you?"

She lay on the hard, cold earth, panting, gasping for breath, and trying to hold back the sobs tearing at her throat. She moaned—though she wasn't sure if it was because of the way her body hurt or from the blinding pain that stabbed at her heart. She blinked the smarting tears from her eyes and, with a shuddering sob, grasped at a tree trunk and pulled herself to her feet. Rubbing her eyes, she looked around.

The foliage was dense, closing in around her like a dark, dank prison. Fighting the claustrophobic panic that threatened to settle over her, she looked up, aching to see the sky, the sun—but the towering canopy of trees almost made her dizzy.

God, God, where are you?

Silence was her only answer, and she rubbed a fist across her eyes, her sorrow a bitter taste in her mouth. *What have I done? If only I'd listened to You…if only I'd asked for help…but now it's too late.*

Teeth clenched against the fear tearing at her, she moved forward, pushing aside branches furiously. If only she could get out of the woods, if only she could see clearly, maybe find a landmark…

With a mighty shove she pushed her way through a large bush and stopped, her breath catching in her throat. She was in a clearing. For a moment hope pounded wildly in her heart and then plunged again. The clearing was only thirty feet wide or so, and not ten feet in front of her was a drop-off. Moving to the edge, she peered down. Dismay filled her at the sight of the rocky gorge. The river below rushed and tumbled, channeled by the rocky walls on either side of it. Climbing down would be impossible. Mist from the roiling rapids bathed her hot face, and she closed her eyes, willing the river to wash away her tears…and her shame.

"Mady!"

She spun, jolted by the harsh cry. She had just enough time to register the horror on Jason's face before her awareness honed in on her feet. On the fact that they were slipping.

She scrambled and flailed her arms but to no avail. Her world tilted crazily as her feet went off the rocky edge, and suddenly she was airborne. For a brief, frozen moment, she thought she was floating, suspended in air, and then she was falling.

She screamed, the sound following her all the way down, until it was cut off by the icy impact of the river.

"No!"

Jason ran to the edge of the gorge and knelt, looking down in horrified disbelief. Quick relief swept him when he realized she must have gone into the water. That just might have saved her life. His eyes scanned the surging river, looking for any sign of her—and his pulse jumped when she bobbed to the surface. She barely had time to grab a breath, though, before the rushing current pulled her under again.

"God…!" The plea for mercy, for intervention was wrenched out of Jason as he realized what he had to do. He jumped up and ran back a few paces. He closed his eyes for a moment, then nodded. "God, have mercy on us."

Then he ran and jumped off the edge of the cliff. Mady was not going to face this trial alone.

❧ 18 ❧

Doubt is the shadow cast by faith.
HANS KUNG

The freezing water took Mady's breath away.

Frantically, she clawed her way to the surface, dragging great gulps of air in as her face broke free from the rushing water's smothering hold. Arms flailing, legs kicking for all they were worth, Mady fought to escape the speeding rapids pulling her along in a half-swim, half-tumble. But it became painfully clear that, like it or not, she was going along for the ride of her life.

She tried to scream but only succeeded in swallowing what she was sure was a gallon of water. Coughing, gasping, she struggled to keep her head above the water more than it went under, but her clothes, boots, and pack were working against her. Terrified that her pack would weigh her down, she clawed at the shoulder straps, trying desperately to press the release clip, but all she managed to find was a zipper. With a frustrated cry, she pulled at it, then let go. She couldn't do it. She couldn't fight the rapids and her pack at the same time.

It wasn't until she gave up the struggle that she realized her pack was actually acting like a float. The baggies. She'd followed Earl's suggestion and sealed them with air inside, so they would make the items lighter. That must be making them more buoyant. Well, she'd take whatever help she could get!

She kicked as hard as she could, fighting to see the bank of the river, desperately seeking something—anything—to grab on to, to halt her headlong plunge down the river.

A large boulder suddenly loomed out of the frothing water, right in front of her.

That's not what I had in mind!

Frantically, Mady spun, trying to avoid what she knew would be a punishing impact, but apparently the river had other ideas. She slammed into it, taking the brunt of the hit with her shoulder and the side of her face. Sharp pain screamed through her body and stars exploded in her head. Her hands dug at the rock face, but she couldn't find a handhold. Mady felt the water tugging at her, trying to spin her away from the boulder, back into the current—even as her vision grew darker.

She was going to pass out. *No! Please, no...*

Just then her grasping fingers closed around something rough, and Mady forced her heavy lids open. A thick branch! It was lodged in a crack in the boulder. She tightened her grip, the ache in her head almost unbearable, and her vision blurred...then grew darker.

God! Help me!

She felt the end of the branch slipping through her hand. She was so tired...so very tired, yet she felt strangely warm.

Through the haze that seemed to have cloaked her mind, Mady felt a deep calm settle over her. She knew she was once again being carried by the roiling water, but it almost felt more like she was floating above it rather than in it...as though strong arms encircled her and held her close, sheltering her from further harm.

"Mady! Mady, can you hear me?"

The voice came from someplace far away and was so filled with alarm that Mady wanted to reach out and comfort whoever was speaking. "Don't...worry..." She wasn't worried. She was safe now, held close in heavenly arms.

"My angel..."

Who said that? Had she? Mady wasn't sure, but she felt a smile cross her face. And then, with a shuddering sigh, she gave herself up to the darkness she could no longer resist.

"Great. Just pickin' great!"

Jason gave several powerful kicks, propelling himself out of the water enough to get a good grip on Mady's pack. It was going to take all his strength and concentration to keep her head out of the water that now carried both of them at breakneck speed.

She could thank her lucky stars, though, that her arm had caught on that branch. That's what had finally slowed her down enough for him to catch up with her.

"The LORD is my rock, and my salvation."

He pushed the words away with an impatient shake of his head. He was just grateful she'd hit it. It was no wonder she'd passed out, though. She'd connected hard enough to knock anyone cold. He was just glad he'd caught her before she went limp.

He'd thrown all caution to the wind when he hit the water and done all he could to use the current to propel him after Mady. When he saw her heading for the rock, he'd known what was coming—and he'd known it might be his only chance. He grimaced as she struck the rock, and he heard her cry out—a sound that had twisted his gut—but he hadn't hesitated. As the river swept him past the boulder, he lunged for her, exultation filling him as his fingers tangled in her shirt.

He'd gathered her into his arms, almost weak with relief as he glanced down at her. Then, of all the crazy things, she muttered something about angels... *my angel*, to be exact. And she said it with an odd, tender smile crossing her face.

Of course, that was just before she passed out cold. Obviously she hadn't been thinking too clearly.

Well, no time to think about the smile or the comment now. He needed to focus on what he'd spotted a few moments ago. A fallen log just ahead. From what he could see, it was half on land, half jutting out into the water. If only he could maneuver the two of them to the right, he just might be able to grab hold of it. Or run into it. Of course, he'd have to make sure he connected between the branches so he didn't end up skewered....

Not exactly an ideal plan, but it would have to do, because Jason wasn't sure how much longer he could keep the two of them afloat.

Kicking, reaching out in powerful strokes with his free arm, he struggled against the current. Mady's dead weight was no help, but at least she wasn't awake and frantic or fighting him.

My angel... He shook his head. Pretty obvious she hadn't realized it was him.

He kept kicking, ignoring the ache in his muscles from the cold and the battle against the current. Keeping one arm locked around Mady, he propelled the two of them to the right. He tried to time his gulps of air with being plunged beneath the water's foaming surface and hoped that Mady wasn't inhaling half the river. Blinking water from his eyes, he watched intently as they drew closer.

The log was low in the water…and Jason swallowed. This was going to hurt.

Gritting his teeth, he tried to shift Mady to the side, hoping to take the brunt of the impact himself. She'd been banged around enough.

They drew closer…closer…

Whomp!

With a grunt, he landed against the log. Sharp pain shot through his side, but he ignored it, grabbing a branch and kicking to pull himself and Mady further out of the current's pull. As the tug of the water lessened, Jason paused, breathing heavily from the exertion. His grip firm on the protruding branch, he let himself relax for a moment to catch his breath.

As he relaxed, his feet came in contact with the soft river bottom. He sank to his ankles, but he didn't care. It was ground. Shifting Mady higher on his shoulder, Jason dug in, looking to the side. The bank was only ten feet away. They were going to make it.

Relief swept over him, so powerful it threatened to buckle his knees. But he didn't savor it long. It wasn't time to relax. Not until they were on solid, *dry* ground.

Pulling his foot from the muck it had sunk into, he took a step, and sank again. So it went for seemingly interminable minutes: step, sink, pause. Pull, step, sink.

He grasped the branches on the log with his free hand, pulling himself along, gritting his teeth. Soon the water was only waist deep, then barely over his knees. The river bottom was firmer here, covered with rocks and pebbles. With a grunt he hefted Mady's inert form into both his arms and climbed up the bank.

Kneeling, he set her gently on the soft grass, reaching out to slip her free of her pack, then laying her back. She seemed to be breathing normally, and relief swept over him again. He moved to set her soggy pack next to his, then frowned slightly. The zipper to the main compartment was half open. Frustration swelled up within him, and he looked away, biting his upper lip. *Don't think about it. You have more pressing concerns at hand. Worry about what was lost later.*

Right. Later. Besides, whatever supplies were still there would be helpful.

He set the pack next to his own, then went back to kneel beside Mady. She still hadn't moved. Not a twitch or a groan. She was out cold. Running through the symptoms and treatment for concussions, he began, with gentle, probing fingers, to reassure himself Mady was in one piece. Carefully, he felt her shoulders, ribs, arms, and legs, then settled back on his heels.

No broken bones. Not that he could tell, anyway.

He grimaced at the nasty bump on her forehead. Feeling in his back pocket, he found his handkerchief still there and pulled it out. He chuckled as he held it up. He didn't even have to get it wet; it was already soaked through. He went to pull an antiseptic pad and a small tube of antibiotic ointment from his pack. As gently as he could, he cleaned the scrapes Mady had on her hands and face, applying the ointment and a dressing.

Thank goodness she's wearing jeans. They'd probably

made swimming more difficult, but they'd given her protection and a modicum of insulation in the cold water.

He did his best to make her comfortable, moving her as little as possible. Better to leave her alone until she woke up. Then he'd see if she had any other injuries.

Looking down at her, seeing the way her wild, damp curls framed her white face, Jason felt a flash of rage. What good did all of his experience, all of his skill and knowledge do now? Mady was lying there, unconscious, possibly seriously injured, and what could he do about it? Nothing. A big fat zero.

"Do not be anxious about anything, but in everything, by prayer and petition, with thanksgiving, present your requests to God."

"Knock it off!" Jason rubbed the aching spot between his eyes. He dropped his hand, then touched Mady's hair with one finger. Maybe it would help to talk to her. Maybe the sound of his voice would get through to her enough to bring her back to consciousness.

He didn't know if that were true or not. What he did know is that it would help him. He wasn't sure why, and he wasn't going to waste energy analyzing it.

"That's the problem with the Bible, Mady." He caressed one damp curl between his fingers. "Once you let it into your mind, your heart, it keeps cropping up, whether you want it to or not."

He could almost see the sparks in her eyes at that, hear her response. He chuckled. "I know, I know. You think I trust it, I just won't admit it to myself." He gave the silken strand of gold a light tug. "Come on, Mady. Wake up. Wake up and tell me how wrong I am."

He watched for a movement, for any sign that she was hearing him, and saw none. He shook his head. "Well, who knows? Maybe you're right...."

Leaning forward, he cupped her face with his hands, but at the contact, he frowned. Her skin was so cold it was almost icy. Once again the words from the Bible flooded his mind. *"Do not be anxious...present your requests..."*

Forcing back the wave of resistance that clamored at his heart, he offered the closest thing to a prayer that he could manage: *Help her. Please.*

His throat tightened, and an aching stab of pain pierced his heart. To his chagrin, he felt a sudden stinging in his eyes. "Whoo, Mady. You're gonna be sorry you slept through this." He passed a hand over his eyes again. "Just think how much you would have enjoyed seeing me like this." Taking her chilled hands between his, he rubbed them. He had to get some warmth back into her. "But I think you'd recognize it as a hollow victory. I'm tired, that's all."

Tired...and worried. His gaze roamed her still face.

Four minutes. That was all it took, if the water were cold enough, for hypothermia to set in.

Jason looked at the river, then back down. It was plenty cold. And they'd been in the water a lot longer than that. At least fifteen, twenty minutes.

He started to stand, then winced as sharp pain cut through his side and ricocheted through the rest of his body. He pressed a hand to his side, feeling, and winced again when his fingers made contact just below his armpit.

Apparently his close encounter with that log had left

him with some bruised ribs. Just to be sure that was all it had given him, he stripped off his wet jacket and shirt, removed the miniflashlight from his pack to help him see the spot more clearly, and checked his side. No bumps or bulges. Good. Didn't look like anything was broken. After he took care of Mady, he'd check to see if they had any tape, anything he could use to bind his ribs and provide some support.

But his first concern was getting Mady warmed up.

Fortunately, it was the warmest time of the day, and they were in a spot where the sun had free access. As he buttoned his shirt he could already feel the warmth making its way through the damp fabric.

That would help, anyway. He glanced at Mady, studying her clothes. Her jacket, which had been tied around her waist, was gone. She wore a denim shirt over a T-shirt. Best to get that denim shirt off of her. It would take the longest to dry.

He knelt to unbutton it, slipping her out of it as gently as he could. Then he pulled his extra jacket from his pack, lifted Mady, and laid it beneath her. He couldn't hold back a small smile at the way the jacket all but engulfed her. He wrapped it around her, tucking the arms under her sides, watching her face closely.

She looked…serene. Like she was sleeping and having an especially pleasant dream. He hoped that was the case because she probably would have one whopper of a headache when she woke up—if not from that crack on the head, then from the reality awaiting her. *That* was a nightmare.

Jason felt his jaw tense as he looked back up the river. How far had the current carried them…a mile and

a half? Two? Even more? His eyes scanned the banks of
the river, which, not fifty feet upriver, gave way to rocky
walls. No wonder the water had carried them with such
speed. Rocky cliffs on either side had effectively fun-
neled the flow through a twisting, winding gorge. From
the looks of the area, the spot where he and Mady were
was about the only section level with the river. A kind of
secure little cove.

While that was good news for now, it also meant
there was no way they could just follow the river back.
They'd never be able to scale those walls of moss-covered
rocks. He glanced at the woods behind them, taking in
the thick brush and foliage. If worse came to worse and
no one found them here, their best bet would be to hike
out to a high spot, someplace where they'd be seen more
easily, someplace the radio would transmi—

He turned with a jerk. The radio!

Two long strides took him to Mady's pack. With any
luck, the radio was still there—and hadn't been smashed
when she'd hit the boulder. Holding his breath, he
opened the zipper and peered inside.

It looked like a baggie convention in there.
Apparently she'd taken Earl's instructions to heart.
Everything was safely ensconced in a sealed baggie.
Everything, that is, but the radio.

Well, at least it was still there.

Jason pulled the device out, feeling his hopes wash
away as water ran off of it in little rivulets. Still, he gave
it a try. Depressing the talk switch with his thumb, he
lifted the radio to his mouth.

"Earl, this is Jason. Come in please…. Earl, this is
Jason."

Nothing. Just a lot of static. Jason closed his eyes, fighting the disappointment. Mady was always talking about God's care. It sure would have been nice if He'd seen fit to keep the radio dry.

His lip twisted and he shook his head. "Not that I expected it of You. You haven't exactly gone out of Your way for me in a long time, now have You?"

You haven't exactly asked for it, now have you? his conscience whispered, and he turned impatiently to set the radio on a flat rock. He'd try it again later. First he'd better build a fire and get their clothes dried out before night and lower temperatures hit.

He took a quick inventory of the rest of the contents in Mady's pack. She'd lost her matches, knife, and compass. He couldn't restrain a rueful grin at that discovery. Oh, boy, Mady was going to be flat heartbroken over the loss of that compass. He was just sure of it.

Now if she'd just wake up so he could test his theory...

She will. Soon enough. He pulled the extra pair of socks from the pack, then went to pull Mady's soaked shoes and socks off. As he slipped dry socks onto her feet, he looked at her still form and forced another smile. *Best enjoy the quiet while it lasts, Tiber.*

But he knew he wouldn't. What he wanted right now, more than anything, was to hear Mady's voice, to see her open those green eyes and tell him she was all right.

He pushed away the anxiety trying to rise up inside him. Worry was a waste of time. Better to focus on doing what needed to be done. Like getting a fire started.

A shiver ran up his back, drawing his attention to

the fact that for all the warmth of the midday sun, his clothes were still definitely damp. He pulled his change of clothes from their protective plastic bags, then moved behind a bush to change. Odds were good Mady wasn't going to wake up anytime soon. But if she did, he had no intention of sending her even further into shock by finding him standing there in such a...revealing moment.

Pity he didn't have an extra pair of boots, but he was glad he'd had enough forethought to slip two pairs of socks into his pack. They'd help keep his feet warm and dry, despite the dampness of his leather boots.

Adding his wet clothes to the pile, Jason moved into the woods, never going so far into the trees that he couldn't keep an eye on Mady. There was an abundance of dry wood lying about, and soon he had a substantial pile of sticks, twigs, and small logs. Dry leaves would work great for kindling and send up some smoke as a signal as well—though Jason was pretty sure no one was looking for them yet.

He glanced at his watch. No, it was barely four in the afternoon. They weren't even due back until between four-thirty and five. It would take another half hour or so beyond that before Earl would try contacting them on the radio.

The thought sent Jason to where he'd set the radio. He picked it up and slid it into his back jeans pocket. Best to keep it close at hand, just in case it decided to start working.

He went back to the fire, sobered by the realization that it would be at least a couple of hours before anyone even started looking for them. Which would give them

little more than an hour or so before dark. Seeing as the
last checkpoint he and Mady had made was a two-hour
hike from camp, that wasn't going to do them any good.

They were going to spend the night out here.

Maybe even two.

"Hey there...partn'r."

Jason spun, and his heart leapt in his chest when he
saw a very confused, but blessedly awake, Mady staring
up at him.

❧ 19 ❧

*And what a delight to make friends with
someone you have despised.*
COLETTE

Excitement surged through Jason, and he almost reached out to pull Mady into a relieved hug. But since he still couldn't be sure she didn't have a neck or back injury, he settled for a broad smile. "Well, hey there. Welcome back to the land of the conscious."

She licked her lips and looked around slowly. "Where…?" But the question faded away as, with a deep sigh, her lids fluttered shut again. Jason tensed. *No, not again. Don't go out on me again.* He touched her arm lightly. "Mady?"

Thankfully, she opened her eyes and looked at him. "Are you thirsty?"

She started to nod, then winced. "Oooooo…"

He touched her shoulder. "You're going to have a doozy of a headache, partner."

"Keen…sense of th' obv'ous," she managed, and he grinned. Not even a run-in with a rambunctious river and a belligerent boulder could dampen this woman's spunk.

"Just lie still, Mady. I'll get you some water. And don't—" he added quickly, putting a restraining hand on her cheek—"bother to nod."

She patted his hand where it rested, then gave a limp thumbs up.

When he came back with the canteen, he held it poised near her mouth. "I don't want you to lift your head just yet, Mady. Just open your mouth and I'll pour it in."

"Tryin'…t' choke me, par'ner?"

He grinned. "Never even crossed my mind. This time."

A dry chuckle was her only response as she obediently opened her mouth.

With infinite care, he poured the water, pausing as she swallowed, then pouring again when she was ready.

"Amazing how good that tastes." She smiled up at him again, and he was relieved. She didn't sound like she was talking through a mouthful of oatmeal anymore, and that was good.

"So I take it I've been out awhile?"

Her eyes were alert and questioning, and Jason hesitated. But he knew Mady would want the whole truth and nothing but. "About fifteen minutes, give or take a few minutes either way." He made the words as even as he could. "My guess is you've got at least a slight concussion."

"Twenty minutes is a long time for a slight concussion." Her gaze on him was steady and calm.

He inclined his head. "You got up close and personal with that boulder, Mady. And you did it with a good deal of force."

"I didn't exactly have a lot to say about it."

"Well, you've got a regular memento of the encounter." He laid a gentle finger on the side of her face. "You've got a good-sized lump on your forehead. Some scrapes and bruises."

"Hmm. Something tells me I'm glad I don't have a mirror."

"You look great." The words came out before he could stop them.

She gave a short burst of laughter. "I'll bet."

Too late to take it back now. Besides, it was true. For all of her bumps and bruises, she was beautiful.

Beautiful? When did she go from cute and attractive to…beautiful?

He didn't know for sure. He just knew she had. And he wasn't going to let her tell him otherwise. He held her dubious gaze silently, and soon her eyes lowered and a wave of pink tinged her cheeks.

"Yeah, well…I'll take your word for it."

His only reply was a smile. "The good news, though, is that your pupils are responsive and even. And so far you haven't shown signs of being confused or disoriented—" He flashed her a quick grin.

"I know, I know—" she held up one hand to forestall his words—"any more than usual."

It felt good to laugh. He leaned his elbows on his knees. "Anyway, what I need you to do is tell me how you're feeling. How bad is the headache?"

Her eyes shifted and grew a bit unfocused. Alarmed at first, Jason relaxed when he realized she was doing an internal systems check, so to speak. He waited quietly.

"It's dull and throbbing, but I've had worse."

"Any numbness anywhere?"

Mady slowly wiggled her fingers and rocked her feet back and forth. She moved her arms and shoulders, her legs, then looked at him again. "No. My shoulder hurts, where I hit the boulder, but everything else feels fine. No tingling, no numbness."

He hadn't realized he was holding his breath until it came out in a whoosh. "Thank God for that."

Drat! Where had *that* comment come from?

Your heart.

He wasn't going to argue the point. He was just hoping that Mady had been distracted, hadn't heard what he'd said….

One glance at the astonishment touching her face and he knew he was sunk. At the look in those emerald eyes, Jason felt heat flooding his cheeks. Again.

He'd blushed more in the last three days than he had in the last three years!

Chewing the inside of his lip, he waited. There was little doubt in his mind that she would jump on what he'd said. But she surprised him yet again by staying silent.

Clearing his throat, he went on. "Do you feel nauseous?"

"Depends."

He gave her a quick look, and this time it was her face that lit up with a grin. An irresistibly mischievous one. "On what you've got planned for dinner. I'm not eating bugs or grubs!"

He held out his hands, laughing with a mixture of amusement and relief. "I promise, nothing that crawls for dinner." Which reminded him…"Mady, I've got to gather some wood to keep the fire going. Your dry clothes are gone, courtesy of the river. We need to get you dried out before nightfall. And I think a hot dinner would be helpful for both of us."

"So what are you waiting for, bucko. Get moving."

He snapped her a salute. "Yes *sir!* Your servant, *sir!*"

Her giggle was marvelously contagious, and he found himself laughing along with her. He started to rise, then hesitated. Narrowing his eyes, he gave her his best stern father look. "Listen, I don't want to alarm you, Mady, but I don't think you should try getting up or moving around much. Not until you have to."

Her somber expression told him she was digesting that "not until you have to." Quickly, he clarified. "I'm betting they'll find us tomorrow." He waved a hand at their location. "If they look for us along the river, they've got a clear view of us here. So we can wait it out, even until noon tomorrow."

"And then?"

"And then we'll try something else. Find high ground, see if the radio will transmit there without the trees and walls of rock around us."

"So...you're saying you aren't going to carry me?"

His lips twitched. "Ah...no. Not unless I have to."

"Well, then, I'll just be all recovered by tomorrow. Okay?"

He knew she was worried, even frightened. And that made it all the more moving that she spoke with such humor and calm determination. "It's a deal. As for me, it's firewood a'hunting I go." He hesitated again. Better to be overemphatic than sorry.... "You're going to be a good girl and stay put, yes?"

Wide eyes filled with innocence gazed up at him. "I'm going to be a good girl and stay put, yes."

There was something warm and enchanting in their gentle banter, and Jason felt almost lighthearted as he went to gather more wood. It didn't take long to have a pile he felt could take them through the night.

He glanced at his watch.

"What time is it?"

With a hard swallow, Jason turned to Mady. The desire to fudge the truth, to protect her, was powerful, but he pushed it away. As before, he knew she'd want a straight answer. "A little after four in the afternoon."

At the flicker of anxiety in her eyes a band had tightened around his heart. Her next words only cranked up the tension.

"They aren't even expecting us back at base camp until between four thirty and five."

He nodded.

When her lips trembled, his determination not to sweep her into his arms…not to make himself a barrier between her and the cold, hard facts…melted like a snowman sitting on a stove. But he wouldn't be helping either of them if he did that. They both needed to know what they were facing.

"When will they start looking for us?"

The question came out in a small, tight voice, and Jason moved then. He knelt beside her, gently taking her hand in his, rubbing his thumb across it in slow, calming circles. "Mady, we're going to be okay."

She bit her lip, then gave him a slow nod. She tried to say something, but he could tell she was almost in tears. Drawing a shuddering breath, she tried again. "I know. I really do know that. I'm just…just…"

Tears made a trail down the sides of her face as her words dwindled away, and when she muttered a choked "I'm sorry," jagged pain tore at Jason's heart. He leaned forward to wipe the dampness from her temples, his fingers lingering there. Offering her what reassurance he could, he leaned down to press a soft kiss on her forehead.

"It's okay, Mady. It's normal to be emotional after a head injury." He looked around them. "Add to that the only slightly stressful situation we're in…." He let his gaze drift back to hers. "I think maybe you're entitled."

She gave him a watery smile. "You can be a nice guy when you try, you know that?"

A burst of laughter escaped him, and he cupped her face. "Maybe I should have tried sooner."

When she studied him, searching his eyes, he had the sense of a tenucus connection—like a lacy, filigreed web stretched between two blades of grass—being formed between them.

"You aren't the only one who wasn't really trying. I'm sorry, Jason. For all of it." She reached out then, and her fingers were soft and warm as they touched his arm. "And I forgive you." The gaze that held his was sincere. Guileless. Vulnerable. "For all of it."

Forgiveness. He'd had no idea how much he longed for it, needed it…that he ached for it like suffocating lungs screamed for a gasp of air. Forgiveness from Mady. And from so many others….

How had she known? With four simple, tender words, it was as though Mady had reached inside him and wrapped her arms around his wounded heart. A heart he'd been sure was well fortified and armored against any entry by those he no longer chose to let in….

Until now. And suddenly, like the first signs of thaw after a long, long winter, hints of hope crept in.

Forgiveness…

Easy enough for her. She hasn't known you very long. How much can you have hurt her? Nothing compared to what you did to—

Jason turned away quickly, closing his mind to the thought. *Shut up. Shut up…*

Remember how he looked at you? The grief in his eyes? The disappointment?

"Jason."

He turned abruptly to look down at Mady, and for a moment it was another face he saw…another pair of warm, piercing eyes…another concerned smile…

"Jason " her hand squeezed his wrist gently. "It's all right."

With a start, Jason focused on the sweet face looking up at him. "I…what is?"

Compassion reached out to embrace him in her gaze, her words. "Whatever is hurting you…haunting you. Whatever it is, Jas, you don't have to face it alone. It will be all right."

Sitting there, held by those clear eyes, a soft breeze caressing his face, her hand warm on his wrist, he almost believed her. He wanted to. Lord in heaven, how he wanted to.

"If we confess our sins."

The words came back to him slowly, like a creaking, rusty door that hadn't been opened in a long, long time.

"If we confess our sins, he is faithful and just and will forgive us our sins…"

Forgive. There it was again.

"And cleanse us from all unrighteousness."

Cleansed. His throat tightened on the sob that

wanted to escape. Dear heaven. What would it be like to feel cleansed? To be restored. Free. Unhindered by regret...sorrow...grief...self-condemnation—a cursed confederacy that had held his heart bound for what felt like forever but had only been...what? A year?

Closing his eyes, he bowed his head. He didn't know how it would feel. Couldn't even begin to imagine it.

"Come unto me..."

I want to. I want to....

His jaw tensed. His teeth clenched. He put his hand over Mady's where it lay on his wrist and willed himself to give in.

But he couldn't. The anger...the betrayal...the fact that he'd been such a trusting fool...he couldn't let them go.

As though sensing his struggle—and his defeat—Mady wove her fingers with his and tugged gently. "I'm here."

He met her eyes—those wonderful eyes—and nodded. "I know." His voice was low and choked as he saw tears glittering in her eyes.

"Don't worry, Jason. We're not alone."

He managed a low laugh. "You can say that again. There are more critters buzzing and creeping around here than you can shake a stick at."

Her expression was pointed. "That's not what I meant."

Jason let his eyes caress her face. "I know."

She patted his arm softly. "And I know you don't like talking about this. But if it's okay with you, I'll keep talking with God about it all. Okay?"

Seeing as she was the one He was most likely to listen to, that was fine with him. But he just took her hand and gave it a small shake. "Deal. You do the praying while we're out here, and I'll do the rest." He slanted a roguish look at her. "Which, to my way of thinking, is a much easier load."

As he'd hoped, she laughed. "Which just goes to show how much help your way of thinking needs."

He looked down at their joined hands and tightened his hold. "Mady, you know we're going to have to stay here at least for the night, right?"

"I know. Earl probably won't even try to contact us—"

She broke off suddenly, and he saw the same spark of excitement in her eyes that must have shone in his earlier. He hated to douse it, but he did so. "The radio's not working."

He wasn't sure how he'd expected her to react, but it wasn't by squeezing his hand as though she were trying to encourage him. He pushed on. "Anyway, you're right, Earl probably won't try to contact us until we're a half hour late or so." He gave a rueful smile. "He's cautious about embarrassing people unnecessarily."

"Never thought I'd say this, but curse that man's compassion."

"Shoot, I've been saying that for days."

She swatted at him playfully, and Jason let go of her hand and rose to tend the fire.

Mady watched him, not speaking until he was back beside her. She lowered her chin, narrowing her eyes in a mock scold. "Sooo, didn't I hear someone mention something about dinner?"

"You did, indeed."

As he moved to pull the food from their packs, he couldn't help shaking his head with wonder. These were without a doubt the most dire circumstances he'd ever faced. But he wasn't afraid. Instead, he had the strangest sense of…anticipation. He couldn't explain it, but he had the clear feeling they were here—he and this small, maddening, delightful woman with a golden halo of curls and a faith that challenged him—for a reason.

And though a part of him scoffed, calling him every kind of fool for letting such feelings in, he didn't care. Time enough tomorrow to analyze…to scrutinize and dissect with reason and rationale.

Right now, all he wanted to do was enjoy the sensation warming him from the inside out. It was something he hadn't felt in a very long time…something absurd, improbable…but he welcomed it all the same.

Hope.

❧ 20 ❧

To change one's life: start immediately;
do it flamboyantly; no exceptions.
WILLIAM JAMES

Mady shifted slightly on the hard ground, wishing for the umpteenth time that she had more padding on her backside.

She'd considered asking Jason if she could move just enough to fold some kind of cushion under her, but she didn't want to distract him. She enjoyed the show too much.

He almost made it seem the most natural thing in the world to be lost in the middle of the mountains. He'd gone about feeding wood to the fire, whistling the entire time. Whistling! Like he was having the time of his life.

Renewed respect for the man's knowledge and skills filled her as she watched him. The happy, crackling sound of a fire filled the air. Along with a very welcome warmth. The air was already starting to cool, and Mady's clothes were just damp enough to send her into chills every time a breeze blew over her.

"That feels wonderful."

Jason had looked at her again, and she saw the light of appreciation in his eyes. Amazing how even small words of gratitude or kindness could stir a heart.

"Pleasant words . . . are sweet to the soul, and healing to the bones."

I know, Lord. I know. She let her eyes drift shut. *So why don't I follow that more often? Why do I jump into the emotional fray, fists and verbal jabs at the ready?*

"You okay?"

She turned her head carefully. Jason's concerned gaze rested on her, and the smile that filled her face came from the center of her heart. "I'm great."

Something warm and slightly disturbing smoldered in the depths of his eyes. When he spoke, his voice had a raw edge to it. "I'll go along with that."

As though he'd surprised himself with the comment, he pulled back slightly, then turned and went to gather up several long sticks.

"What are those?"

"Our dryer."

She stared at him. "You're kidding."

Chuckling, he began stretching the wet clothes out on the sticks. "Oh, ye of little faith," he muttered, and Mady stuck her tongue out at him.

His burst of laughter was uninhibited, and Mady couldn't hold back a responding giggle. Her heart filled at the sparkle in Jason's eyes. He looked like a man set free.

If only that were true....

She watched in wonder as Jason dug the ends of the sticks into the ground in front of the fire. She heard the material of the clothes sizzle quietly as the moisture evaporated.

Her grin widened. "Forgive me, Mountain Man. I never should have doubted you."

"And don't you forget it."

Dinner that night was a meager affair. Jason divided up the food they both had and doled it out accordingly. It wasn't much. All they had were their lunches: a sandwich, an orange, and two power bars each. So Jason cut off half of their sandwiches and a few slices of one of the oranges. But it tasted wonderful.

Jason told her he would keep the fire burning low, for heat and to discourage any animals from paying them a visit. "It won't give us a lot of light, I'm afraid, but it will be something."

"That's fine." But Mady knew it wasn't. Not by a long shot. She wanted a bonfire. Something with flames shooting ten feet into the sky. Something that would hold back the curtain of darkness that was slowly but surely taking over the sky.

And as the last remnants of daylight melted away, Mady's peace seemed to follow suit. She lay there, watching the black, black night descend, swallowing up both Jason's meager fire and the calm Mady had been so proud of just a few hours earlier.

It wasn't so much the dark that frightened her. It was what was hiding in it.

Prickles of apprehension traveled over her as her eyes adjusted to the now inky world. During the day, the surrounding trees had been beautiful. Now they hovered there, blackened silhouettes arching over them like vultures watching for an opportunity.

Turning her head, Mady looked toward the river, but that was a mistake. If anything, it seemed even darker there. And the sounds drifting toward her were oddly ominous.

Frogs, she told herself. *Insects.*

A perfect draw for snakes, a nagging voice deep within added. *Looking for a warm place to sleep, a warm body to snuggle next to—*

Mady closed her eyes tightly, willing herself to stop trembling, willing her mind to stop echoing over and over with the same frantic cry: We're going to die out here!

"I am with you…I am with you…I am with you…" She whispered it quietly so Jason wouldn't hear her. But it didn't seem to stop the trembling that had taken hold of her. Terror as impenetrable as the night settled over her.

Trust me.

Don't You think I want to? She gritted her teeth together. *Just tell me how when I'm in this place, vulnerable, powerless….*

You're always powerless, Mady. I am in control. Not you.

That was evident. What wasn't so evident was how that fact was supposed to help her. Was realizing her inability to protect and save herself supposed to make her feel better?

Rest in Me.

How can I rest out here?

She let her eyes drift again to the dark shapes of the trees. So many things could be out there…what had Earl said? Bears? *Grizzlies?* And here she lay, unable to move.

Laid out like an hors d'oeuvre for a hungry beast.

Squeezing her eyes shut, Mady bit her lip against the shivers traveling up and down her spine.

There's nothing out there, reason told her dryly. *Open your eyes and see for yourself.*

But she couldn't. Her eyes refused to cooperate. Instead, she was sure she could hear the creature snuffling near her…feel its hot breath as it leaned close, lifting a giant clawed paw over her—

"Wow!"

Mady gasped and her eyes flew open at Jason's startled exclamation.

"*What?*" Frantically she looked around, but all she saw was him, sitting nearby, his head tipped back, the fire sending shadows playing across his form.

Following his gaze, Mady felt a sense of wonder wash over her.

Stars. Millions of them. Like tiny pinpricks letting the light escape a black, enveloping sheet. She stared, following the flow of light as it washed across the night, and found herself studying the moon. It hung there so large and bright Mady was sure she could reach out and take it in her hand.

"God made two great lights—the greater light to govern the day and the lesser light to govern the night…and saw that it was good."

Mady smiled. She'd thought the darkness surrounding her was impenetrable, but no darkness, no matter how dense, how far-reaching, could hold back God's light.

I'm sorry, Lord. I forgot.

I am with you….

This time she heard it. Really heard it.

She wasn't alone.

Jason looked down at her, and he was grinning too. "Talk about a night-light," he murmured, and she laughed.

Suddenly, Jason smacked his palm against the side of his head. "Good grief! What an idiot!"

"What—?"

But instead of answering Mady's question, he jumped and went to pull something from his pack. He turned and came back, holding it out for her to see.

The strobe light.

Mady grinned. "Our night-light."

Jason's responding smile was hopeful. "With any luck, one that will bring our friend Earl running."

"Oh, Lord, let it be so."

Jason paused, looking down at her, then moved to set up the strobe and flip on the switch. But Mady could have sworn, as he walked past her, that she heard a quiet, "Amen."

As the strobe came to life, Mady whooped at the way the blinking light pierced the night sky. "If they don't see that, they're blind!"

"Or they're not looking."

The words dampened Mady's excitement. "Not looking?"

Jason pulled his shirt from where it had been drying, then walked back to her and knelt beside her. "Mady, they'll look nearest our last known location first, then spread out. It may be too early for them to look this far afield."

Her disappointment must have shown on her face because he gave her shoulder a squeeze. "Don't worry. We'll be fine. And if they are looking anywhere near here—" he jerked his chin at the strobe—"they'll find us."

With that he leaned over to drape his shirt across Mady. She looked at him in protest. *"You* need it—"

But he was already shaking his head, tucking it around her, then reaching out to touch her face gently.

"Humor me, will you? I'll sleep better knowing you're warm."

Well, considering the effect his words—and his touch…and the look in his eyes—were having on her, the man should get the best night's sleep he'd had in days.

Smiling at the thought, she closed her eyes, letting the fatigue overtake her, drifting into a place of sweet quietness. But she could swear, as she floated into sleep, that she felt warm lips against her forehead and heard a soft, low voice murmur, "Sleep well, pixie."

The next morning, Mady woke with a shiver.

Grabbing Jason's shirt, she slipped her arms into the sleeves and hugged it close. Sunlight was just bringing a blush of pale pinks and oranges to the sky. Mady scanned the campsite.

A low fire was still burning, but Jason was nowhere to be seen. Which was decidedly unfortunate in light of her promise not to move without his approval. Because if there was one thing she needed right now, it was to move.

Quickly.

Biting her lip, she crossed her legs. "Um…Jason? You out there?"

No answer. Okay, she'd have to handle this herself. Slowly, gingerly, she did a check of her arms and legs, moving them experimentally, flexing the muscles bit by bit, waiting for any pain or numbness.

Nothing. Everything felt normal.

She didn't have a headache, which was good. Slowly

she turned her head from side to side, then up and down. Again, no pain or discomfort at all.

Except, of course, where her poor bladder was concerned.

With a deep breath, planting her hands firmly on the hard ground, she eased into a sitting position, then up onto all fours, then stood.

A sigh of relief escaped her. All systems were go. Her eyes widened. Speaking of which...

Hurrying to her pack, she rummaged quickly until she found the biodegradable tissues she'd packed. Then she made her way gingerly—and rapidly—into the woods.

Jason lowered the radio, fighting the disappointment that pricked at him.

Nothing. He'd been so sure that once he made his way to a higher spot, he'd be able to raise Earl. So he'd walked until he spotted a tree he could climb and scrambled up as high as he could safely go. Hanging there, suspended above the ground, he'd pressed the button.

"Earl, this is Jason. Earl...do you read me?"

Nothing. Not a crackle, not even static. Just silence. The thing was dead.

Fighting the urge to throw it as far as he could, Jason jammed the radio into his jacket pocket and made his way back to solid ground.

At least climbing the tree had given him a good look at the terrain, which answered some questions he'd had. There was no way they'd be able to follow the river back to where they'd fallen in. The rocky cliffs extended as far as he could see. They'd have to head east until they found a place to climb, then head back toward the river to the edge of the cliffs and follow them back toward the camp.

Problem was, they were on the wrong side of the river. The cliff they fell from had been on the west bank, but they'd come out on the east. He played with the idea of trying to cross the river, so they'd at least be on the same side as base camp...but the memory of the power and speed of the current squelched that idea. They'd never make it.

So there was only one option. Head east, find a place to climb to higher ground, then head back west toward the river.

That decision settled, he made his way back to the camp, hoping Mady was still sleeping as soundly as she'd been when he left. She'd need all the rest she could get. This was not going to be an easy trek.

Well, she handled yesterday just fine. A whole lot better, frankly, than he'd believed possible. He wasn't sure how he expected her to react, but the calm she'd shown, the reason and trust, had pretty much stunned him.

It's not like she's trusting you.

No, he knew that. But after what he'd seen in Mady's eyes when she ran yesterday—fear, disappointment, abandonment—he'd thought...

He closed his eyes. He didn't want to think about what he'd thought. Odd. All this time he'd been doing his best to open Mady's eyes, to debunk her insistent faith in a God Jason had long ago stopped trying to follow. And yet...

The pain that had stabbed through him when he'd succeeded—or thought he had—had taken his breath away. It had stunned him almost as much as the relief he now felt that her faith was more resilient than he'd believed.

As their circumstances grew more serious, her trust only seemed to grow stronger. It was as though the flotsam—the squabbles, the sparring, the posturing—had floated away on that river, and they'd been dumped on the bank with nothing but the bare-bones basics, physically and emotionally.

What mattered most was survival. Staying calm until they were found. And he had to admit that Mady's faith—and the knowledge that she was praying for them—gave him a sense of peace and security.

Because you know the One she trusts.

His jaw tensed. *No comment.*

But deep inside, in that hidden place somewhere in his heart, he knew that he did, indeed, know Him. And even more than that, he missed Him.

Roughly twenty minutes later, Jason reached their campsite, and alarm jolted through him.

Mady was gone.

He looked around quickly, was about to call out, then stopped. "What in the...?"

Moving as quietly as he could, he stepped back into the trees and made his way, hidden, toward the river. There, standing crouched in the calmer, knee-deep water near the bank, was Mady. She held her hands below the surface, a look of intense concentration on her face as she stared down into the water.

Jason craned his neck and grinned. The shadows flitting around Mady's legs could only be one thing: fish.

She was trying to catch a fish. With a quiet chuckle, he stepped out of the trees. "Mad—"

But at that precise moment she straightened with a whoop, unleashing a cascade of water—and one wriggling, slimy trout. Right at him.

The water doused him as the fish hit him smack between the eyes. With a yelp, he jumped away, only to trip on something and go flying backward. With a thud he landed sprawled on the ground, staring up at Mady, who'd come out of the water and stood over him, holding a nice, plump, flailing fish in each hand.

"And you call *me* an accident waiting to happen."

With that, she shot him a grin and spun on her heel, heading back to camp.

Jason watched her go, laughing as he wiped the water and fish slime from his face.

Well, so much for a neck injury. That woman was clearly feeling just fine.

After a delicious breakfast of trout, Mady and Jason worked in silence, cleaning up their site and getting their packs ready. Jason appreciated the way Mady went about what she knew to do, not asking him the questions he knew had to be buzzing around in her head.

With a final tug on the strap of her pack, she turned to him. "Okay, so what's the plan?"

He looked up from his pack. "I know I said we'd stay here, but I think we need to head out this morning."

She didn't look surprised. Just inclined her head, her eyes somber. "There's a storm moving in, isn't there?"

Jason's surprise must have shown on his face because she broke into a grin.

"Hey, I may not be Jeremima Johnson, Mountain Woman, but I can tell when the barometric pressure is changing. And not for the better."

He nodded and looked upward. The sky was full of clouds, and they were moving at a fast clip. Clearly the wind was building. And Mady was right on target: The barometric pressure was giving clear signs of a whopper of a storm on the horizon. They had to find shelter before it hit.

"So, we head out." Mady looked around, a small frown pulling her brows together. It was the first sign of uncertainty Jason had seen today. She turned back to him. "Where?"

He nodded toward the woods. "East, just until we can find a place to head to higher ground. We need to get to the top of these cliffs and then follow the river back toward camp."

She nodded again. "We'll make it. If not today, then tomorrow."

"Sure. We'll just take it nice and slow, drink plenty of water along the way, and rest when we need to." He stood, pulling his pack on and securing it in place. "Not a problem."

Mady followed suit, slipping her arms through the straps of her pack. "Absolutely. It'll be a walk in the park."

But he saw the shadows flitting across her face and knew the doubts that pricked at her. For all her brave words, she was as aware as he that right now—with no radio and a storm moving in—the odds were not exactly in their favor.

Mady couldn't remember ever being so thirsty. Or tired.

Step, step, step…

She kept her feet moving, one after the other, matching Jason's strides as best she could. Every once in a while she had to make a quick, little catch-up two-step, but that was okay. As long as she kept her eyes on Jason's pack and her stride in sync with his, she'd be fine.

No matter how much her body was protesting.

Step, step, step…

Every muscle in her body ached. Probably thanks to slamming into that boulder on her wild river ride, she thought as she rolled her shoulders for the hundredth time, trying to ease the sharp ache between her shoulder blades. She'd sidestepped more holes in the ground, scrambled over more fallen logs, woven through more stands of close-growing trees than she ever imagined possible.

But she wasn't going to complain. No way. If Jason could keep going, so could she. The further they walked, the sooner they'd be back with the others. Then back at the lodge.

Safe. Sheltered. With beds and mattresses and pillows…

Out of this infernal, knee-high foliage! Rotten stuff was next to impossible to walk through. And the ground was growing downright damp, as though they were nearing a marsh or something.

Smelled to high heaven, too. Moldy and musty.

But I'm not complaining, Lord. I'm just making an observation.

Mady let her eyes close to slits, focusing on Jason's pack. They'd been walking steadily for hours. The whole morning, anyway. She'd hoped the overcast sky would keep the day from getting too warm, but instead, it seemed to crank up the humidity factor until everything was damp—her clothes, her hair, her skin—everything, down to her bones.

She felt like a wet dog coiled in gloom, longing for a friendly fire.

Pulling the sticky fabric away from her skin, she grimaced at the breeze that continued to blow. No, not a breeze. Not any longer. It was wind. A gusty, almost belligerent wind at that.

Why couldn't it be helpful and blow at her back, for cryin' out loud? Instead, it blasted away at her face, as though doing its level best to keep her from making any progress.

"Time for a lunch break, Mady."

She almost threw herself into Jason's arms in gratitude. Instead, she gave him a bright smile. Or as bright as she could muster. Okay, so it was about as bright as a flashlight with a dead battery, but at least it was a smile.

Mady watched as Jason walked back and forth, looking for a spot where they could sit. She should be helping him, not standing here like a lump. "Can I help?"

His expression as he glanced at her was an odd mixture of amusement and concern. "Yeah, by not falling down. Just hang on—ah. Here we go."

He waved her over, and she forced her feet to move until she reached the fallen log he'd found. Sinking down, she didn't even protest as he pulled her pack free and rummaged around, finally pulling out the last of her sandwich and handing it to her.

Jason settled on the log, chewing his sandwich slowly, his gaze resting on Mady. The frown between his eyes told her he wasn't all that pleased with what he saw.

Well, let's see him look like a fashion plate without a comb and hairspray.

But even as she thought it, she knew that wasn't what bothered him. She could feel for herself that she was pale and sweating. And shivering.

"Are you feeling all right?"

She started to say she felt great but stopped herself. Hiding the truth had gotten them into this mess.

"Hold to the truth in love."

Right. Okay. "Not really."

He stood and came to lay a cool hand beneath her bangs; his brows creasing again as his hand fell away. Without thinking, she leaned forward, letting her fore head rest against his thigh. His hand came to cup the back of her head.

Oh, Lord, please…don't let me get sick. Not now. Not out here.

The urge that hit her then was so powerful that her eyes widened in disbelief. The message was clear, as clear as if someone had leaned over and whispered the instruction in her ear: *Ask Jason to pray for you.*

Mady just shook her head. How could she do that? *You know how he reacts to just the mention of You…how resistant he is, even angry…*

She could ask him to pray *with* her. That she could do. But to pray *for* her? It didn't make sense....

Do it.

She wanted to argue, wanted to ask why, to ask that it at least make sense...but bottom line, she knew that didn't matter. Obedience. That was what mattered.

"Jason?" A shiver wracked her, and she fought back weary tears. "Would you pray for me?"

She felt his fingers tense, and an apology sprang to her lips. But she held her silence. She'd only done what she knew she was being asked to do, and she wouldn't apologize for that.

The silence stretched into seconds, even minutes, and then, much to Mady's surprise, Jason's low voice drifted around her.

"God, I know we haven't exactly been on speaking terms for a while..." He stopped, and when he started again his tone was rough. "A long while. And I know there's no earthly reason You should listen to me on anything. But Mady—" he cleared his throat—"she's Your daughter. That's plain. She loves You, and I know You love her. I see it in her face all the time. So please, God. Help her. Touch her. Don't let her get sick. And don't let her be afraid."

They stayed as they were, a kind of stillness wrapped around them, until Mady murmured a low, "Amen" against Jason's leg.

She looked up, blinking back tears. "Thank you."

His smile was self-deprecating. "I don't know how much good it will do."

The smile that came to her then was one of simple joy. "It's already done wonders." And it had. Hearing

Jason pray for her had moved her in a deep, profound way. As he spoke, she'd had the powerful sense of God's presence—and His pleasure. With each low, cautious word, she felt enfolded, cradled in heavenly arms, and lifted to the throne of the Great Physician.

Jason's hand moved from the back of her head to cup her cheek, and she saw a flicker of surprise in his eyes. He frowned, then put his hand on her forehead, and then frowned again. "I could have sworn you had a fever a minute ago."

Mady smiled. "'He delights in the prayers of the upright.'"

Stepping back, Jason's features reflected his doubt, and Mady held her silence. Now was not the time to push. But she'd discovered something.

Jason was no stranger to God. He was not a man who'd never encountered the Savior. She was sure of it, and not just because of his words. Something in the way he'd prayed, in the tone of his voice, had told her this was a man who knew God. Intimately.

Mady was sure of something else, too. Whatever it was that had turned Jason's heart cold, God was at work.

And like it or not, a thaw had begun.

❧ 21 ❧

Love is not gazing at each other, but
looking together in the same direction.
ANTOINE DE SAINT-EXUPÉRY

Studying the sky through the canopy of trees, Jason figured they had about four hours of daylight left.

There was still a solid wall of rock beside them as they walked along. He'd been so sure they'd find a break in it, a place to climb to the top of the cliffs and then head back toward the river, but no such luck.

He swallowed his disappointment. They'd done the best they could. If only the map showed the area they were in, but it didn't. So while he knew the direction they were heading, knew where they needed to end up, he had no idea how they were going to get there.

It hadn't helped that after lunch, he'd slowed their pace considerably. Miraculous healing notwithstanding, Mady's pale face and listless walk before their lunch break had flat scared him. The heat he'd felt burning at his palm when he'd laid it against her forehead sent his heart plunging into his shoes.

She'd had a fever. Was getting sick. Big time. And there was nothing he could do about it.

Or so he'd thought. Then she asked him to pray. At first he almost pulled away from her, but he'd been afraid she would have toppled over onto the forest floor.

So he stood there, arguing with himself, teeth clenched tightly together.

No way. It won't do any good. Why should I?

Because she asked you to.

That and the fact that she had to be feeling lousy—and probably scared—to do so. So he'd done it. Gone against all the promises he made himself a year ago and spoken to the One he'd sworn he'd never speak to again.

He hadn't expected it to do any good. Why would it? A shiver ran though him at the memory of feeling Mady's forehead again—and finding it cool.

Just like that. Asked and answered.

Mady had taken the whole thing in stride. What had she said? *"'He delights in the prayers of the upright'"*? The upright. That was a laugh.

Jason gave an impatient tug on the straps of his backpack, almost glad for the twinge of aching pain in his ribs. *That* was reality. Hurting and overcoming and fighting your way through.

Not miracles in the middle of nowhere.

Those made no sense at all—not when they happened in response to a prayer from him.

Face it, Tiber, you don't like things that you don't understand.

Oh he understood it. He understood it just fine. He'd prayed; God had answered. Sure, it could have been coincidence that Mady's health had turned around the way it had just after he prayed. That her fever had just disappeared. That the color had come back into her cheeks, and her trembling had stopped. Maybe she'd just needed to rest. To eat.

But he didn't buy it. That had been no coincidence.

He'd seen it too many times in the past to doubt what he knew: God had reached down, even as Jason was asking him to do so, and touched Mady.

Healed her.

No, his problem wasn't that he didn't understand it. It was that he didn't like it. Not one little bit.

Mady sent up another prayer of thanks. She felt stronger with each step. Despite the fact that the undergrowth was still dense, the trees still thick, the day still humid, she felt better as each minute passed.

Lord, You're amazing.

Jason had asked her several times if she needed a break, but she'd just grinned and told him the truth: She felt fine. Great, even.

He glanced back at her now. "How you doing, partner?"

Mady shook her head, a smile twitching at her lips. "Still fine, Jason. Just like I was when you asked me fifteen minutes ago." She took in the tenseness around his mouth and reached out to pat his arm. "Sorry, partner, but the answer to your prayer is still working."

He opened his mouth to reply, then stopped and glanced around. "What was that?"

Heat rushed to Mady's cheeks, and she planted a hand in the middle of his pack and propelled him forward. "I didn't hear anythin—"

"There it is again." His frown was replaced by a dawning realization, and he started to chuckle.

Mady stopped and put her hands on her hips. "What?"

Her miffed tone just made him grin as he angled a look back at her. "Either your stomach is grumbling, or there's a dog following us." His grin broadened. "A *big* one."

She pressed a hand to her midsection. "My stomach is not—"

But another rumble sounded, bringing her up short. Jason laughed out loud this time, and Mady gave a sheepish shrug.

He stretched his shoulders, one hand on the strap of his pack. "Well, I think we've each got half of a power bar left…." He paused, and Mady figured she knew what he was thinking. He didn't want to use them up yet. Just in case. Earl would have notified search and rescue by now, so surely someone would find them before too much longer. Still, better to be safe.

"We should probably save them, if we can."

He smiled at her comment and nodded. "If we can." He looked around them, his gaze sweeping the area. "Besides, this area looks pretty promising for finding something edible."

"Oh, yeah?" Mady studied the trees and weeds and bushes surrounding them, then gave him a dubious look. "You see Nikos's golden arches, do you?"

"No…" He spotted something and moved forward quickly.

Mady padded after him, wondering what treasure he'd found—then came to an abrupt halt when she saw what was on the ground in front of Jason.

A moss-covered, decaying, fallen log.

He couldn't be serious. She looked at him, saw his expression. Oh yes, he could. Shaking her head, she stepped back.

"No way, Tiber."

"You heard Earl. Never pass up any reasonable source of nourishment when you're in need."

"I'll never be *that* much in need! At least, I'm not right now."

His expression was sober. "Mady—"

She swallowed, then closed her eyes. "I can't. I just can't."

Jason fell silent, and Mady waited...knowing he'd insist...knowing he was right....

Then Jason stiffened, tipped his head.

Maybe she could convince him. "I'm not that hungry, real—"

"Shh!"

She *shhed*, then jumped when he grabbed her sleeve and tugged at her, pulling her along as he walked rapidly through the brush.

"Do you hear that?"

Mady jerked to a halt, pulling her arm free. "I can't hear anything with you stomping through the brush!"

He paused, waiting as she listened. She really hated to disappoint the man, but..."All I hear are frogs."

His grin filled his face. "Exactly." He started walking again, Mady on his heels, and suddenly they stepped out of the dense trees and knee-deep ground cover, into an open area.

Mady stood there, staring at the pond in front of them. A pond full of lily pads. And algae. And green floating things with eyes.

A pond full of big, fat croaking frogs.

It took a moment for it to sink in, then Mady jerked to stare at Jason, her mouth gaping. "Tell me you're not suggesting what I think you're suggesting!"

He crossed his arms. "It's either that—" he glanced back toward the trees—"or the bugs."

Pressing her lips together, Mady turned to the pond…then rolled up her sleeves and waded in. "How many of the little hoppers do we need?"

Jason leaned back against the wide tree trunk at his back, let his eyes drift shut, and sighed contentedly.

"You don't have to look so pleased with yourself, you know."

He opened one eye to peer at Mady, watching her lick her fingers daintily. "Was I right, or was I right?"

She paused, glanced down at the now empty shish kebab stick in her hand, and broke into a mischievous grin. "You were right." She licked her lips. "Frog legs are delicious."

This was too good a moment to let it go by too quickly. "Better even than chicken."

Her nod was without hesitation. "*Much* better."

The grin splitting his face was so wide it almost made his jaws ache. "Well then—just keep that in mind for next time."

Mady caught herself at that, and her eyes narrowed ever so slightly. "Next time?"

"Next time I tell you something will taste good."

"Something…?"

He waved a careless hand in the air. "Out here? Shoot, there's a whole smorgasbord for us to try! Snake, fish, bird, rabbit—" he gave her a sideways glance— "bugs—"

"Oh my, will you look at the time!" Mady's forced cheerfulness cut him off cold. She directed an overly enthusiastic smile at him and stood. "If we're going to make it to higher ground, we'd better get going again, hadn't we?"

Okay. Fine. He wouldn't talk about eating bugs. Not until he absolutely had to.

His amusement faded at the thought, and he found himself directing another plea heavenward as he tugged his backpack into place.

Please, for Mady's sake, let them find us tonight.

But even as the prayer was formed, Jason didn't hold much hope of it being answered. They were too low, too close to the trees, to be spotted easily.

They really needed to find their way back to the cliffs above the river. He glanced at the sun—and there was precious little chance of that happening anytime soon.

They'd been walking for about a half hour when Jason stopped dead in his tracks.

"Hey!" Mady squawked. "Get your brake lights fixed, buddy!"

"There it is!"

Mady came to stand beside him. "There *what* is?"

Jason laughed, about to do a victory dance right then and there. He pointed, his smugness only increasing when he saw Mady's face light up.

The rocky wall that had held them at bay all day long had finally given way. There, in front of them, was a slope leading upward.

Mady grabbed his arm. "Well, what are we waiting for?"

He gave a whoop and swept her up into his arms. "Absolutely nothing!"

Laughing, he ran, ignoring her squeals and demands that he put her down. Within minutes they were halfway up the hill. Then Jason stepped wrong, and the next thing he knew, they both were pitching forward.

He heard Mady's cry of alarm as she flew out of his arms. He clutched at her but grabbed only empty air. Rolling to land on his shoulder, he grunted in pain as his already bruised ribs complained at the hard impact.

Jason pushed himself up and looked around frantically, then felt his heart constrict. Mady lay a few yards away, sprawled facedown on the leaf-and-twig-covered ground.

Surging to his feet, he ran over to her side. "Mady?"

The only response he got was a low moan. "Oh hon, I'm so sorry. I never should have... I was being an idiot...."

Her shoulders were shaking now. She was crying! His heart tore into shreds at the sight—and the knowledge that he was responsible for the pain she was in.

Heaping condemnation on himself, he pulled her pack free and tossed it aside. Then, as carefully as he could, he grasped her arm and hip and rolled her onto her back.

Mady's breathing was coming in wheezes and coughs, and her hands were flapping at Jason like a bird caught in a snare struggling to take flight. Her eyes were clenched shut, but that didn't keep tears from running down her face as she tried to speak. "You…I…you…"

Jason plucked twigs and leaves from her hair with trembling fingers. "Mady? What is it? Where do you hurt?"

She opened her damp eyes, stared up at him wide eyed, and grabbed the front of his shirt in a surprisingly strong grip to pull herself up. He put his hand over hers just as she threw her head back and let out a whoop of belly-deep laughter.

Jason's mouth fell open.

Mady let go of his shirt and rolled on her side, clutching her stomach, overcome with snickers and hoots of laughter.

Jason's mouth shut. And his lips thinned into a grim line. "Mady."

She buried her face in her hands, laughing so hard she was hiccuping.

"Mady." Apparently the heated tone of his voice got through to her. She pushed herself up on one elbow and faced him. "Oh…Jason! (*hic!*)…y-you should have (*hic!*) seen your face…."

"Are you hurt?" He ground the words out, and she cleared her throat and drew in a steadying breath.

"Um, no." She wriggled her arms and legs, then gave him a bright smile. "I don't think so." Her smile faded at the look on his face, though when she spoke the laughter was still painfully evident. "Not unless you plan to help me up the incline again?"

He shot to his feet then, standing rigid and glaring down at her. She scrambled to her feet, a swift apology on her lips.

"Don't bother!" He started to stalk away, then spun back to her. "Are you *nuts?* You lay there laughing your head off while I'm standing here…I thought you were—"

He reached out to grab her and give her a shake. "You scared the *life* out of me!"

"I know, I know. I'm sorry, Jason. I couldn't help it. I mean, there I was, Miss Accident-prone, airborne courtesy of Mr. Caution and Athletic Grace. And then I look back to see this dumbstruck look on your face…." Much to his utter disbelief, she almost started laughing again.

"Mady, I'm warning you…"

She swallowed the laugh before it escaped, bit her lip, and slanted him a wide-eyed, puppy dog look. "I'm sorry. Next time you fling me through the air, I'll be sure to be appropriately injured." She put her hand on his chest, patting it reassuringly. "Scout's honor."

Jason's anger melted at her touch, and he looked down at her hand where it lay against him, then back at her face. The laughter was gone from her eyes now. Instead, he saw something else there…something infinitely tender…infinitely appealing.

Without thinking, he pulled her to him, closed his arms around her. She didn't resist, just buried her face in his shirt.

He felt the warmth of her filling his arms, felt her hands spread out against his chest—and gritted his teeth against the havoc being wrought on his emotions.

Dumb, Tiber. Dumb move.

Maybe so, but necessary. He had to do it. Needed her close, to feel for himself that she was all right.

"You're sure you're okay, Mady?"

The raw sound of his voice surprised him, but Mady

just nodded against his chest. "I am now." She turned her face up to him. "Thank you for finding the way up the cliff, Jason. I…I was starting to think we were just getting more and more lost."

He let his fingers massage her shoulders gently. Just to comfort her, to let her know she didn't need to be afraid.

"We'll be okay, Mady. Even if we don't make the river or the cliff's edge above it before dark, we'll be okay. Don't worry."

A small sigh escaped her as she looked from him to the trees around them. "I just hope we find some kind of clearing soon. They'll never find us in these woods."

She was probably right, and swift anger washed over Jason. They were headed for a second night out here—maybe in the face of a storm—and he couldn't change that. But someone could….

God…how can You let her be frightened like this? Don't You care that she's afraid?

Follow Me.

Jason stiffened. What? What was *that* supposed to mean.

Mady picked at his shirtfront absently. Clearly something was bothering her.

"Mady?"

She wouldn't look at him. She stared at his button, and her lips trembled. "It's my fault. For being so slow earlier."

He gave her a little shake. "You were sick. And you've done great since lunch. It's not your fault."

No, it wasn't Mady's fault. It was his. He'd pushed her yesterday when she was confused, wanted to punish her for the things she'd said. For the things she trusted so implicitly.

"I'm scared."

The admission was small and weary, and his hold on her tightened. "I know. Me, too."

Mady pulled back at that, looking up at him, eyes wide. "You?"

He smiled at her surprise and brushed a curl away from her brow. "You'd be surprised how many things scare me."

"Like what?" Her eyes held his, and it was as though she looked into the very heart of him. His head swam with answers, with words he ached to speak but knew he wouldn't.

Like you. Like how perfect you feel in my arms and the fact that I don't want to let you go. Like the way you make me believe again in possibilities…the way you make me long to be close to God again, to listen to Him, to do what He's asking….

His hand moved of its own volition to cup her face. She leaned her cheek against his palm, her eyes drifting shut. Slowly, reverently, he lowered his head, and the words he'd been fighting for what felt like a lifetime escaped at last.

I love you.

The words whispered through him as he covered her mouth with his, and she settled against him with a soft, whispering sigh.

I love you.

Her lips were warm and sweet, and for a moment, there was nothing but this. No woods, no danger, no storms threatening, no fear….

Only the two of them. Together.

When he finally lifted his head, he stared down at her, drinking in the sight of her face, exulting in the admission he read in her eyes—and then he saw it, deep in those green depths. Mixed with the love was an aching sadness. And as reality washed over Jason, he drew her close again, resting his chin on her head as she nestled against him.

He loved her. And she loved him. No point in either of them trying to deny it.

But this was as far as it could go. He knew it, and so did Mady.

"A home divided against itself is doomed."

For all that Jason had felt drawn back to God…for all that he'd sensed the Father calling him to reconciliation, restoration—he knew he wasn't ready. Wasn't ready to surrender himself again to what surrender, true surrender, would demand of him.

Follow Me.

He couldn't. Not yet.

With a will Jason hadn't known he possessed, he took hold of Mady's arms and stepped back from her. Meeting her eyes as she looked up at him, he offered her the only thing he could. The truth.

"There are things I want to say to you, Mady. Things I want to tell you and ask of you, but I can't."

"I know."

Her simple response surprised him, as did the peace he saw on her face.

"I'm not the kind of man you can love—"

Her fingers covered his lips, halting the words. "It's too late for that, Jason. I already do." Her smile was so sad he thought it would tear his heart apart. "But I understand. My first love will always be Christ. And if that's not true for you, then it wouldn't work."

He could deny it. Tell her he'd given in to God, opened himself to His leading again—or that he was close to it. But that wasn't good enough, and he knew it.

Loving a woman like Mady would be a whole-hearted endeavor—and loving God beside her would be nothing less. And Jason wasn't there. He just wasn't. He felt the tugs on his heart, his spirit...heard the whispered words of eternal love...but he couldn't do it. Couldn't let down the protective wall he'd put up.

He'd been hurt too deeply....

As he acknowledged that hard truth, he couldn't stop the dull ache of loss. Loss of Mady, of what could have been.

And on the heels of that, loss of what used to be....

He uttered a soul-weary sigh. "No. It wouldn't work."

She looked away, blinking against what Jason was sure were tears. Then she faced him again and, lifting her chin a fraction, gave a small nod. "So, if we're going to make it back to the river before dark, I suppose we'd better get started."

Jason held her gaze for a moment longer, then inclined his head. "I suppose so."

"Right. Okay, then." She managed a semblance of a grin. "But this time I'll go under my own steam, thanks." With a wave of her hand, she motioned him to the lead. "You first, I'll follow."

He touched his forehead lightly in a mock salute. "Yes, ma'am. Whatever you say, ma'am."

The sound of her laughter as it drifted around him was a balm to his tortured heart, but Jason knew it only eased the pain that clawed at him—a pain that wasn't going away anytime soon.

If ever.

"We've done everything we can for the day, Earl. It's getting too dark and too windy to keep go—"

"I know, Carl." Earl stared down at the cup of hot, black coffee in his hands. *God, where are they? Please…they're running out of time.*

Carl Aimes zipped his rain jacket and laid a large paw of a hand on Earl's shoulder. "We're gonna find 'em. Sooner or later, we're gonna find 'em."

Letting his breath out, Earl stood to shake Carl's hand. "I know that, too." He mustered up a lopsided smile. "I'd just been hoping for sooner."

As Carl headed out the door, Earl turned to study the map of the area again. He took a sip of coffee, eyes fixed on the shapes and swirls on the paper before him. "Where are you, Jas?"

Two days. It was going on two days. He'd really expected to find Mady and Jason before now. Jason didn't know the area well, but he knew the outdoors. He'd faced worse terrain than the Cascades had to offer.

Not without supplies. Without food.

Didn't matter. Jason knew what he was doing. As for Mady…she may not be experienced, but she had spunk. And she was strong in body and, more importantly, in faith.

She and Jason weren't alone out there. That was the

only thing that kept Earl from going nuts.

He rose from the chair and paced. If at all possible, Jason would keep them safe. But there was a lot that was out of his control.

Earl paused by the window, taking in the dark clouds gathering and boiling across the skies. *Jesus, this storm's not going to hold off much longer. Tomorrow morning, maybe afternoon. And when it breaks...* Earl felt his heart sink in his chest.

When it breaks, it is going to be a killer.

Sitting again, Earl set aside his mug and reached for the only tool he had that would help Mady and Jason. Opening his worn Bible to Psalms, he started reading out loud, the words becoming a prayer from the depths of his heart:

"I am praying to You because I know You will answer, O God. Bend down and listen as I pray. Show Jason and Mady Your unfailing love in wonderful ways. You save with Your strength those who seek refuge... Guard them as the apple of Your eye. Hide them in the shadow of Your wings and protect them...."

Bowing his head, Earl finished on a whisper. "Please... keep them safe."

❧ 22 ❧

If you ask why we should obey God, in the last resort
the answer is "I am." To know God, is to know
that our obedience is due Him.

C. S. LEWIS

Once they topped the incline, their progress was amazing. Mady knew both she and Jason probably were operating on adrenaline now that they were headed back toward the river, but she was still surprised at how much ground they'd covered in the last few hours and how neither of them seemed tired.

It helped that the terrain up here was more open. They seemed to be on a wide path of sorts. "A game trail, most likely," Jason said.

To the right was the edge of the rocky wall that they'd been following the opposite direction all day. To the left were small hills, jagged rock formations, and piles of boulders. Trees were scattered here and there, but the ground was rocky and less tangled with ground cover and brush, which made the going easier. Good thing, since the wind was picking up again.

Mady sped up until she was beside Jason. He slowed his strides, and she smiled at him, then looked up at the sky.

"Jason, if the storm hits, will they keep looking for us?"

His grim expression wasn't very comforting. "It will

depend on how severe it is. And what kind of storm. If there are strong enough winds or if it's an electrical storm, probably not." His gaze swept from side to side. "We should probably keep our eyes open for any kind of shelter, Mady." His jaw tensed. "Just in case."

Mady scanned the area, wondering what kind of shelter they could possibly find, when her gaze fixed on something. She frowned, peered more closely, then felt a grin easing across her face.

There, not thirty feet away, was an opening in the rocky hillside. A big, black hole in the rocks. She grabbed Jason's arm. "You mean like a cave?"

He nodded. "Sure, that would work. But I don't know that we'll find—"

Pulling his arm, Mady pointed. Jason just stood there, looking from her to the cave. She lifted her shoulders. "I just looked and it was there."

"Uh-huh." His tone was wry. "Why am I not surprised." Turning back, he started toward the cave. "Well, might as well check it out."

As they drew near, Mady saw that boulders and rocks of all sizes were all around and above the opening. She closed her hand around Jason's arm, apprehension making the hair on the back of her neck stand up.

"I don't know, Jason. It doesn't look safe."

He studied what looked like a veritable mountain of rocks now that they were up close to it, then shrugged out of his backpack. Unzipping a compartment, he pulled out a small flashlight.

"I'm going inside to check it out. Wait here." He crouched and shone the light inside. "Looks like it goes back a little ways…I can't see to the end." He started to enter, then hesitated. "Better yet—" he gestured to a tree about twenty feet back—"wait over there."

Mady started to argue, but he held up a hand. "Look, there could always be some kind of animal in here."

"You mean a bear?" The question ended on a squeak.

Jason uttered a patient sigh. "Not necessarily. But if I do happen to disturb some snoozing critter, I'd prefer not having to worry about you being in its path, okay?"

"Okay, okay." She trotted over to the tree and stood there, tapping her foot. In just a few minutes, Jason popped back out.

"All clear. I don't see any sign that it's been inhabited recently, and it's even tall enough in the main chamber that we can stand up. So we should be okay."

"So we stay here tonight?"

Jason stared down the path, chewing his lip pensively. Then he nodded firmly. "Makes the most sense. If that storm hits, we'll be glad for the shelter." He hefted his pack. "We stay here tonight."

It didn't take long to get everything set up. Jason cleared a spot just outside the cave for a fire, and Mady went about scrounging as much fuel as she could find. When she returned with her arms full, she saw that Jason had set out the tarps, reflective side up again, and was kneeling between them, holding the strobe and muttering.

"What's wrong?" She dropped the wood in a pile near the fire area.

The look on Jason's face as he stared down at the

strobe light in his hands was pure frustration. "It's dead."

Dismay twisted around Mady's heart. "Dead? Are you sure?"

Jason's head came up swiftly, and Mady stepped back.

"I'm sorry. That was dumb. Of course you're sure."

A shadow of disgust crossed his face as he stared down at the strobe and released a huff of air. "Just when we're about to reach a point where it can really do some good..."

Keep it.

Mady hesitated for a second, confused. *But if it's broken...*

Keep it.

Jason pulled back to pitch the strobe, and as though shoved by some invisible hand, Mady lunged forward and plucked it from his fingers.

"No!"

Jason spun to glare at her. "It's busted! Why haul something that's no good?"

"I—" Mady met his glare, chin up, eyes wide—"I don't know!"

His open-mouthed stare was almost comical. "You...don't know."

"It's—it's just a feeling I have."

"A *feeling.*" He crossed his arms. "Let me guess. God is telling you to hold on to it?"

Mady's fingers itched to flick his nose. "I don't know." Her gaze dropped to the ground, then came back to meet his eyes. "I think so, yes."

Jason threw his hands up in the air. "Of course. Makes perfect sense. Can't throw away something just because it doesn't work anymore. So the battery's dead. So what? We're bound to need it for something." He held up a finger, as though he'd just thought of something. "I know, a doorstop!"

Mady spun on her heel and went to stuff the strobe into her pack, then lifted her pack and marched to the cave entrance.

She spun back to Jason just before she went inside. "I'm going to get some sleep. When you're done being sarcastic, I hope you'll do the same." Her look was pointed. "I think we both could use some rest."

"What about dinner?"

Mady's stomach churned at the thought. "I'm too tired to eat anything." With that she started into the cave. But she didn't get very far. It was pitch black. Great. Just great. And Jason had the flashlight. She lowered her head and let out a sigh. So much for a great exit.

But before she could turn and go back out, a light shone from behind her, illuminating the way.

"I'm sorry." Jason's voice came from right behind her, and his hand rested briefly on her shoulder. "You're right. We both need some rest."

She managed a nod, despite the tightness in her throat, and made her way down the corridor to the sleeping area Jason had set up.

Please, Lord, let the night pass quickly. As she punched her backpack into a pillow, she wasn't sure what was most weary: her body or her spirit.

"Here."

She glanced over her shoulder to find a chunk of power bar being waved at her. Jason's face, though partially concealed in the shadows, was determined. "You need to keep up your strength, Mady. I'd feel better if you ate something." He waggled the bar again. "Just a little?" His tone was wheedling now. "Please, huh?"

Her sense of humor took over, and she laughed as she reached up to accept the proffered bar. "Okay, okay—" she infused the words with longsuffering— "anything to make you happy."

When he held on to the bar for a moment, she found her eyes captured by his, and what she saw in those blue depths took her breath away. Her whole being seemed filled with waiting as she watched emotions flit across his rugged features: warmth, tenderness, longing...and then resignation. His mouth quirked.

"Well, almost anything, eh, partner?" He let go of the bar but still held her gaze.

Mady nodded, wishing for the hundredth time that things were different. Cocking his head, he leaned back against the side of the cave. "So, ready for lights out?"

She nodded again, and he smiled, then flicked off the flashlight.

Mady curled on her side, taking a bit of the power bar and doing her best to get comfortable on the hard ground. *And Lord, if at all possible, let them find us tomorrow. I'm ready to go home.*

The next morning dawned as humid as the last—but looked a good deal more stormy.

Jason looked skyward as they stepped from the cave, and the tight line of his lips looked troubled.

"What is it?"

He shrugged, then offered her a small smile. "I just

wish the storm had cut loose last night, that's all. When we had shelter."

She fell into step beside him. "You think it's still brewing?"

His nod was firm. "I know it is. We're not out of this yet."

A half hour later, Mady knew he was right. Her clothes hung from her like damp rags, and she shifted as the straps of her pack rubbed the dank fabric of her shirt into her skin.

To take her mind off of what she was sure was a whopper of a heat rash getting started, she stared at the trees all around them. They were walking through a grove of alder trees. She'd thought they were birch, what with the whitish, peeling bark. But when she commented on how close the birch were growing together and how dense the stand was when they'd seen so few trees to this point, Jason set her straight.

"They're alder."

Mady looked at the trees with a frown. "Older than what?"

His eyes peered back at her over his shoulder. "*Al*-der." He pointed at a tree as they walked past it. "Alder trees."

Her lips twitched. She shouldn't. She knew she shouldn't. But she couldn't resist. "All der trees are what? Birch? Yeah, I know."

Jason slapped a hand to his forehead. "I don't know why I even try."

She brought a hand up to stifle her laughter, and he stopped, hands planted on his hips, giving her the chastising look of a Sunday school teacher who'd caught a child in a prank. "Mady…"

Quickly she bowed her head, doing her best to look duly repentant. "I know. I'm sorry. I couldn't resist." She raised her eyes to him, letting her bottom lip stick out. "I tried, I really did."

A glint of humor returned to his eyes, and he gave her a half-lidded, considering look. "Yeah, I'll bet you did. For all of two seconds."

"Hmpf. Shows what you know. It was three. At least."

He laughed and shook his head, turning to start walking again.

Mady fell in behind him. "So, anyway, isn't it amazing how close all these birch trees are growing?"

Her only answer was a deep groan.

Mady was constantly amazing him.

Jason didn't know how he'd expected her to handle all of this, but it sure wasn't with an impish sense of humor and an unshakable reliance on the God she was so sure was watching over them. And as much as he wanted to cling to his determined denial of that fact, he was starting to feel that he was the foolish one, not Mady.

Every time they'd needed an answer or some help, it had come. Maybe not in the way they'd expected, but something had come to supply their needs.

Their needs. Not their wants.

What about being found? That's a need, isn't it? And that sure hasn't happened yet.

No…but it wasn't exactly a need yet. Not really. Not until today. They'd had sufficient food, even this morning. They'd no sooner started walking than Mady had spotted a bush loaded down with ripe berries.

It was as though their every step was being prepared…guided….

Follow Me.

He flinched.

"Are you okay?"

Mady was looking up at him, her eyes creased with
concern.

"Just something buzzing around my head." He
made a show of waving his hand at the air. "Irritates me,"
he finished with a mutter. Especially since with each rep-
etition of the call, Jason found himself more and more
drawn to answer….

"Follow Me." He knew what it meant. Knew Who
was speaking. Knew what it would cost him. And his gut
wrenched at the thought of going down that path again,
laying everything on the line. And for what? To be taken
for granted? Ignored by the very people you served?
Treated like some kind of holy doormat—

"Jason! Look!"

Mady's fingers dug into his arm, and her voice rang
with excitement as she pointed in front of them. There,
roughly twenty-five feet beyond the woods, was the
clearing. And the cliff's edge.

"Thank God! Oh, thank God!"

Jason's heart echoed Mady's sentiment with more
sincerity than he'd have believed he possessed. They ran
out of the trees and went to gaze over the cliff, down to
the raging river below. The white, foaming water tumbled
and boiled over logs and past boulders, pounding with
such power that a rumble filled the gorge and a mist of
water rose to pelt their faces.

Mady's eyes widened and she swallowed, then met Jason's eyes. "We...we went down that?"

A grin split his face. "That we did, partner."

Her eyes once again fixed on the rapids they'd survived. "God is good." She said it quietly, in a low, dazed, utterly sincere tone.

When Jason didn't reply, she looked up at him. Why deny the obvious. He nodded. "I won't argue with you on that one, Mady."

Suddenly she moved behind him, tugging at his pack. "Mady, what—?"

The radio was shoved at him, and he took it silently. If it was going to work anywhere...

He turned it on, pulled up the antenna, and hit the button. Please...

"Earl, this is Jason. Earl...come in."

They waited, eyes on each other, and Jason saw how Mady's hands trembled despite the fact that she clenched them together in front of her.

Silence. There was no response. He glanced down at the river, afraid to see the disappointment on Mady's face. But a gentle hand came to rest on his arm.

"It's okay, Jason. If they can't hear us, we'll just have to make sure they see us."

He turned to her, and it took all his willpower not to pull her to him, to crush her in his arms and kiss her until they were both breathless. Instead, he slipped his pack from his arms and moved to the middle of the clearing. He started pulling the tarps free, excitement growing inside him.

Even before he asked her, Mady set her pack next to his so he could pull out whatever he wanted. He shot her a look of appreciation. She scanned the area, and Jason saw the hope stirring on her face. Heard it in her voice.

"They have to spot us up here. They have to." Her green eyes sparkled. "We're going home today, Jason."

"As you're so fond of saying, Mady—God willing."

Her response to that was a beautiful smile. With a spring in her step, she turned toward the woods. "I'll gather firewood." She gazed up at the sky, squinting her eyes—and he knew what she was watching for: the glimmer of a plane or helicopter in the bits of sun that poked through the clouds.

When Mady returned, everything was ready. The tarps were laid out, reflective side up, the mirrors were set close at hand, and Jason had prepared a spot for the fire. Mady dropped her collection of twigs, leaves, and sticks, and went to find more.

By the time she returned again, he had a fire blazing. And smoking. Mady grinned. "They've got to see that!"

Jason straightened, brushing his hands. "I'd say the odds are pretty good, partner."

With a squeal, Mady ran over to engulf him in a hug.

"Hey! You trying to knock me off the cliff before we're rescued?"

Laughter bubbled out of her, and she just hugged him fiercely. He let his arms close around her for a brief moment. *I'm only human, Lord....*

Then he gripped her arms and set her away from him, moving to throw more damp leaves on the fire. "Take that," Jason said, feeling a sense of elation as the smoke billowed into the sky.

"So…now what?"

Mady's face was so eager, so excited that he had to force his own tones to be calm and reasonable. They couldn't let themselves get too excited. Not yet.

"Now we wait."

❦ 23 ❦

Be silent, and God will speak.
FRANÇOIS FÉNELON

Mady hated waiting.

She hadn't realized just how much until this moment, until they'd sat here, all day, continually feeding this stupid fire with sticks and leaves and evergreen needles, and…and…

Nothing.

She hugged her knees to her chest, fighting the tears—and the anxiety gnawing at the edges of her heart. She'd been so sure someone would come. But all that had shown up was thunder. Loud, ominous rumbles that started out far away, rocking the sky and the distant mountains. But with each passing hour, the sound had come closer. And now the very trees around them trembled with each clap that split the air.

The air had grown even more humid and heavy. From the pounding behind her eyes and the pressure at her temples, the barometric pressure had to be going crazy. Mady shivered. *They have to come soon. They have to.* She closed her eyes against the rising agitation.

She couldn't do it. She couldn't spend another night out here.

"Move closer to the fire. You'll warm up some."

"I don't *need* to be warm. I need to be home!"

"Well, don't yell at me about it."

His voice was hoarse with frustration, and Mady responded in similar fashion. "I'm *not* yelling at you."

"Then you're doing a darned good imitation of it."

She surged to her feet, facing him, her hands on her hips. "Where are they? Why haven't they come?"

Jason rose, too, and they squared off, anger sparking between them like a power line gone nuts.

"How should I know? I'm not the one in control here, remember?"

With a sound that was part terror, part wrath, she kicked at the fire, sending sparks flying in every direction.

"It shouldn't be this hard!" The words hissed out of her, and she closed her eyes against the shaking that was taking hold of her.

"Mady—"

She spun to face him. "No! I *mean* it!" She stepped toward him. "You step out into the wilderness, you keep going and following. You take the risk, right?"

Jason's gaze was intent. "We didn't take anything, not on purpose."

"Oh yes, we did. We came on this trip. God called, and we followed."

He was shaking his head and Mady stepped closer, hands clenched at her sides. "Stop it! Stop acting like this is just some little jaunt you came on to kill time. You came because you had to. Because something drew you." Her eyes narrowed. "Because *He* drew you."

Denial flickered in his eyes, then he looked away. "I don't know why I came." The words were tight. "It wasn't what I expected."

Mady flung her hands into the air. "Is it ever?" She rubbed a hand over her eyes. "*Follow Me.* He whispers it over and over until you think you're going crazy—" Jason's eyes were fixed on her now, pinpoints of glittering, blue light—"and you do. You follow. And you end up in some crazy place, doing everything you know to do—"

Her voice broke as tears clawed at her, but she shoved them away, forcing her point out. "And He *brings you through.* It's over. The dark night gives way to joy, right?" A sobbing laugh escaped her as she held out her hands. "So where's the joy?"

She was shaking, but not from the damp or the cold. Her emotions held her, and she couldn't keep the tremors from her body or her voice.

"God promised to watch over His children like a shepherd watches his sheep. Well, the sheep are getting creamed here, so why isn't He doing something?"

"He is. He's doing the same thing He always does."

The low, bitter retort stopped Mady cold.

"Letting those who are foolish enough to follow Him suffer. They get led into the wilderness and left there. They get dumped in pain and struggles and despair and death. It's part of the package, Mady. Follow Christ and suffer. Pour yourself out, remember? Make your life *an offering.*"

The last two words were almost spat at her, and Mady shook her head.

"No...."

His lips twisted. "No? What about Abraham? Counted God's friend, for all the good it did him. What did God tell him? Sacrifice your son. Leave everything you know. And for what? To wander around, be taken prisoner, have your wife stolen…some deal, huh?"

"But—"

Jason wasn't listening. "Then there was good old David, God's chosen. There was a *real* success story! Spent years running from a man who wanted to kill him. A man who was supposed to be his friend. Betrayed. Afraid. Read Psalms, kiddo. Heck, read *most* of the Bible and you hear God's children whining. Job. Solomon. The disciples." His hard eyes held her gaze relentlessly. "Especially the disciples. The men who walked with Jesus. They ran for their pathetic lives when He was executed. Hid in dark rooms. Sat around wringing their hands."

"But God was there…Christ came to them—"

He dismissed the words with an angry gesture. "So what? What good did that do? They were hounded, tortured, murdered. Paul, the *great apostle*—" the contempt in his voice slashed at her—"spent his life in chains!"

She held out her hands as though to ward him off, and he stopped. His tortured gaze held hers for a moment before he turned away with stiff, abrupt movements.

But his words remained. They were true. *Your followers, Lord…your children…you let them suffer so much. Why?* It didn't make sense. Didn't fit the God she'd always known…

You promised to take care of us.

Numbly, she turned from Jason, moved away, toward the trees. *"Fear not, for I am with you." That's what you say, God. But how can we not fear…how can I not fear*—she raised her face to the sky, pleading—*when there's so much suffering…so much unanswered…*

Pick up your cross.

The words breathed across her mind, her soul, and she blinked.

Pick up your cross…and follow Me.

"Follow Me"? Where?

The answer came in pieces, in flashes of pictures playing in the corners of her mind.

A man…a simple man led by love, walking miles and miles through dusty, dry country, surrounded by crowds who reached, clung, pled…Christ healing, touching, loving…reaching out to restore, speaking words of truth that marked Him for death.

The Son kneeling in the garden, weeping, crying out, "If this cup cannot be taken away until I drink it, your will be done." Drops of blood, red sweat falling on the hands clenched in prayer…and then the cries, the clatter of shields and swords…

The Lord of heaven, standing as He was betrayed by a beloved, sold out…derided in a kangaroo trial…spat on, slapped at as His enemies delighted in His downfall…thorns shoved into His scalp…blood, warm and sticky, trailing down His face, and He couldn't wipe it away because His torn, scratched hands were full of the cross He carried as He staggered up the street.

Toward the hill of the skull. Toward death.

Mady gasped. *No…dear God, no.* She wanted to stop it. To save Him. But she couldn't, so she closed her eyes, feeling the tears that washed through her lids and coursed down her cheeks as she watched the vision that would not release her.

Jesus was mocked…the robe ripped from His

body...the nails pounded in, each strike of the hammer sheer agony...muscles convulsing as the cross was lifted, set in place...the jeers pelting Him, sorrow piercing Him as He hung there, even as the spear was thrust into His side...pain...terrible pain that wrung those words from holy lips...

"My God, my God, why have you forsaken me?"
Oh, Jesus...

Her tears were a river now. He knew. Knew her struggle. Knew her fear—and more. Far more than she could ever imagine. The Lord of life surrendered Himself to suffering, to ridicule, to death...

For her.

She lowered herself to the ground, pulled her knees to her chest, buried her face in her arms. *For me. Oh, forgive me.*

Jason was right. Obedience brought hardship. It had led the Master to the cross. And following the Savior meant laying everything down, surrendering it to God for His use, His purposes. Purposes that didn't always make sense, wouldn't always feel right. *"Let this cup of suffering be taken away from me...."*

Jesus.

His name. It was all she could think as she saw him taken from the cross, wrapped by tender, trembling, grieving hands...placed in a borrowed tomb...

And then...

Her heart seized, gripped her, took her breath away. Oh...then! The stone rolled way. The angel smiled, amused and compassionate. "He is not here."

"He is not here!"

Alive. Risen. Restored. The Savior had overcome life

and death and stormed the very gates of hell to bring freedom and life to those whose hands opened.

Those like Mady.

"For the joy set before him, he endured the cross."

Jesus...

"He was despised and rejected...we turned our backs on him...he was whipped and we were healed...we are healed...My purpose is to give life in all its fullness."

And then, the words that cleaved her very soul in two: *"I have told you all this so that you may have peace in me. Here on earth you will have many trials and sorrows. But take heart, because I have overcome the world."*

And so he had. Overcome death. Overcome sin. Overcome all that held her apart from God. And she was restored. Sheltered. Protected. Always.

But not exempt.

She breathed it in. No, not exempt. Her faith wasn't some magic wand to wave away life's hard times. Nor was it some spiritual, supernatural force field, an impregnable barrier against attacks, against the onslaught—the consequences of being a human living in a broken, sinful world.

"I have told you...here on earth you will have many trials and sorrows."

God, forgive me. I didn't want to accept that part. Didn't want to face it.

Follow Me.

The words came in a gentle whisper, and she nodded, letting her tears carry away the last remnants of her regret, accepting the call and the forgiveness that came with it. He was there, faithful as always. She could see that now.

And, at long last, she let herself rest in the arms of

One who knew, far more intimately than she ever could, the cost of obedience.

The touch of a hand on her shoulder brought Mady's head up. Jason knelt beside her. She grew aware that the wind had picked up, was blowing Jason's hair across his eyes—eyes filled with a grief so deep that Mady reached for him instinctively.

He started at the action and she stilled.

"I..." His tone was harsh. Raw. "I'm sorry. I shouldn't have...didn't mean to dump all that..."

"Jason, you were right."

His head came up at that, his eyes, narrow with confusion, seeking hers. "What do you mean?"

She struggled to put into words all that still raced through her mind. "Everything you said about faith and obedience, about God. You were right."

Doubt. Disbelief. They stared at her from his eyes. And something else.

Despair.

"I was right?"

She nodded. Vaguely, Mady realized she had to raise her voice above the wind whistling around them, realized she should be concerned, but she wasn't. The storm didn't matter.

Jason did.

"You know Him, Jason. You see God more honestly than I ever have. I saw Him as some kind of lucky rabbit's foot. But you see Him for what He is." She willed him to understand. "Master. Creator. Almighty God." As she spoke the words, she felt them ringing true within. God was all of that. And more. "You met Him, Jason. You met the I Am."

She took his hand then, held it to her heart. "And you showed Him to me. Now. Today." Tears filled her eyes. "For the first time."

He jerked his hand away and stood. "Don't."

She frowned. "Don't?"

"I didn't show you anything, Mady. How could I? I stopped looking for God, stopped listening to Him a long time ago. Right after I found out the real story: Follow Christ and the ending is always the same. You suffer. You lose. The end."

No, oh no...that wasn't the end. She rose to her feet, stepped toward him. "Jason—"

"Don't you get it, Mady?" He was yelling now, his words were fierce, desperate. "God doesn't want me anymore. And I don't want Him!"

A streak of lightning pierced the sky, lighting up the sky around them like a million strobes. The clap of responding thunder stunned Mady with its speed and nearness. It made her ears ring it was so close.

Jason swept a tense look at the sky, then grabbed her arm. "Mady, we've got to get out of here."

"*What?*"

He threw a hand out. "Look around! We're sitting ducks here. Perfect targets for lightning. We've got to get cover."

She knew he was right. And she knew what to do. "We can go back to the cave."

Rain started falling, pelting them like small missiles, driven almost sideways by the banshee winds. Jason drew her into the protective circle of his arm, yelling over the storm. "Assuming we can find it."

Mady didn't even hesitate. "We'll find it."

She grabbed her pack just as another flash of lightning made the hair on Mady's arms tingle. The distinctive odor of ozone filled her nostrils.

That one was close.

Their clothes whipping wildly, Jason grabbed Mady's hand, and they started running. Rain pelted them so hard it stung—and then Mady realized it wasn't rain at all. It was hail.

They ran, staggering against gusts that threatened to toss them to the ground, holding their packs over their heads for some protection. A flash of lightning backlit the woods around them, momentarily blinding Mady with its stark brilliance.

Jason pulled her to a halt, one arm locked around a tree to steady them in the gale. He looked around hopelessly. "We'll never find the cave in this!"

Mady took his hand, pulled him from the tree, facing him with determination. She didn't know where the cave was, no. But she knew which way to go. Forward. With God.

They started moving again. A powerful gust struck her full force, and she staggered back against Jason. As his arms closed around her, his cheek rested against hers, she grabbed at the sleeve of his shirt.

"Pray with me, Jason!"

"Mady—"

She spun to face him. *"Now!"*

His eyes told her he thought it was useless, but he did it and their voices joined against the howling of the wind as they stumbled on. "God…help us," Jason offered.

"Help us, Lord," Mady added, and the sense of

God's presence was so powerful within her that it almost took her breath away. "Show us the way."

They finished together: "Amen."

Mady blinked against the rain and hail, peering ahead of them, keeping her feet moving in the direction she felt so sure they needed to go. Then a clap of thunder shook the very ground beneath them, and Jason's grip on her fingers tensed, but still she kept going...listening....

Follow Me.

Mady stiffened, her hand convulsing on Jason's. "Did you hear that?"

His stunned expression told her he had, and her heart leapt.

"It was the wind—"

She wanted to shake him. "It was *not* the wind!" It came again, around her, through her... *Follow Me.* Mady pulled Jason's hand. "This way. I know it."

He followed her, staggering against the blasts of wind until another flash split the sky. Then he jerked them to a halt.

"Mady, this is crazy! We've got to find some other—"

"We're going to the cave."

He grabbed her arms and shook her. "You don't know where it is!"

"It's right over here, I know it—"

"You're going to get us *killed!*"

As though to prove him right, another jagged strike slashed the sky, surrounding them with light, and Jason gaped, his mouth open. Mady looked, and her heart sang with relief and gratitude.

The cave was right in front of them.

❧ 24 ❧

In His will is our peace.
DANTE ALIGHIERI

Jason held his small flashlight high as they entered the cave.

He still couldn't believe they'd found it. But then, things had stopped making sense days ago.

Fleetingly he wished he'd thought to grab up the tarps from where he'd anchored them. They would have given them some modicum of warmth, but wishing was useless. No amount of it ever changed anything.

"Set your pack against the wall so you can lean against it, Mady." He shone the light, helping her see what he meant. She did so, then reached out to lay her hands on his arm.

"Turn around. I'll pull your pack free."

He did as she instructed, then watched as she shoved it against the wall next to hers. At his raised brows, she just settled onto the ground and patted the spot next to her.

"No fire, our clothes are soaked—" her brows lifted primly—"I think a little closeness is only common sense."

"Uh-huh." He couldn't hold back the grin as he moved to sit where she'd indicated. The packs weren't exactly soft, and they only came up to the middle of their backs, but they were some barrier against the cold wall of the cave.

He slipped the flashlight into a side pocket of his pack, leaving the small zipper open so that the dimming light shone on the roof of the cave. Shadows danced around them, giving the cave a cozy, almost dreamy feel.

A soft punch against his arm made him chuckle, and he lifted it to drape it around Mady, pulling her close. When he felt her shiver against him, Jason rubbed her arms briskly to get some warmth back into her.

Mady gave a contented sigh and relaxed against him. "A refuge in the storm." She smiled. "Talk about just what the doctor ordered."

Hugging her close, Jason rested his chin on her damp hair and voiced what had been nagging at him.

"How did you know, Mady?"

"Where to find the cave?"

He nodded. "I couldn't see much of anything, wasn't even sure what direction we were going, and you go and lead us here."

She shifted against him. "I didn't know where it was, Jason. I just followed a feeling, a voice—" her finger made a small circle against his chest, above his heart—"in here."

They huddled together in silence. He knew what she was talking about. Hadn't he heard it himself time and again? The voice, calling. But he'd followed it before…and he hadn't liked where it led.

"What did you mean…when you said the ending was always the same?"

The question startled him, and he leaned his head back against the wall. He didn't want to talk about this. Not now.

"Forget it, Mady. You won't like what I have to say, and I don't want to fight. You want me to think one way, but I've seen the facts too many times. If the Bible isn't enough evidence, I'd still have plenty to go on."

When she didn't speak, he angled a look down at her. He'd expected an argument, but she was just looking up at him. Waiting.

"Why?" The ragged sound of the question startled him, but Mady didn't flinch. Instead, her hand came up to touch his face, to bestow a gentle caress along his cheek.

"Because I want to understand."

He stared into those eyes in the muted light—eyes so full of care, of mercy—and he knew he didn't have a prayer.

His mouth twisting at the irony of that thought, he leaned back against his pack, shifting his weight slightly. If he had to go into this, he might as well get comfortable.

"Just remember, I warned you, Mady."

"I know. It'll be all right."

The words were soft and trusting, and Jason looked away. Wishing he could believe her. Wishing it were over.

Wondering where one started with a story that was going to break someone's heart.

Mady leaned back in the circle of Jason's arm so she could see his face. And she waited.

She could see what a struggle it was for him even to begin.

Father, have mercy on him.

"I knew a man once, Mady. A man who believed everything you do. A gifted, wonderful, godly man—" Jason's face twisted at the words—"a man dedicated to serving God."

He looked around the cave, and Mady had the sense he wanted to be up, pacing. But he stayed where he was, his arm draped loosely about her. "This man could preach, Mady." Jason paused, closing his eyes as though savoring an elusive fragrance. "Oh…how he could preach. His sermons were alive with wisdom and humor and truth, and all who listened were moved and blessed."

He opened his eyes at that, and there was a hard edge to his expression. "All who listened. But there weren't many there to do so. Precious few." Jason's jaw tensed, and Mady could feel the muscles beneath her hand flexing as he looked away.

She longed to say something, to calm him, but a small voice held her.

Be still…be still and listen.

Jason went on, an odd aching in his tone. "He should have been a leader of multitudes. He should have been speaking before hundreds…thousands." His hand clenched on her arm, and she winced. "Don't you see? This man was special. Gifted! And you know how God—the God he served with all his heart and mind and soul—used him?" Derision was so thick in Jason's voice it practically dripped out. "He gave him a tiny church. A congregation that was so small there were days when the only ones there to hear all he had to share were his wife and son—"

He broke off, the words choked with a grief so palpable it almost had physical form. Mady longed to wrap him in her arms and comfort him...but still she was held silent, motionless.

Swallowing hard, Jason went on. "This man's son watched him, listened, saw all his father was...and he adored him. He grew up watching how his father longed to serve, longed to touch hearts, longed to be used by his God, and he found himself wanting the same things. One of his favorite things to do was kneel at night with his father and talk to God together. Slowly, the boy's heart was filled with one determination: to find a place where he could shine for God. And he knew, when he found that place, he would see to it that his father had the place *he* deserved. No matter what.

"So the son went off to college, where he was top of his class. Then onto seminary. Ostensibly following in his father's path. But somewhere along the way, serving God got a little confused with serving his...agenda." Jason's eyes came to hers, and she saw the regret there. "Not that it was all bad. He just wanted people to hear his father, to see all God had given him, to appreciate him. But to do that, the son decided he had to become the best orator, the most charismatic leader, the most desired shepherd anyone had ever known."

Jason's expression as he turned his face to her was defiant. "And he did it. Apparently there was something of the old man in him. When he spoke from the pulpit, those listening were moved and changed and drawn to him. They loved to listen to him. Loved to come to him with their troubles and squabbles. He endured it all, put up with the foibles of the flock, knowing he was working for a goal that mattered: giving his father the platform he deserved."

He wanted to honor his father, Lord. It was a good desire, surely an honorable one.

"My Father will honor those who serve me."

Her heart ached at the truth as Jason went on.

"The young minister received several calls when he graduated from seminary. He accepted the most promising and stayed only as long as it took to receive another, even more promising call. And so it went. He'd accept a call, serve the church with all his ability, and then move on to bigger and better things. He pushed on, refining his skills, following all the guidelines."

Jason counted them off on his fingers. "He expanded his audience with a tape ministry, then a radio ministry. Next came invitations to speak, and finally to start a television ministry. His father watched it all and was so proud. His son was serving God."

As though he couldn't sit still any longer, Jason rose to his feet in a fluid motion. He paced back and forth in the small confine of the cave, and Mady knew she was watching a man on the edge.

"Then our successful young shepherd's time came. He received two calls at once. One to a huge church, one with thousands of members, an enormous building, and extensive ministries. A dream come true."

When he let the bitter words drift into silence, Mady shifted against the packs, drawing her knees to her chest, resting her arms on her knees. "And the other?"

He angled a look at her. "The other? It was to a small church, a church much like his father's, where the faithful were few but devoted. Of course, our hero couldn't be blatant in his acceptance of one over the other. He had to explore both calls, seem to be seeking God's will. But there was no way this guy was getting caught in the trap that had banished his father to oblivion. Oh no. So he went to both churches. *Candidating*, they call it. And in the end—" Jason's laugh was harsh and bitter—"I knew where I was supposed to go."

Mady closed her eyes. "The small church."

The choked sound of Jason's surprise was answer enough. After a moment, she opened her eyes to find him staring at her.

"You really are amazing, you know that?"

She smiled. "I'm just learning how God works to refine us, that's all."

He slipped his hands into his jeans pockets and leaned against the wall of the cave. "Yes, the small church. I sat there, looking at the faces of those good, honorable people, listening to them tell me they felt God had called me to be their pastor, knowing in my soul that this was where God wanted me...and I lost it."

Mady frowned. "Lost it?"

He reached out to rub at some spot on the wall. "I was seeing all my plans, all my hard work just swirl down the drain, Mady. I thought God was mocking me. Mocking my father and his life of sacrifice. And I decided it was enough."

She sat up straighter.

"I laughed in their faces. Told them I was so far beyond a church like theirs that it wasn't funny. Told them God may have spoken my name to them, but he hadn't even mentioned them to me. I'd come out of obligation, but that was it. And as they stared at me, white faced, open mouthed, I threw their letter of calling on the table in front of them and walked out."

"Oh...Jason."

His head came up at that, and he gave her a hard look. "Oh no, no pity yet. I'm far from finished. Do you know what happened, Mady? Do you know what became of all my grand schemes? I went back to that enormous church and accepted their call on one condition. That they let me choose my own associate pastor. Of course, they agreed."

Mady bit her lip. She had a feeling she knew where this was going, and her heart wanted to weep.

A mocking smile twisted Jason's mouth. "Picture it, Mady. The triumphant minister marches back home, a mega church in his pocket, back to where his father is still working at a humble ministry—a ministry where the arrogant, young fool thinks his father's gifts are being wasted—and announces, 'Dad, pack your bags, you're finally going where you belong. You can kick the dust of this place from your shoes and see how it feels to be used by God in a place where it really matters.'"

Grief, sharp and intense, pierced her. "Oh, Jason..."

Something flickered in the depths of his eyes at her low words, and he fell silent. She saw the muscles in his jaw work as he clenched and unclenched his teeth, saw evidence in his features of the emotional struggle raging inside him.

She moved toward him then. Laying a hand on his arm, she asked a gentle question. "What did your father say?"

He looked away, his mouth working as though it were taking every ounce of control to restrain his emotions. When he spoke, his words were thick. "At first? Nothing. He just stared at me."

His eyes moved to meet hers, and the pain she saw there, the shame and regret, tore at her heart.

"I'd just ground his entire life, his ministry, his service to God under my foot. Dismissed it as a waste of time and told him I was here to be his savior. Me. The almighty Jason." He swallowed, shook his head. "I don't think he knew what to say. Not at first. And then…" He tipped his head back, blinking rapidly. But the tears came despite his efforts, and Mady felt responding tears gather in her eyes and overflow.

"Then my father told me I was a fool."

Jason looked at her, and she saw the confusion he'd felt then…still felt. "He said it so gently, with so much regret. Like it broke his heart to say it." His eyes drifted shut, as though he couldn't bear to see any more. "I remember every word as it stabbed into me. "I have a Savior, Jason, and He's much better than you could ever be. And I *am* where I belong. This is where God has placed me, where He's using me. And He *is* using me. In His way.'"

Mady was sure that Jason's emotions in that moment were mirrored in his eyes now. Abandonment. Betrayal. Desolation.

"The look on my dad's face made me want to crawl under a rock, but he wasn't done. He told me how much he loved his church. How they were his flock, the extended family God had given him. He said he cherished them, and the fact that God put him right there, in that place. To be a shepherd. And that's what he was."

She couldn't hold back any longer. "Just like his son."

Blue eyes jerked to collide with hers, and the red of anger seeped into his face.

"I...am *not*...a shepherd."

The rejection, the near-violence in those words slapped at her, but Mady didn't back down. She couldn't. She had to hold to the truth. For Jason's sake.

"Yes, you are. And nothing you say is going to change that."

His hands clenched at his sides, and for the first time since they'd met, Mady wondered if Jason would strike her.

Jason's fury was so deep it almost choked him.

He wanted to grab Mady, to shake her until she cried out for mercy, cried out that she was wrong.

But it wouldn't do any good. She could take the words back a million times, and it wouldn't change the truth he already knew. And hated. He *was* a shepherd. Like his father before him.

He turned his back to Mady. "I argued with my dad. Told him he deserved better. Told him he should be speaking to hundreds, blessing multitudes, that God had *gifted* him—" Jason shook his head as the angry words echoed in his memory. "Told him I had done everything for him, for God."

"What did he say?"

At Mady's quiet question, Jason flinched. "Two words. Quiet, even words that stopped me cold: 'That's enough.'" He turned a rueful smile back to Mady. "It was what he said when I was a kid and got out of line, when I'd gone off some deep end and was heading for trouble.

'That's enough.' Just like that. Suddenly, I was ten years old again, a ball bat in my hand, staring at a shattered window."

He turned back and saw the startled surprise in her eyes when he grabbed her arms, gripping them firmly in his hands. How could he make her understand? "I wanted to save him, Mady. To pull him out of the oblivion *God* had stuck him in. I wanted to let him shine! Let everyone see how amazing he was."

"Jason…"

He heard the pain in her tone and dropped his hands, releasing her abruptly. "I'm sorry. I didn't mean to hurt you." Watching her rub the circulation back into her arms, he let out a bitter sound. "But then, I seem to have perfected that. Hurting people without meaning to."

Her eyes came to meet his, and he pushed on. She needed to know it all. "I hurt my dad, Mady. With what I did. With what I said. He looked heartbroken when he said he'd thought I was serving God, but the only one I was serving was myself. My pride."

Anguish mixed with the bitter taste of anger in Jason's mouth.

"I could tell how devastating it was for him to say those things, but say them he did. And he pointed out that being a shepherd doesn't depend on the size of the flock. It depends on God's call and the shepherd's obedience to that call. He said there was only one measure of success for a shepherd."

When he didn't continue, Mady cocked her head. "One measure?"

The words almost stuck in Jason's throat, but he

forced them out. "Am I a good and faithful servant. Not numbers or acclaim or a platform. A shepherd's success is measured by obedience. Day in and day out. Loving the flock God has given him."

Tears sparkled in Mady's eyes. Her hand moved, as though she wanted to touch him, to soothe him, but then it fell to her side again. "He's right, Jason."

He nodded. "I know. I saw it that day, as clear as having mud wiped from a window. Being a shepherd means serving where God calls and staying there until He sees fit to say otherwise. I saw that my father was more of a success, more of a man of God than I could ever hope to be. And as I watched my dad fix me with those blue eyes, and I saw the sorrow there and knew I'd caused it…I wanted to die."

"Everything you'd done…it was all empty."

Grief, as sharp now as it had been that terrible day, slashed at him. His smile was wry. "'Meaningless. A chasing after the wind.'"

He saw the understanding in her face, saw the sorrow, and wanted to lay his head on her shoulder and weep. "And that's when I knew."

Mady frowned. "Knew?"

"I couldn't do it anymore. Serving God, being a so-called shepherd, obeying…all of it was a waste of time. Everything I'd done, everything I'd accomplished had been a waste. My father was happy. Honored in ways I couldn't begin to fathom. And I was a fool."

Silence fell between them then, and Jason felt an exhausted kind of emptiness, like he had nothing left to share. But Mady wasn't quite finished.

"So you walked away."

He didn't deny it. "As fast as I could. Left the megachurch to manage on its own and walked. I'd managed to stash away a good bit of savings. Enough to live on for a year or so." At her surprise, he gave a shrug. "My pay was decent, my living expenses covered, my home supplied. What did I have to spend my money on? Nothing. Not for several years. So I stuck everything I made in savings and short-term bonds, and it paid off. At least it gave me enough for the last year, to do what I wanted when I wanted. Without worrying about anyone—" he cast his eyes heavenward—"or anything else."

"And now?"

Meeting Mady's gentle gaze wasn't hard. Holding it was. There was a strange, hollow sense within him, and looking into her eyes only seemed to make it more noticeable...more uncomfortable.

"Now, I don't know."

He took her hands in his and pulled her gently into the circle of his arm, both because he wanted to feel her close and because he didn't think he could stand the searching look in her eyes.

"You've ruined me, Mady. I hope you know that."

She made a sound of protest, and he smiled down at her. "You have, don't deny it. I was content with my version of God and faith and Christians. And then here you come, bounding into my life—"

"Almost knocking you out." There were tears in her laughter.

"And bringing a faith I've seldom seen before, never had to face day in and day out. Every time I thought you'd given up on God, you just bounced back, stronger than before. You questioned and doubted and agonized...and ultimately let go and trusted." He shook his head. "And that only made you stronger."

"Hey, when you're as overflowing with weaknesses as I am, God has plenty of opportunities to show His strength."

Jason grimaced at her half-playful, half-serious words. "In the process, you made me face some facts I wasn't thrilled about facing. I'd been so convinced I was serving God and serving my dad, but I see now what I was serving was myself, my pride like Dad said. And you showed me that trust and acceptance are real, not just pipe dreams. As evidenced by the fact that even now, after hearing what I've done, how I walked away from what many consider the most holy calling of all...the only thing I feel from you is compassion. Acceptance."

He studied her face, savoring the peace he felt when she was near.

She traced the back of his hand with her finger. "Who am I to condemn another for turning from God when I've been doing the same in my own way for so long? I heard His call, Jason, knew what He wanted of me, and I wouldn't follow." Her smile was wistful. "We're facing the same things, Jason. God has created us for one path, and we want to take another."

She chewed her lip, clearly trying to sort through her thoughts. "But that's what I finally came to see. I am what God made me to be, with the gifts and talents and quirks that are all uniquely Mady. And refuse all I want, I can't change who and what I am in His eyes."

Her fingers laced with his. "Any more than you can."

Jason stilled, taking in her words, turning them over

in his mind. "I can't go back, Mady."

"You can't do anything else."

He jerked to stare at her, and her smile was as tender as her touch on his face. "Ah, Jason, don't you see? Like it or not, you're a shepherd. It's in your heart, your spirit. Just look at all the things you've done since you've come on this trip."

Jason frowned. "On this trip?"

This time she counted the items off on her fingers. "You helped Lea when her horse spooked."

"If I remember correctly, you weren't particularly impressed with that."

She gave him a sideways look. "Lea's need may not have been real, but your desire to help was." Her fingers resumed the count. "You helped Brian and Heather that morning while they were fishing. You served Earl every step of the way..."

"And we won't even *try* to count the ways I've saved your lovely hide in the last few days."

"Or the many ways you enjoyed yourself in the process." Her smile was too sweet, and he chuckled.

"Jason, don't you see? God has built you a certain way to fill a certain need within His family. And He's been calling to you, holding up a mirror to help you see yourself more clearly, outside of your anger and hurt."

Looking down at their joined fingers, Jason pondered her words. He longed to give in, to say she was right, to surrender to the pull in his heart and mind and spirit. Certainly he had to admit God had been watching over them these last few days, keeping them safe in the face of amazing odds.

But could he try it again? Could he open himself to

all that being a shepherd meant? Could he…

"What is that?" Jason shifted quickly, looking behind him to figure out what was poking him in the side.

Mady leaned forward, glancing down with a frown. "It's something in my pack."

She knelt beside her pack and started to rummage in the compartment, then, with a sheepish look, pulled out the strobe light.

Jason cast his eyes heavenward. "Of course." As they turned around to sit again, he punched the backpack back into shape.

"I don't know, Mady, I can't deny that some of what you're saying makes sense."

He paused. She wasn't listening. She was messing around with that stupid, dead strobe. "Mady—"

"Jason, could you shine the flashlight over here?"

"What? Why?"

She peered up at him from beneath her still damp curls. At that look, he huffed and reached for the flashlight.

"If you'd just thrown the silly thing away when I—"

"Oops!"

With that, the back of the strobe popped off and pieces went flying. They scrambled to find them, Jason muttering the whole time. His hand closed around the battery, and he leaned back against the pack, staring belligerently down at it.

Then he paused. Turning the light on the battery, he stared more closely.

"Hey! Who turned out the lights?" Mady's complaint came from where she'd gone to grab the back of the strobe.

"Mady, come here."

She did so, looking down, then her wide-eyed gaze came back up to him.

"Corrosion."

He nodded. Moving quickly, Jason pulled a rag from his pack and went about cleaning the battery, then the inside of the strobe. He knew Earl usually checked his equipment thoroughly. But this one must have slipped through.

Mady watched in silence as Jason fitted the light back together, and they both held their breaths as he flipped the on switch.

The strobe blazed to life, blinding them both.

"Aak!" Jason's fingers groped for the switch and turned off the light. Blinking like barn owls, he and Mady stared at each other, and then they started laughing. Peals of it. Ringing out of the cave, bouncing off the walls.

The strobe had been dead. Jason was sure of it. Until he looked further than his eyes could see. And now? Now it was alive and working and ready to split the sky with shafts of light.

Like his dad had been doing all his life. Serving, shining in the darkness.

Just as I'm calling you to do, My son. My call isn't easy. Nor is it for just anyone. It is for you, My chosen shepherd. Stop running, son. Come back to Me. Follow Me.

Jason didn't answer. A soft, small hand slipped into his, and he looked down at Mady, then reached out to pull her close.

"I want to."

She didn't question him. "I know."

"I just…I'm just not sure."

Her arms slipped around his waist, holding him tightly as she leaned her head against him. And he knew, with startling clarity, that she was praying for him.

Closing his eyes, he did the only thing left to do. He joined her.

❧ 25 ❧

For broken dreams the cure is, "Dream again, and deeper."
C. S. LEWIS

The next morning, Mady eased from the cave opening, cautiously, wondering what she would find.

Her eyes widened at the answer awaiting her: a wonderland.

The air was no longer heavy and oppressive. Rather, it was clear and fresh, as though all the dirt had been washed away from the world, and everything was new.

True, trees were bent, some even blown over, and leaves and evergreen needles scattered the entire area. And yet, it didn't have the feel of a scene of destruction as she'd feared. Instead, it looked like—

"Renewal."

She glanced over her shoulder at Jason. He gave her a gentle nudge, and she moved the rest of the way out into the morning light.

Stretching her arms above her head, she reached for the bright sky. "It's like a whole new start."

Jason's expression was smilingly tolerant as he pulled his backpack on. "It always feels this way after a storm, hon."

She let the endearment envelop her, wrapping arms of warmth and near giddiness around her. *Hon.* She loved the sound of it from his lips.

I don't know where You're taking us, Father, but thank You for where we are. Right now. This moment.

"I know, but that's what makes it so exciting. You think everything's going to be destroyed, and instead it's made fresh and clean." Her smile was triumphant and she knew it. "New."

"Hmm, gee. What point could you be trying to make?"

Laughter bubbled out of Mady, and she stuck her tongue out at him. "Okay, Mr. Theological Wiz Kid. So I'm not very subtle."

"Very?"

"At all! Happy now?"

His smile was smug. "Implicitly."

She reached down to grab a handful of soggy leaves and fling them at him. Looking around, she grinned. The storm may have shifted some things around, but the direction they'd gone yesterday morning to the cliff's edge was still clear.

Turning on her heel, grabbing the straps of her backpack firmly, she started to run, weaving through the grove of trees as quickly as she could without slamming into one.

"Race you to the river!"

Jason's laughing voice followed her. "Are you *nuts?*"

She didn't even pause. "Last one to the cliff is a rotten egg!"

A sudden sound of rustling and stomping behind her told her Jason had taken the challenge—and he was hot on her heels. With a yelp, Mady felt adrenaline surge through her and she ran faster, barely missing the white trunks all around her as she flew past them.

Then, just ahead, she spotted a welcome sight: their berry bush. There were still plenty of berries clinging stubbornly to the branches, and her stomach growled in anticipation.

"Breakfast!" she hollered over her shoulder. Giving a whoop of victory, she headed for the bush until the uneven ground reached out to grab her foot, and suddenly she was flying forward. She barely had time to get her hands out in front of her before she landed on the damp, rocky ground.

Mady lay there, panting, snorting with pained laughter as her muscles complained at their mistreatment. "Mady! Are you okay?"

Lifting a hand to wave at Jason, she called out, "Peachy. Just—" she groaned—"peachy." Moving slowly, she pushed herself up so that she was on her hands and knees. That was when she heard it. A soft whuffing sound. Like someone blowing air out of his lungs.

She quickly looked up, scanning the area around her. "Jason?"

"What?"

She jumped at the reply that came from right behind her. He was shaking his head at her again, eyes bright. He slipped his pack from his back, setting it on the ground. "Woman, you need a keeper."

Mady grimaced. "Are you applying for the job?" Deep emotion glittered in his eyes, and he knelt beside his pack, pulling the compartment zipper open.

"What are you doing?"

His expression was eloquent. "Getting the first-aid kit out, though why I ever put it away in the first pla—"

The whuffing noise came again, and Mady glanced

to the side with a frown, her eyes scanning the scattered trees, the rock formations above them…the berry bush. "Jason, did you hear that?"

He didn't answer. He was staring at something, eyes wide, jaw tense.

"Jas—?"

He held out one hand, cutting her off. "Shh!"

She stilled, and her mouth went dry as day-old zwieback toast when Jason whispered one word: "Bear."

Suddenly her veins were flowing with ice water.

"Mady, listen to me carefully."

She nodded at his low command.

"Don't stand up. Just crawl toward me, slowly."

With the utmost care, she did as he said. When she reached him, he lowered a hand to help her to her feet. As she rose, she followed Jason's intent gaze.

Not fifty feet away, peering from around the berry bush, its mouth stained with juice, lumbered a huge mass of thick, silvery brown fur and claws and teeth and beady, black eyes. Even on all fours, the bear stood a good foot taller than the thick bush. Its head was the size of a beach ball, and silver-tipped hair stuck up like alarmed spikes on the hump of the animal's back.

"Please don't tell me that's a grizzly." Her plea came out in a rasping whisper.

Jason's gaze was resolute. "It's a grizzly."

She closed her eyes. "I asked you not to tell me that." Looking at the animal again, she took in its wary stance. Head lowered, ridiculously small ears flattened against its massive head, the bear rocked back and forth. It kept those sharp, black eyes trained on the two of them, and it was blowing air out in those soft puffs she'd heard a moment ago. The beast had to weigh over three hundred pounds.

Her hand moved to clutch Jason's. "Tell me our berries aren't its breakfast."

"They're its breakfast."

She tightened her grip on his hand and hissed at him, "You're not *listening* to me!"

Jason turned his hand so that his fingers laced with hers, and he drew her close, putting his lips right next to her ear. "We need to stand very still, Mady. Show him we're no threat. That we're not going to horn in on his meal."

No problem. She figured she couldn't make her legs move if she had to. She leaned back against Jason, drawing strength from the warmth she felt through his shirt, her hands clenching his.

With a ripple of massive muscles, the grizzly raised up to stand on its hind legs, snout pointing to the tops of the trees as it opened its mouth and let out a deep, blood-curdling roar that made Mady's knees go weak.

Jason's arm slipped quickly around her waist, and she breathed a prayer of gratitude. She was sure she would have folded into a quivering pile on the ground without the support. She'd never heard anything so terrifying in her life.

"Don't move!"

Jason's low command jolted through her, and she felt as though she turned to stone, except for her breath, which came in short, shallow gasps.

The bear continued to roar, waving its mammoth paws, slicing the air with claws that had to be at least three inches long. Mady knew she should be screaming.

Should be blind with terror. Instead, one phrase kept going through her mind.

Jesus, be with us.

Fear not.

The reassurance filled her, and she took it in, holding it fast. Still, she had to admit she thought she just might faint when the bear dropped back down on all fours and started toward them.

They had nowhere to go. They couldn't outrun it. And even if they tried, their options were sadly limited, what with cliffs on two sides of them.

Again, she whispered a prayer, amazed that she wasn't panicked. Just…emphatic. "God, help us."

The next thing Mady knew, she was facedown on the ground. She tumbled forward, only to be enveloped by a tall form. For one stilled heartbeat, she thought the bear had her.

But it wasn't the bear at all, it was Jason.

"Play dead." He whispered next to her ear. "Don't move a muscle. It's our only chance. Please, sweetheart, don't move. Don't make a sound. You hear me? No matter what."

She nodded, pulling her knees up, gripping them with her arms and curling as tightly as she could, burying her face in her knees.

They lay there, motionless, and Mady asked God to still her ragged breathing. *We are in Your hands, almighty God….*

Then a roar exploded right over them, and the bear bellowed over and over until Mady thought she'd never stop hearing the sound. But she did because another came, low and intense, to replace it.

"Shh. Shh."

Jason was curled around her, encasing her in the shelter of his body. His lips were next to her ear, and his low voice comforted her, cautioned her, reminded her she wasn't alone.

"'The LORD is my shepherd, I shall not want…'"

His barely audible whisper washed over her, and she dug her face deeper into her knees.

"'He maketh me to lie in green pastures, he leads me beside the still waters, he restoreth my soul…'"

Like a protective cloak, the words settled over her, flowing into her mind and spirit, blocking out what was happening, lifting her into a place of other-worldly calm.

Jason went on in a voice so low that at times she wasn't sure if it was him or her mind reciting the psalm. She was dimly aware of the bear walking around them, and once she felt hot breath fanning the back of her arm. Forcing away the yelp that clamored to escape, she honed in on Jason's voice.

"'Yea, though I walk through the valley of the shadow of death, I will fear no evil…'"

None, Lord. Nothing this world brings against us.

"'For Thou art with me—'"

He broke off, and Mady felt him stiffen when something nudged at them. She felt him bury his face against the side of her head, felt his arms tighten about her.

"'Thy rod and thy staff, they comfort me…'" Mady took up the prayer, for that's what it had become, keeping her tones as low as Jason's had been. Another nudge came, this one at their backs. Jason's voice melded with hers as they kept on with the psalm.

"'Thou preparest a table before me in the presence

of mine enemies. Thou anointest my head with oil. My cup runneth over.'"

Slowly, Mady grew aware that the sounds of the bear had disappeared. No growls, no snufflings, no heavy steps of large, padded paws. Nothing.

"'Surely goodness and mercy shall follow me all the days of my life, and I will dwell in the house of the LORD forever. Amen.'"

Jason's grip eased slightly and his body, though still curled around her, relaxed a fraction. "Wait…" His caution came to her, and she obeyed.

Mady didn't know how much longer they lay there, her in her protective cocoon, every sense tuned with each movement to any sign that the bear was still there.

Nothing.

She turned her head slightly to peer at Jason's face. "Is…is it gone?"

He moved slowly, like a slug with a hangover, lifting his head to peer around them. At long last Mady felt him release her, rolling slowly onto his back. Straightening, stretching the cramped muscles of her back, she leaned up on one elbow and made a quick scan of the area.

Jason's hand eased over hers where it lay on the ground. "Not yet."

She looked from him to the rocks above them, and her breath caught in her throat when she saw the bear moving away from them, up the rocks, with a rapid, shuffling gait. She stood watching until it ambled out of sight, and then she fell back on the ground with a whoosh of utter relief.

Turning her head on the hard ground, she met Jason's stunned, though smiling face. "It nudged us!"

He nodded. "Twice." His eyes roamed her face. "Are you all right?"

She rested her hand on his chest, feeling the beat of his heart beneath her fingertips. "Thanks to you."

The warmth of his smile echoed in his voice. "Just call me a hero."

Leaning forward, Mady let her fingers trail his cheek. "No, I think I'll just call you a shepherd." At the wry resignation in his eyes, she smiled, then leaned over slowly, pressing her lips to his forehead in a soft kiss. "My shepherd."

He waggled his brows. "Now *that's* a calling I think I could go for."

Then, as though sensing they were in dangerous territory, he rose to his feet, reaching down to pull her up as well. He cast a look at the bush, then gave her a shrug. "I believe we have a table free now, if you're still hungry."

Mady licked her lips, slipping her arm into his. "Believe it or not, I'm even more hungry than I was."

"Must be the company you're keeping." Jason threw a glance in the direction the bear had taken.

Mady didn't answer. She was too busy popping berries in her mouth.

Jason sat on the ground, legs crossed in front of him, watching Mady add more damp leaves to their fire.

As unbelievable as it was, they'd actually found one of the reflective tarps still in the clearing when they reached it. It had wrapped itself around a tree, and though they'd had a dickens of a time getting it loose, it was laid out now, glinting in the late morning sun.

Follow Me.... I will supply your needs.

The strobe was flashing away as though it had never been off. Never seemed broken, useless...

Follow Me.... I will restore you. Heal you. Use you beyond your imaginings for My good purpose.

Mady glanced at Jason from time to time, her gaze curious, but she didn't break the silence between them. It was as though she knew he needed time. Time to think.

Time to pray.

Was the bear just to make a point, Father?

"The stubborn are headed for serious trouble."

Jason laughed. Well, the point had been made. Mady was right about him. He'd seen the bear, and the only thing on his mind was sheltering her.

Of course, he loved her. But he knew it was more than that. He would have done the same for Earl. For Heather. For one of those white-haired saints he treated so poorly....

For anyone given to his care.

Face it, Tiber ol' man. Your heart beats to serve, to lead, to encourage. You want nothing more than to know you're being used, to know you have a home, a family....

A flock.

His mouth twisted. He was his father's son. And like his father, his chest beat with the heart of a true shepherd. And for the first time in his life, Jason understood that it had nothing to do with him and everything to do with the One who had made him.

And called him.

Jason didn't choose this path. Oh, he could choose not to take it, but he wasn't the one who set out on it in the beginning. God had called him here. Like He'd called Jason's father, and that reality overwhelmed Jason.

I'm not like Dad. I'm not a natural at this....

"Don't be afraid or discouraged."

He's such a good man, so suited to what he's doing.

"I will equip you with all you need for doing My will."

I want to honor him. Tears stung at Jason's eyes. *I want to honor You.*

Follow Me, my son.

The call rang out, echoing within him, bouncing across every inch of his spirit, his soul.

Follow Me...and I will make you whole.

Jason bowed his head, the last bit of resistance falling away. He didn't know where it would lead. Didn't know what it would mean for him. For Mady. But he couldn't deny any longer what was inside him. What he knew he wanted. Had wanted from the moment he'd walked away from it.

Peace. Restoration. Fellowship with the One who loved him above all others.

Follow Me.

Yes. Yes, Father, I will follow.

At first, Mady didn't know what it was.

She tilted her head, listening. And then awareness jolted through her, and she surged to her feet, her heart pounding so hard she thought it would break free from her chest.

"Jason!"

He jerked, looking up from where he'd been sitting,

head bowed. Quickly, he looked around, obviously seeking the danger that had alarmed her.

She ran to him, grabbed his hands, and pulled him to his feet. "Listen!"

Mady knew she was screaming, but she couldn't help it. And when Jason did as she commanded, the light in his eyes was brighter than any they'd seen in the storm.

"A helicopter!"

He engulfed her in a hug, then let her go and raced for the signal mirror. But it wasn't needed. The 'copter was floating up, over the trees on the other side of the river, and from the way it was hovering, it was clear the pilot had spotted them.

Mady's breath caught in her throat as the chopper blades pounded the air, and she ran to throw herself in Jason's open arms. He buried his face in her hair, and she heard him saying over and over, "Thank you, God. Thank you."

"Well, hello there, you rascals!"

Tearful laughter escaped Mady as she looked up to see Earl hanging out of the helicopter, megaphone in hand. She and Jason waved like a couple of goons, and Earl's laughter drifted down to them.

"It's about time, you two." Earl's laughter was tinged with a deep relief. "It's about time."

"No—" Jason's arms tightened around Mady, and he looked down to smile at her—"it's the perfect time. God's perfect time." Then a frown creased his brow. "What are you crying about, woman? We've been rescued!"

She caught the sob of joy on a hiccup, gripping his shirtfront in her hands. "Have we really, Jason? Really?"

The flicker in his eyes told her he knew exactly what she was asking, and with a smile that warmed her from head to toe, he swept her into his arms. Holding her tight, he pressed his mouth next to her ear.

"We have indeed, Mady girl. Now and forever."

And she knew the rejoicing that would take place back at Earl's was nothing compared to what was happening right now among the angels. And in her heart.

❧ 26 ❧

Tomorrow…comes to us at midnight very clean.
It's perfect when it puts itself in our hands.
It hopes we've learned something from yesterday.

JOHN WAYNE

Jason stood watching as the others loaded their gear onto the small plane. Nikos, Lea, Heather, Brian, Mady…they stood together, talking and laughing.

When Jason and Mady stepped out of the rescue helicopter, they were met by a wave of hugs from the group. Nikos, Brian, and Heather told them over and over how they'd been praying for them, hoping against hope that they were safe.

Jason had met Nikos's eyes with a start. "Praying?"

The other man's shrug was noncommittal. "Desperate times call for desperate measures, do they not? And it seemed to help. Us as well as you."

"Hmm." Jason eyed him. "And now that you're no longer desperate?"

Nikos lifted his hands in an eloquent gesture, his mouth curving in a thoughtful smile. "One can never tell, Jason." His smile broadened. "One can never tell."

Even Lea had thrown her arms around Mady, tears sparkling in her eyes.

"I was so jealous of you, I wanted you to disappear into the woods. And you did! Then I was afraid I'd never have the chance to apologize." The simple words were delivered with a downcast gaze, and Mady wrapped Lea in her arms and hugged her tightly.

"It's okay. I understand."

Lea's eyes widened. "You do?"

Mady's nod was as firm as her smile. "Absolutely. You're a beautiful woman, and that was pretty hard to take sometimes."

Mady glanced at Jason as she said this, and Lea's eyes twinkled. She slipped her arm through Mady's and led her away—but not before Jason heard her murmur, "So, tell me. What was our Jason like, out there in the wilds? And don't spare the delicious details."

Later, after Jason and Mady had gotten cleaned up and had a rest, they'd all gathered for dinner. Earl bowed his head to offer grace—and heartfelt thanks for their safe return—and when he finished, the group had erupted into applause and laughter.

It was a night Jason would not soon forget. The care and concern he felt from the others still warmed him. Which probably explained why it didn't bother him now to see Mady's golden curls disappear into a hug from Nikos. Well, not much, anyway.

Amazing how much life could change in a few short days.

"You ready to go, buddy?"

He turned to find Earl standing behind him, that smug smile on his face. "That goofy grin of yours is driving me nuts. Just hope you know that."

Earl slapped him on the back, chuckling. "It just feels so blasted good to be right, Jas."

Jason laughed at that, leaning down to hoist his backpack. "Won't argue with you there." He lifted one brow. "After all, I'd hate to take away from something that happens so seldom for you."

They started walking toward the plane. "Have you told Mady your plans yet?"

He shook his head. "I just told her I knew what I needed to do, but that I couldn't explain it, couldn't give her details." Jason chewed his lip. "I want to, Earl. God knows I want to. But I can't. It's as though He's holding me back."

Earl's large hand closed over Jason's arm and he pulled him to a halt. "Listen to me, Jas. God brought you two together for a reason. I know it deep in my bones. So you listen to what He tells you and leave the details to Him. He'll take care of you. And that delightful, though decidedly dangerous, woman you've fallen for."

Jason soaked in his friend's words, recognizing them for the solid counsel of someone who cared. He turned to gaze after Mady again, watching her, hearing her laughter floating to him on the breeze, making him ache deep inside.

"Ever notice, Earl?"

"What's that?"

"God's call isn't easy." Jason stepped out again. "It may be clear as the nose on your face, but it sure as shootin' isn't easy."

"That's why it's gonna feel so good when it works out, buddy." Earl patted his shoulder. "You just wait and see."

Jason smiled at that. He didn't have any other choice.

The flight back to Seattle had been remarkably smooth. Mady sat next to Jason, and though neither of them said much, the feel of his hand cradling hers had spoken volumes to her heart.

I trust You, Lord. She blinked away the tears. *It's not easy, but I trust You.*

When the plane landed, she and Jason spent some time bidding farewell to the others in the group. Nikos had taken Mady's hands in his, gazed deep into her eyes, and then raised her hands to plant a soft kiss on the back of each.

"May your God lead you to your dreams, sweet Mady."

She put her arms around his neck and hugged him close. "Amen, Nikos."

"What was that all about?" Jason asked when she went to join him again.

"A friend saying good-bye."

"Hmm." He looked after Nikos's retreating form, then down at the ground. Silence fell between them, and Mady waited. She knew Jason was struggling, trying to find the right words to say.

When he finally spoke, his words were rough with emotion. "I want to tell you something, Mady. But I can't. Not yet."

She nodded as his eyes scanned her face. She understood. Knew that only one thing would keep him from speaking the words that overflowed from both their hearts.

He studied her, as though committing her features

to memory. "Just know this…when God sets me free, I will find you."

She nodded, letting him fold her into his arms, hold her against his heart. She knew they both had things to do. The promise was enough.

For now.

Jason stood before the wooden door, staring down at the knob, trying to make his hand reach out and turn it.

"Let me help."

He stepped aside as a wrinkled hand reached forward to open the door, throwing it wide. With a deep breath, Jason stepped over the threshhold. No going back now.

He moved to the head of the table, pulled out the chair, and then leaned back. They were all there, the people of the pastoral call committee. Six gentle-natured members of this small church family who had made themselves vulnerable to him.

Six life-tested saints whom he had mocked.

And yet, as he scanned each face, met each person's eyes, Jason saw no condemnation. Only waiting. And peace.

God, give me Your words….

"Be strong and courageous, and do the work. for the LORD God, Your God, is with you. He will not fail you or forsake you."

Drawing a deep breath, Jason plunged in. "First, I want to tell you all how sorry I am for the way I treated you before. I was arrogant and insulting. I was wrong. And I ask your forgiveness."

There were nods around the table, and one tall, lean

man spoke up. "Thank you, son. That means a lot to us. And we do forgive you."

Gratitude moved over him, and Jason didn't even try to hold back the grin that started deep in his heart and ended on his face. He gave a small shrug. "I know you were surprised to hear from me."

"Not really, son."

This came from Mr. Clark, the man the others seemed to consider a leader—a tall, lean man with a kind face that looked like he smiled often.

Jason blinked. "You—you weren't?"

"No, sir. You see, like we told you when you came here before, God made it real clear to us that you were the fella to fill our pulpit. Now, I won't say your parting words didn't come as a bit of a puzzler—"

Heat filled Jason's face, but he held the man's even gaze.

"—but even after that, we all prayed over it and came to the same conclusion."

Jason waited. If there was one thing Mady had taught him, it was the value of silence.

Mr. Clark went on. "We all felt we were to wait for you. So we've been doing that this last year."

Jason's confusion must have been plain on his face. "You...waited?"

The little man sitting next to him bobbed his head up and down. "Been using lay leadership, Pastor Jason. Been working pretty well, too."

"We've each been taking turns, leading worship time," another woman chimed in. "It's actually been kind of fun. Maybe you can let us help you with the services sometimes?"

"Now Agnes, that's up to Pastor Jason," Mr. Clark cautioned, and Jason held out his hands.

"Wait, please. I need you to help me understand all of this." He looked from one smiling face to another, wonder washing over him. "Are you saying you still want me here?"

"No, son." Mr. Clark's words sent Jason's heart into a nosedive. Until he continued. "We're saying God still wants you here. Made it clear as the peeling paint on the parsonage walls."

Jason didn't know what to say.

Mr. Clark rose from his seat and came around the table, extending his hand to Jason. "Jason Tiber, we issued a call to you a year ago, asking you to come here and be a part of our family. To be our pastor. Our shepherd. God has made it clear that He wants you here, so we ask you one last time, sir. Will you come?"

Swallowing the tears that choked him, Jason pushed back his chair and took the hand extended to him.

Grace. Restoration. Would he ever get used to it?

Jason hesitated, uncertain what to say. Or, more accurately, how to say it. "Mr. Clark, before I can answer you, I have one request."

The older man's gaze was steady. "Speak it, young man."

"I—I don't feel ready. That is, I think God has some things to teach me before I come here. Before I can serve you." He shook his head. Was he making any sense? "I've felt very clearly that I need a time of prayer and preparation before I do anything else."

The older man was already nodding. "From what I see in Scripture, God generally leads his teachers and prophets into the wilderness for a time of preparation."

A burst of laughter escaped Jason at that, and he held up his hand to forestall the question in Mr. Clark's eyes.

"I'm sorry. Remind me to tell you what happened to me not long ago. It was, as you said, a wilderness experience."

"Well—" Mr. Clark sent a look around the table, and Jason watched as each person offered a nod—"I'd say we're amenable to your condition, Jason. So, will you come and serve here in this place?"

"Yes, Mr. Clark. I accept the honor. With thanks."

The man's handshake was firm; the gladness in his eyes sincere.

Jason cleared his throat. "I won't let you down."

Mr. Clark grinned. "Son, I believe you."

The sun was just dipping below the horizon when Jason pulled the car into the driveway. He sat for a moment, staring at the steps leading to the front door of the parsonage.

Leaning his head on the steering wheel, he prayed for guidance. Peace settled over him, and he pushed open the car door, stepping out into the cool evening air. There was nothing like the country at sunset.

"Nothing like the country at sunset, eh, son?"

At the echo of his thoughts, Jason turned. His dad was sitting in a chair on the porch, a mug of coffee in his hands.

"No, Dad, there's not."

He walked forward, went up the steps, feeling as

though this was the longest walk he'd ever made. As he drew near, his father indicated another chair against the wall.

"Pull up a seat, Jas. Want some coffee?"

Jason did as he was told, shaking his head as he sank into the comfortable old chair. "No coffee, thanks." He studied his father's face. He'd aged in the last year, and yet he still looked the same. This was a face that told of wisdom and life and experiences that Jason could only imagine.

The face of a man of God.

Lord, let me be such a man.

"Did you know I was coming, Dad?"

His father turned to him then, and Jason's throat caught when he saw the tears in the older man's eyes.

"Someday. I knew you'd come home someday."

Jason covered his father's hand where it rested on the arm of the chair, and they sat in silence for a while. And as the night grew around them, Jason began to talk, telling his father all that had happened...about Mady, about the wilderness, about being lost in so many ways.

And about being found.

"I was so sure I was serving God, serving you, but all I was serving was myself. My pride. And I couldn't face that for a long time."

"God's refinement takes time, Jason. I've always known you had a heart for Him. I just had to take my hands off of you and let Him have His way, no matter how hard that was." His father's blue eyes turned to him again. "And it was the hardest thing I've ever done."

Jason put his hand on his father's shoulder. "Thanks, Dad."

Tears overflowed his father's eyes at that, and he stood, pulling Jason to his feet. Arms that Jason knew well from his childhood encircled him, and he pressed his face into the chest that had caught so many of his boyhood tears. Gentle hands that had soothed the fears of his youth rested now on his head, trembling with emotion.

"Welcome home, son." His father's voice cracked. "I missed you."

Jason's arms closed around his father's lean form. "I missed you, too, Dad. More than you'll ever know."

They talked into the wee hours of the morning, laughing, reminiscing, letting God restore all that had been lost and more.

"What will you do now, Jason?"

It was a joyous thing to be able to answer him. "Serve where God has sent me."

Understanding dawned in his father's eyes. "The church in Tarnation?"

Jason nodded. "That's the one. And I'd like you to help me, Dad." Jason turned to him, then glanced at the parsonage…and at the small church that sat just off the road. "Will you teach me? Help me learn what it means to be God's shepherd?" Jason had to clear his throat to finish. "To be like Christ…like you."

His dad's voice was choked with emotion. "I'd be honored, son."

Finally, stretching and yawning, Jason stood from his chair. "I guess I'd better go. But I'll come back this weekend, if that's okay? To start our study together?"

"That's more than okay, son." Now it was his dad who had to clear his throat. "I'll be waiting."

They walked together toward the car, and as Jason's dad pulled open the car door, he stepped back, then held out his hand. "I'm proud of you, son."

Jason took his dad's hand, unable to speak as tears coursed down his face—and the wonder of restoration bathed his heart.

Mady managed to grab the phone on the last ring before her answering machine picked it up.

"In His Image, this is Mady Donovan, may I help you?"

"Ooooo, I love how professional you sound!"

Mady dropped into her chair. "Eva, you brat! I thought it was a client. What are you doing calling me on my business phone?"

"Actually, dear, I've got work for you. Got a call today from a church with a parsonage to be redecorated. Seems the pastor's getting married and wants the place done over *Mady Donovan-style,* according to the sweet lady who called me."

Flipping open her calendar, Mady felt the little jolt of amazement that hit her every time she saw how full it was.

You're amazing, Lord. It's only been six months, and I've got more work than I can handle.

She listened as Eva gave her the details, flipping her shoes off as she did so. It had been a long day, but a good one. She'd never imagined it could be so complicated and confusing and utterly fulfilling to have her own business.

"Gotta go, Ev. I hear a bubble bath calling my name." She wriggled her finally free toes.

"Uh-huh, so you probably don't want to hear about Earl's visit with Jason, then?"

Mady paused, her pulse jumping as it did every time she heard Jason's name. She forced nonchalance to her tone. "Well, I suppose, if you must…"

"Yeah, right. From what Earl says, he's really doing great, Mady. He's been at the church for about three weeks now, and everyone there loves him." There was a snicker. "Especially the women. Earl says they're mad for him."

"More likely mad because of him," Mady muttered around the fingers of jealously that were tangling inside her.

There was a pause, then, "You know he's kidding, right?"

"Of course. Don't worry. I'm fine. Jason and his place in my life are in God's hands. And I'm okay with that."

"Uh huh. Yeah. I believe that."

"Eva…"

At the warning, her friend changed subjects. "So be sure to call that woman from the church. The place needs to be done by next month. You can do it, yes?"

"Barely, but since it's for a friend of yours, I'll fit it in."

She bid Eva good-bye, then dropped the phone in the cradle. But her sense of contentment and fulfillment had vanished as completely as a balloon caught on an updraft.

He said he'd find me, Lord. So where is he? She dug her

toes into her carpet. *It's not like I'm asking for that much. Just to have someone love me....*

"My gracious favor is all you need."

She stilled. Was it? Was it enough? Even if Jason never called?

A tiny part of her heart cried out in protest, kicked and screamed and pitched a royal tantrum, but even as it did, Mady knew the truth. She loved Jason, as deeply as any woman could love a man. But even if they weren't meant to be together, she wouldn't be alone.

Yes, Lord... You're enough. More than enough.

"Oh, my dear, it's simply stunning!"

Mady stepped back to survey the object of Mrs. Coffman's admiration and found herself grinning.

The older woman was right. The house was a wonder. When she'd first come to the small town to work on the church parsonage, she'd been amazed to find a beautiful little cottage nestled among tall evergreens and wildflowers dancing in grass. Walking inside she'd felt as though she were entering a sweet place of rest.

"Are you sure the work needs to be done?" She looked at the little woman, uncertain. "It's already a beautiful home."

Mrs. Coffman's head had bobbed back and forth. "Oh no, dearie. We've been given strict orders. It's to be redone, all right."

Mady frowned. "Will I meet the new owners? I'd really like to spend a little time with them, get to know their tastes a bit—"

"They're not coming until the house is ready." The

woman's gloved hands fluttered in the air. "They said to tell you to do what *you'd* like with it. To make it a place you would love. They've seen the articles about you, all those lovely pictures, and they trust you."

So Mady had gone to work, following the only guidelines she'd been given. And as the place took shape, she found herself making the thirty-minute drive from Seattle with more and more excitement. And frequency. This little place really had become the haven she'd always dreamed of. So much so that as she stood in the doorway now, ready to turn the keys over to Mrs. Coffman, she felt as though she were leaving a part of her heart behind.

Turning quickly, Mady muttered something about checking one last detail, hoping against hope that the sweet, old woman hadn't seen the tears running down her face. She moved into the airy living room, sinking into the overstuffed chair, folding her legs beneath her, slogging in her misery.

God…what are You doing?

As though in answer, a hand came to rest on the top of her head with a touch that was infinitely gentle. "I told you I'd be back."

Mady's heart stopped. Slowly she turned, looked up, and found her gaze captured by a pair of ice blue eyes. Eyes filled with laughter and love and promise.

Without a word she went into his arms, letting him hold her close, listening to the uneven beat of his heart.

After a moment, he took her hands and drew her into the room she'd come to love the most: the sun porch. Sunshine streamed in the windows, nurturing the plants and flowers scattered about the room. Jason led her to the loveseat, pulling her down beside him.

Mady blinked at him, lifting a hand to his face. He laughed.

"I'm real, sweetheart."

She shook her head slowly. "What are you doing here?"

His smile was as sweet as the early morning sun. "This is my home. The parsonage to the church I'm pastoring." His gaze captured hers and held it. "Now what I need to know is if it will be your home as well."

A smile trembled over Mady's lips, but she wouldn't let it come out. Instead, she crossed her arms, pinning him with as severe a look as she could muster.

"Well, I don't know."

The alarm on his face only made her feel guilty, so she let the smile peek out a fraction. "First, I think you should answer one question."

His eyes narrowed slightly. "Such as?"

With an exclamation of pure joy, she launched herself into his arms. "What took you so long?"

Jason caught her, and his laughter rained down around her, the joyous sound filling her heart to overflowing. He set her back against the cushions, then took her hands in his and lifted them to his heart.

"Everything is restored, Mady." Wonder rang in his words, shone in his eyes. "Everything I thought I'd destroyed, God has given back to me, blessed over and over again. We're a small group here, but the heart among these people is amazing. And I've never been more at home, never felt more right with anyone... except..."

She licked her lips. "Except?"

"Ah, sweet Mady. Don't you know my heart isn't whole without you?" He lifted one hand, kissing the back with slow, tender care. "How can I shepherd these people with all my heart when part of it is missing?"

He raised her other hand, opening it to place a warm kiss in the palm, and Mady felt dizzy from the feel of his lips against her skin.

"You own it, Mady. It's belonged to you from the first moment I looked into those amazing eyes, the first time I felt your hand against my chest—"

"I almost broke your back!" She choked the words out through the laughter and joy bubbling up in her.

I love you. Oh, I love you.

Pulling her into his arms, Jason cupped the back of her head in his hands, looking down into her face. "I love you, Mady. Broken back and all. And everything that God has given me, I offer now to you."

Her skin tingled where he touched her, and she wove her arms inside his jacket, around his back, reveling in the feel and warmth of him—this man God had given her.

Jason kissed her with his eyes, and then leaned forward, kissing her with his lips, lingering, savoring every moment. When he drew back, Mady wondered if she would ever think straight again.

"Marry me, Mady Donovan. You asked me once if I were applying for the job of your keeper. Well, I am. I want to keep you now and forever, to grow old with you, to spend our lives discovering the wonders God has given us. Ah, Mady, you've already made my house your home. Now I'm asking you to make my heart your home as well."

An unaccustomed shyness gripped her as she finally spoke the words she'd been holding back until it was right…until now. "It already is, Jason. I love you, wholly and completely. I knew God had something in store for me on this venture, believed He had a perfect reason for me to come—" tears choked her words, and Jason's fingers tightened on hers—"but in my wildest dreams, I couldn't have imagined the wonder God had in store for me. The wonder of finding you."

Smiling impishly, Mady reached up to lace her fingers at the back of his head, pulling his mouth down to within a fraction of her own.

"I just have one request."

Jason's tender smile warmed her from head to toe. "Only one?"

"Can we go back to Earl's place in the mountains for our honeymoon?"

Jason almost choked on his laughter. "You really do like living life on the edge, don't you?"

Her smile was smug, and she pressed a small kiss at the side of his mouth. "Look at it this way, it's great training for being a pastor's wife. I mean, if I can face down a grizzly, the church board won't have a prayer!"

The smile that lifted his lips was lazy and utterly enticing. "So I take it that's a yes?"

She didn't answer. She was too busy kissing him. And he was far too busy kissing her back to care.

*Justice will rule in the wilderness and
righteousness in the fertile field.
And this righteousness will bring peace.
Quietness and confidence will fill the land forever.
My people will live in safety, quietly at home.
They will be at rest.*

ISAIAH 32:16–18

Dear Readers,

I've struggled with what to say in this letter. *Wilderness* is a reflection of so much of my heart. I grew up in a small church where my father has been a faithful pastor for forty years. I've been so blessed...Mom and Dad made my brothers and me their first ministry. They were always there for us, filling our home with love, laughter, and honest faith. As a result, my brothers and I grew up loving the church, following the God our parents serve, and devoted to these two who nurtured and taught us what love means. My mom and dad are, to this day, two of my most treasured friends and counselors.

As a child, I thought such a childhood, such a family life, was normal. Now I know better. Many families in ministry struggle, even break apart. And that grieves me.

I see ministers battle feelings of failure, of inadequacy when the pews aren't overflowing—but my dad has shown me success to God's call isn't measured in numbers, but by obedience, by being faithful where He's put you, by giving yourself to the flock God has entrusted to you. Look at Jesus. Whom did He have left at the end of His earthly ministry? No one. They'd all fled. And yet, when those few faithful returned, seeking forgiveness and restoration, He welcomed them. And empowered them. And look at what happened! Just a few men touched by the Savior changed the world.

I see ministers' children grow resentful, wounded when their parents give all to the ministry, leaving little for at home. And my heart cries out. For I've seen that being a shepherd, a *true* shepherd, begins with the way you treat your children, your spouse.

I've known two true shepherds: My dad and Len Davis, who has taught a Bible study for the twenty years I've known him. Like my dad, Len has offered himself wholly to God's call, submitting when it would have been easier to walk away, speaking the truth when it would have been easier to remain silent, loving and leading when it would have made so much more sense, in the world's eyes, to be distant.

These are the shepherds' hearts that have touched and taught and blessed me. These are the kind of men I wanted to honor in this book.

And I wanted to remind myself, and anyone who reads this story, that we *all* are called by God, crafted by an Almighty hand as individuals who bring our own unique gifts to the world. Often we struggle with our call—I know I did at times. And that was when God, in His wisdom and love, led me into my own wilderness where I had to rely on Him to survive. And it was there—in that place of terrible beauty, of fearful discovery—that I met the God I'd known all my life. Really met Him. And I can tell you, He is sufficient.

While it's not always easy to give ourselves to those calls, I know this much: The blessings when we let go, when we follow the gentle voice of Love, are overwhelming. Like Mady and Jason, when we finally surrender to the One who knows us better than anyone, we will find our dreams, our hopes, our joy. In Him, the questions are put to rest, and the future holds promise. It won't always be easy—life seldom is—but it will be a wonder.

May God speak His love to you. May He whisper His call to your heart, showing you who He created you to be. And, if need be, may He lead you into your own wilderness. And when you come out, may the truest joy fill your heart and spirit as never before.

Karen M. Ball

You can write to Karen Ball
c/o Palisades•P.O. Box 1720•Sisters, OR 97759